CÉSAR FRANCK

CÉSAR FRANCK AT THE CONSOLE OF HIS ORGAN
AT SAINTE-CLOTILDE, 1885

Jeanne Rongier

Photo Braun et Cie, Paris, by permission of Soho Gallery, Ltd, London

Fr.

CÉSAR FRANCK

by
Léon Vallas

Translated by
Hubert Foss

GREENWOOD PRESS, PUBLISHERS
WESTPORT, CONNECTICUT

Library of Congress Cataloging in Publication Data

Vallas, Léon, 1879-1956.
  César Franck.

  Translation of La véritable histoire de César Franck.
  Reprint of the 1951 ed. published by Harrap, London.
  1. Franck, César Auguste, 1822-1890.
ML410.F82V33 1973   780'.92'4 [B]   73-5210
ISBN 0-8371-6873-2

First published 1951 by George G. Harrap & Co. Ltd., London

Reprinted with the permission of George G. Harrap & Company, Ltd.

Reprinted by Greenwood Press,
a division of Williamhouse-Regency Inc.

First Greenwood reprinting 1973
Second Greenwood reprinting 1976

Library of Congress Catalog Card Number 73-5210

ISBN 0-8371-6873-2

Printed in the United States of America

Preface

TO César Franck and his music his ardent disciple Vincent d'Indy devoted an excellent study in his book of 1906. It was a work of devotion, informed as much by hagiolatry as by the true history of the man. And it was by this means that the golden legend of the great saint in music was given to the world.

Twenty-four years later Maurice Emmanuel brought this golden legend into closer focus. His short but affecting study of Franck sought to lower the composer down from heaven, back to his Franco-Belgian earth, so as to present a broader and more truthful portrait of him.

In this book it is our endeavour to complete the first labours of our predecessors and friends.

We have tapped all the available sources, public and private, in France and Belgium; we have used (with proper judgment) the numerous reminiscences of the Franck family, as well as those of his colleagues, pupils, and disciples; we have constantly referred to the authentic documents that the Master's granddaughter, Mme Jean Chopy-César-Franck, generously opened to our vision at Nemours before she gave them, in 1947, to the Library of the Paris Conservatoire. By such means we have attempted to establish a detailed and definitive biography of César Franck, the first part of which may appeal to the reader as containing new material.

The biographical record of César Franck is here mingled with the study of his works, in continuance of the direct chronological plan adopted by the author in his *Claude Debussy et son temps* (Paris, 1932; London, 1933), and in the first volume of his *Vincent d'Indy* (1946).

It is our hope that this book will establish without any distortion the complex picture of César Franck and make known to all, in place of the pretty d'Indyist legend, the true history of one of the most fascinating composers in nineteenth-century music.

That hope is in some part illusory, we are aware. In the

memory of the public Franck the composer will never cease to be the uncanonized saint—canonized, that is, solely by the powerful devotion to him of Vincent d'Indy. For ourselves, we make no personal complaint about such an idealistic view.

Since this book was completed a number of studies of César Franck have appeared, of varying value. One is a romanticized biography by a Belgian literary man, not himself a musician (Maurice Kunel, *César Franck; l'homme et son œuvre*, Paris, 1947). Then there have been two admirable short volumes, both plainly titled "César Franck" and both written by musicologists of the first order: the Belgian Charles van den Borren and the Frenchman Norbert Dufourcq (Brussels and Paris, 1949). The latest is the musical study published in London in 1949 by the English composer Norman Demuth.

César Franck's elder son, Georges, expressed the intention of writing a biography of his father in collaboration with Julien Tiersot; no word of it has yet appeared. There remain a number of unpublished notes and documents which the Master's grandson Robert Franck, brother of Mme Chopy, has declared over a period of thirty years that he was about to use in a personal study of the man and the composer.

LÉON VALLAS

Contents

Chapter I. Childhood at Liége (1822–35)   *page* 11

II. First Years in Paris (1835–37)   19

III. The Paris Conservatoire (1837–42)   26

IV. Teaching and Concert-giving during the Conservatoire Period (1838–42)   35

V. The Trios (1842–43)   46

VI. Concerts from 1842 to 1845   59

VII. *Ruth* (1845–46)   70

VIII. Idyll: Betrothal and Marriage (1840–48)   81

IX. Life in Obscurity: The Young Organist (1848–58)   94

X. The Organist at Sainte-Clotilde (1858–70)   112

XI. The War (1870–71): The Société Nationale   129

XII. Professor of Organ at the Conservatoire (1872): *Rédemption* (1873)   137

XIII. The Conservatoire: *Les Éolides*: *Les Béatitudes* (1872–80)   151

XIV. The *Quintet* and *Rébecca*: Two Symphonic Poems: A Scheme for an Opera (1880–84)   166

XV. *Prelude, Chorale, and Fugue*: *Hulda*: The *Symphonic Variations*: Trouble in the Société Nationale: The *Violin Sonata* (1885–87)   183

XVI. Piano Pieces and Songs: *Psyché*: The *Symphony* (1887–89)   201

XVII. *Ghiselle*: The *Quartet*: Improvisation: Chorales: Death (1889–90)   217

XVIII. The Man   237

XIX. The Teacher   252

XX. The Composer   265

Note   276

Index   277

Illustrations

César Franck at the Console of his Organ at
    Sainte-Clotilde, 1885   *frontispiece*

César Franck's Father (Nicolas-Joseph)   *page* 14

César Franck's Mother   14

César Franck's Brother (Joseph)   15

Franck's Autograph Dedication to Spontini   15.

Title-page of *The Three Exiles*   144

Part of the Sketch-manuscript of *Les Éolides*   145

César Franck in 1848   160

César Franck in 1889   160

Concluding Lines of Franck's Manuscript of the String
    Quartet   161

Part of a Letter written by Franck in 1884 to Pierre de Bréville   161

Childhood at Liége
(1822–35)

LOVE and admiration for their master have led the pupils of César Franck to distort the facts of history. The object of the following pages is to establish the truth.

There has been, to begin with, an effort to prove Franck a Frenchman not only by naturalization, which he wanted to be and was, but by origin, which he never was. Vincent d'Indy pronounced in his lectures that Franck "was born at Liége by accident"; another disciple, Paul de Wailly, building on the loose sand of the historical frontiers of Picardy, has assured us that Franck derived in part thence. Fond advocacy, indeed; but it is far from reality, neither less nor more so than the assertions of certain critics—among them Debussy himself—who imagined that they had discovered Franck's background to be Flemish.

The whole question of nationality seems, in this particular case, to matter not one jot—it is a floating factor, anyhow! For when César Franck first saw light, in 1822, his nation had not achieved independence. After a long domination by Austria, up to the French conquest of 1794, Belgium was still one of the Netherlands. Not till 1830 were the Belgians to be free to constitute a definite kingdom of their own.

His birth at Liége made Franck a Walloon, and so, it would seem, of French language and tradition. Vincent d'Indy, his biographer, holds closely to the point. He even accepted the family theory about a dynasty of Walloon painters behind the composer. This lineage is entirely legendary. In truth, some distant ancestry leads us rather to Austria. As far as can be traced, somewhere in the middle of the sixteenth century the paternal line was settled in the province of Liége, not (as they say) in the region called Campine, but within the neighbourhood of the Dutch Limburg and of Prussia, precisely at Völkerich—a subject-village of Gemmenich, which is the last Belgian station on the railway between Liége and Aix-la-Chapelle, and about a league from the latter. The name of Gemmenich shows that it is not French; the dialect there is Germanic—something between Low German and Netherlandish, but spiced with French words.

Into that community was born the grandfather, Barthélemy, the son of Étienne Franck; there he lived all his life save for his schooling in the Rhineland, at the near-by towns of Aix and Cologne. He held a high place in the village in administration and law; like his father, he bore the title of *Grossmayer*, or Burgo-master. César's father, Nicolas-Joseph, was born on May 30, 1794, at Völkerich, and studied at Aix. Establishing himself at Liége in 1817, he married Marie-Catherine-Barbe Frings on August 24, 1820. She was his senior by six years and he had met her while he was a student in Germany. The daughter of a cloth-merchant at Aix, Mme Franck was a German.

And so we find that César Franck's origin was Germanic through his father, pure German through his mother. The French musician-to-be spoke German with his mother. From this early start he retained all his life (and so did his brother Joseph) the habit of so uttering his prayers: "Vater unser," "Ich heile dich." His heavy voice—which a few rare survivors can remember very clearly—his thick voice and characteristic in-tonation were formed as much by the first language he spoke and learned as by the rough Walloon patois.[1]

A Liégeois by birth, a Netherlander, later a Belgian, later still a Frenchman by naturalization, Walloon by upbringing, French at heart, Franck came none the less from Germany; that is a fact which, long ignored or carefully hidden, should in no way diminish the affection of his compatriots in Belgium or France.

The registry at Liége records his birth thus[2]:

---

[1] These linguistic influences were pointed out to Mlle May de Rudder by one of his fellow-townsmen of Gemmenich, Joseph Lamberts, Professor of German at the Athénée Royal at Brussels, who died in 1905.

[2] The factual particulars of the registration run thus: "December 12, 1822, at noon, before the Burgomaster; Nicolas-Joseph Franck, aged twenty-nine, of independent means, a male child, born on December 10 about 7 A.M. of his wife Marie-Catherine-Barbe Frings, aged thirty-four: proposed names César-Auguste-Jean-Guillaume-Hubert."

There was an elder child born eighteen months before, who died at the age of one year; he was christened César-Hubert-Auguste, which three names were transferred to the newcomer.

The house where César Franck was born has long since disappeared. The memorial plaque of his birth has been set on the front of an old hotel of the eighteenth century alongside which is a deserted open space.

L'an mil huit cent vingt-deux, le douze décembre à midi, devant M. Frédéric Rouveroy, bourgmestre de la ville de Liége, officier de l'Etat-civil, est comparu Nicolas-Joseph Franck, âgé de vingt-neuf ans, sans profession, Rue Saint-Pierre, no 13, quartier de l'Ouest, lequel nous a présenté un enfant du sexe masculin, né le 10 du présent mois, vers les sept heures du matin, de lui déclarant et de Marie-Catherine-Barbe Frings, âgée de trente-quartre ans, son épouse, auquel il a déclaré voulir donner les noms de César-Auguste-Jean-Guillaume-Hubert.

Three years later the birth of a second son was registered—Jean-Hubert-Joseph—also to be a musician and born on October 31, 1825.

César-Auguste used both these Christian names for twenty-four years, but his brother was never known by anything but Joseph.

Nicolas-Joseph, their father, though he styled himself *rentier* of independent means, was, in fact, a 'writer' or scrivener at the bank run by Frésart, who witnessed Joseph's birth certificate. This world of finance was not without its dangers for a man of Franck's temperament—adventurous, greedy, ambitious, and audacious.

Nicolas-Joseph left little behind him except ill repute—in the mind of César, who always spoke of his father with reverence, in the memory of his daughter-in-law, who out of respect said but few words, save to mention his sordid avarice, and in those of his cousins or friends, who, held back by no filial considerations, did not trouble to conceal their view that the composer's father was the evil genius of his son, indeed of both his sons. The photograph reproduced at page 14 gives us indications of the arrogance and harshness of his character. A pretentious egotist, a fierce authoritarian whom even the sweet nature of his wife was powerless to mollify, Nicolas-Joseph suffered from the mediocrity of his position, so different from his dreams. He was a lover of music, perhaps even something of an instrumentalist; one observes in his portrait the immense fingers which his son inherited from him. At Liége he frequented the little world of painters, musicians, and writers, and derived from their company not only self-esteem, but also some connexions that he knew how to use. His stifled ambition he transferred to his children. Though César-Auguste showed a clear talent for drawing, he determined to make both boys into virtuosos, the elder at the piano, the younger on the violin. Both of them exhibited musical promise.

About the age of eight the elder of the sons was entered at the Royal Conservatoire of Liége, and three years later the younger at the same age. The names of the instructors who had the privilege of teaching César-Auguste are known to us; in addition to the director, Daussoigne (a nephew of Méhul), there were Duguet, the blind organist of the church of Saint-Denis (whose name we later find as dedicatee of a *Grand Offertoire* by Joseph Franck), Ledent, Conrady, Delavaux, and Jalheau.

Among the Conservatoire archives are to be found marks and reports earned by César-Auguste in various examinations, all of them high in praise: "Marked ability . . . does good work . . . has keenness and application . . . full of promise . . . is doing well on all sides,"—and the like. This model pupil, who before his enrolment, in October 1830, had already studied the rudiments of music (*solfège*), won the first prize for that subject in 1832. A full score given to him on prize-day bears the date August 25, 1832, and his age, nine and a half years. In 1833 he began to study harmony, and in 1834, at only eleven and a half, he became a pupil-teacher of *solfège* and piano.

Ample proof of the diligence with which César-Auguste, as both child and adolescent, pursued his musical studies, can be found in his exercise books.[1] The clean, neat handwriting shows how carefully the conscientious pupil paid attention to his master's remarks.

From the Liége volume we are able to follow almost day by day the progress of these harmony lessons and to appreciate the methods of the master as well as the aptness of the pupil. The exercises are written in a fair hand, and are carefully laid out on the pages in chronological order. The heading of the book is informative:

Harmony: begun December 2, 1833, by *César-Auguste Franck*, born at Liége December 10, 1822, in Rue Neuve Saint-Pierre, at Maison Thompson (which has no number), in the Parish of Sainte-

[1] They are preserved in various places. The first volume gathers together in 238 pages the harmony exercises worked out at the Conservatoire between 1833 and 1835. The others, written after the departure to Paris in 1835, are discussed in Chapter II. The earlier book was in the possession of M. Victor Balbreck, the viola player, who took part in the first performance of Franck's Quartet, in 1890.

CÉSAR FRANCK'S MOTHER

CÉSAR FRANCK'S FATHER (NICOLAS-JOSEPH)

CÉSAR FRANCK'S BROTHER (JOSEPH)

FRANCK'S AUTOGRAPH DEDICATION TO SPONTINI

15

Croix. *Pupil of the Royal Conservatoire of Music, Liége.* In the class of M. Daussoigne, the Director.

There are dates on many pages, the last being inscribed: "End of my harmony course, Liége, January 29, 1835." We thus discover that fourteen months were sufficient for absorbing this difficult subject. He had no other harmony-teacher than the Director.

As a musician, Joseph Daussoigne-Méhul's experiences in the theatre had been unfortunate except in the production of his uncle's operas. Before his appointment to the Liége Directorship, in 1827, he had for a long time taught *solfège*, piano, and harmony at the Paris Conservatoire. A man of culture and intelligence, interested in art and literature, and an admirable instructor of a large number of students, he employed a method of teaching harmony that differed from the usual Parisian system in being based on counterpoint. César-Auguste seems to have mastered from his eleventh year the somewhat artificial difficulties of that science with both ease and pleasure.

Of the boy's piano-studies we have naturally less direct evidence outside his teachers' reports. He appears to have worked at them as assiduously as he did at his harmony and counterpoint. From one teacher we can get some idea of the expressive quality of his playing, for he praises his aptitude and mentions "a tendency towards warmth of feeling which sometimes becomes mere daubing." The quality was real, evidently, and his professors were forewarned against its excess becoming a fault. Another report approves his application and dexterity, but adds the reservation that he is "less intelligent than one would have expected from hearing his prepared pieces." Nevertheless, he carried off the first prize when aged only eleven years and three months, on February 22, 1834, and received a score of *Robert le Diable* suitably inscribed in letters of gold.

Nicolas-Joseph Franck considered that the moment had now come to launch his eldest son as an infant prodigy, in the dual character of pianist and composer, and to that end organized a short tour for the lad to appear in Aix-la-Chapelle, Liége, Louvain, Malines, and Brussels. The concert in the capital of the newly formed kingdom was given in the Royal Palace, the Belgian King, Leopold I, himself attending the performance. During this trip César-Auguste met a certain girl of his own age, herself an

excellent pianist—the young Garcia, who was destined, under
the name of Pauline Viardot, to become a famous singer. In this
way César-Auguste had the honour of playing before Pauline's
elder sister and brother-in-law, the famous Malibran and her
husband, the violinist Charles de Bériot.

In the programmes of these recitals, of which the last, before
royalty, seemed like an official consecration of his genius, several
of the boy's compositions were included: a *Grand Rondo, Ballade,
Fantaisie, Variations on the theme "Pré-aux-clercs."* Of these the
first and fourth have survived; they are correct in technique,
decorous in style, and altogether a worthy start for a youngster
of eleven.

Not long after, the father brought out his second son, Joseph,
whose gifts as a violinist and musician seemed to him hardly
inferior to those of the elder son as pianist and composer. The
two gave their first joint concert at Aix-la-Chapelle in 1835,
Joseph (then about ten years of age) playing from memory a
concerto by Rode.

Nothing would satisfy Father Franck from now on but the
proper commercial exploitation of his sons, especially of the
elder. It was the time of the triumphs of the young Franz Liszt.
Here was César-Auguste—was he not also a pianist-composer?
Were not his great gifts certain very soon to make his fortune—
that is, his father's fortune? He was put into strict training, with
almost forced labours, to which he submitted partly from
deference and partly from personal inclination. Piano-practice
was well-nigh incessant, broken by the necessity to compose
pieces, not as inspiration led him, but conforming to the utili-
tarian ambitions of the father—virtuoso music designed to
throw a shop-window brilliance over his sparkling piano-
technique. The public's taste at this period demanded fantasias
on fashionable airs: things like the already mentioned *Variations
on the theme "Pré-aux-clercs";* of this two versions exist, one for
piano solo and one for piano and orchestra (was it possibly
played by amateur orchestral societies?); and like the *Variations
brillantes on a favourite round-dance of Gustave III.* Other similar
ear-tickling pieces of 1834 or 1835 paid lip-service to the recent
operas of Hérold and Auber, and were calculated to attract all
amateurs.

We must not look for a trace of originality in these juvenile works, demanded from, and indeed imposed upon, the child by a tyrannical father with a determination to win a speedy success. His undeveloped personality was swamped in every phase by the taste of the 1830's, by the mannerisms of Franz Liszt, and the pianistic tricks of contemporary virtuosos. That is but natural; who at that time could stand up against the domination of the young Hungarian? Other pieces show some acquaintance with the music of Weber and Schubert, and even of the rising young master Schumann. By 1835 some of the last-named's more important piano-pieces had reached a wide public, and had certainly come to César-Auguste's ears, either through his mother's family at Aix or through the Conservatoire staff at Liége; one hears an echo of Schumann in the O Salutaris, dated February 10, 1835, with its expressive vocal line and well-written orchestral ritornellos.

The moment had now come, thought Nicolas-Joseph Franck, when his elder son's talents were ready to conquer Paris. His was an exaggerating mind; his ambition expanded even the title of his son's little concert-pieces, so that 'Fantaisies' and 'Caprices' became 'Grandes Fantaisies,' 'Grands Caprices,' and the first prize for piano the 'premier grand prix.' Thus inflated by him, this last award seemed to him a good spring-board for plunging into the French capital; so he decided to settle his elder son there while leaving the younger at home with his mother.

There was to be no return to the country of his forbears for César-Auguste, save as a bird of passage. He had spent his school holidays at an uncle's house at Gemmenich. Occasionally he revisited the little township during his years of adolescence in the company of his brother and parents, now self-styled Parisians. The simple peasants gave him good welcome and were not slow to hail him as the great musician from Paris. Dressed in a wide blue blouse and straw hat, he appeared to be happy to be once again in the country, far removed from concerts and endless piano-practice. Memories of him were long retained at Gemmenich—of a pale, broad-shouldered young man, with long brown hair, an open and serious expression on his face, and the eyes of a dreamer.[1]

[1] We learn about these visits to Gemmenich from Charles Delchevalerie, in an article in the review *Flamberge* (1894) which was reprinted in *Wallonie* in February 1913 and in the *Intermédiaire des chercheurs et curieux* of March 30, 1913. According to this writer, whose authority in facts seems somewhat dubious, César-Auguste paid his last visit to Gemmenich in 1855 or 1856 and delighted the villagers by playing the organ to them.

One may well wonder, with the Belgian musicologist Ernest Closson, what César-Auguste derived from the neighbourhood of Liége, where he was born and brought up and received his first musical impressions. Was it, perhaps, a part of the impulsiveness, the delicate sensitiveness, the strong emotionalism that characterized his works? His mother may—who knows?—have hummed certain German songs to rock him in his cradle; but his early outpourings must surely have been influenced by the popular songs and dances of the Walloons, by *cramignons* and the like.

CHAPTER II

First Years in Paris
(1835–37)

DESPITE his meagre resources, Father Franck was bent on having only the most celebrated teachers in Paris for César-Auguste; no one else would be worthy of his talents and capable of developing them. Armed with introductions from Daussoigne-Méhul, he approached two of the capital's leading musicians, Zimmermann for piano, Reicha for composition; both, like the Director at Liége at one time, were professors at the Royal Conservatoire of Music.

At the age of fifty-five Zimmermann was held to be one of the outstanding piano-teachers; Reicha, a naturalized Czech, was, at the age of sixty-six, the acknowledged king of the art of counterpoint. The former is now forgotten, but the latter has been to some degree resuscitated by Maurice Emmanuel, who, in his *César Franck*, has shown him to be a fine and original teacher.

As with his harmony studies at Liége, so with his counterpoint at Paris, we know all the details of Reicha's work with his young Belgian pupil, for César-Auguste has recorded his exercises in a series of note-books preserved in a bound volume at the Conservatoire's library (Manuscript No. 1831).

The note-books start on June 24, 1835, in Paris, and bear the title: "Principles and methods of M. A. Reicha, Professor at the Paris Conservatoire." Double counterpoint at the octave or the fifteenth begins on August 12, triple counterpoint on August 29. After the summer recess the studies from October 4 to the end of December are devoted to counterpoint at the tenth or the third. Then, in 1836, comes fugue in all its diversity, and by May 11 the student had reached triple fugue for four voices.

Here the lessons ceased, for a fortnight later he was reluctantly compelled to paste in his book a note saying: "The end of my work with M. Anton Reicha, my teacher, who died at 50 Rue de Mont Thabor on May 26, 1836." The simple text was later corrected by substituting for "my teacher" the words "Professor at the Conservatoire."

The effect of this year on César-Auguste—or, shall we say, the effect at least of several months of intense training under an eminent master of wide general culture?—was to liberate his mind and to provide him with that suppleness of writing which marked all his later works.

Nevertheless, it would appear that Reicha was never able during the ten months when he was teaching this child of twelve or thirteen (twenty lessons, say) to apply the principles laid down in his *Traité de haute composition musicale* ("Text-book of advanced musical composition"). Rather (among other things) Reicha laid the foundation of his remarkable resourcefulness in rhythms and key-changes. Practical skill in contrapuntal writing, in César-Auguste's case, was the result of his three years of study with Leborne at the Conservatoire. According to Maurice Emmanuel, all Reicha's teaching lay dormant in his pupil's brain right up to the period of his masterpieces—that is, for more than thirty-five years. This hypothesis, no doubt attractive to a historian who was overwhelmed by the originality of the Czech-French teacher, does not approach the bounds of probability, much less of certainty.

From the very start of his lessons both Zimmermann and Reicha showed themselves highly contented with their pupil. They went so far as to express their satisfaction publicly when, in November 1835, Father Franck began to prepare for his son's first Parisian concert and wanted to work up some publicity. They even consented to produce flattering testimonials. Zimmermann wrote:

> The youthful César-Auguste Franck has one of the best-balanced young brains I have ever encountered; he combines the most brilliant aptitude with a capacity for hard study which give every promise that he will become a highly distinguished artist.

Nor was Reicha less fulsome in praise. He wrote:

> This young man is gifted with remarkable musical talents, and if he continues his career under the guidance of the best teachers in Paris, there is every reason why he should develop into one of the

most notable musicians, for already he shows powers far in advance of his years.

On these and similar laudatory opinions Nicolas-Joseph Franck based a grandiose scheme of flooding the daily and musical Press of Paris, around November 15, with the announcement of the first appearance in the French capital of the young pianist-composer from Liége. "M. César-Auguste Franck, aged twelve," we read,

> the winner of the first prize for piano at the Conservatoire at Liége, who has already gained a success in Belgium and at Aix-la-Chapelle, is to give a piano recital next Thursday, November 17, at the Gymnase Musical. A number of the most eminent Paris musicians have already expressed their high opinion of his remarkably precocious abilities, and we fancy that it will not be long before young Franck makes a name for himself in the world of music.

Such, at least, was the paragraph that appeared on November 14, 1835, in the *Moniteur universel*, which wisely suppressed certain superfluous details suited only to specialized papers; the *Gazette musicale*, on the other hand, announced that César-Auguste had studied with "M. Jalheau," a musician entirely unknown outside Liége, and Fétis's *Revue musicale* added other details: "First prize-winner for piano, February 22, 1834, from M. Jalheau's class, at the age of eleven."

The paternal vanity was limitless. Father Franck, basking in the warmth of his son's precocity, had visions of a brilliant response on the part of the musical critics; he himself was the author of that imprudent phrase at the end of the notices in the *Gazette* and the *Revue*: "Once we have heard him we shall all be talking about him." Unfortunately the triumphs of Liége seem to have had in Paris none of the effects that Nicolas-Joseph anticipated. As far as we are aware, not a single word was printed about the son. What was the reason? Indifference or disappointment on the part of the critics? Or was it just Papa's blunder in embarrassing them with misplaced importunities?

The shock was unpleasant, in any case, the more so because a large sum of money had been laid out upon this first concert; it was plainly an ill-advised step to disdain the smaller concert-halls and go all out for that vast, modern building on the fashionable boulevards, the Gymnase Musical, which had been solemnly declared open in May 1835 in the presence of Meyerbeer and Rossini, and where on June 2 Berlioz himself had conducted a concert. After so direct a snub Father Franck held off from any similarly ruinous experiments, and for more than a year César-Auguste made no public appearance at the piano, but contented his soul with study and with composition.

After Reicha's death there came up the new idea of entering both the Franck children on the roll of the Paris Conservatoire; for by June 1836 Joseph had also in his turn left his native haunts and settled in Paris. It was a forlorn hope. The Franck family was Belgian. Admittedly Cherubini, the Director of the Conservatoire, was himself an Italian, but he was a naturalized French subject and had no wish for foreigners in his school; had he not, a few years back, refused entrance, in the face of his prodigious achievements, to that Hungarian-born child Franz Liszt? The Francks were thus excluded as aliens.

Without a moment's hesitation Nicolas-Joseph set in motion the necessary machinery of French naturalization. It would be only a matter of a month or two when, properly certified as French subjects, his sons could pass through the open doors.

Meanwhile César-Auguste continued his piano-work under Zimmermann. One may imagine the father debating with himself whether he would not go direct and ask advice from the great Cherubini himself—a rigid director no doubt, but one who as a composer was at this period held to be the rival of Beethoven. On the other hand, Cherubini's support at the moment of the entrance examination would be of priceless value, and that consideration must have weighed heavily in the mind of Nicholas-Joseph, who was not only a shrewd and unscrupulous businessman, but had constituted himself his own children's impresario.

That year of waiting—1836–37—seems not to have been wasted as far as composing was concerned, for César-Auguste wrote (or, at least, began) a number of important works. The first of them was printed as "published by the composer": a sonata for piano, Op. 10; two concertos for piano and orchestra, Op. 11; a *Fantaisie* for piano, Op. 12; two trios, Op. 16 and 22; a symphony for full orchestra, Op. 13. As compositions by a lad of thirteen, they are no more negligible than those of Beethoven at the same age; on the other hand, they are no more interesting.

The "First Sonata for the pianoforte composed and dedicated

to Joseph Franck by his brother César-Auguste Franck of Liége, aged thirteen, Op. 10"—so runs the title-page—is written in the style of the early Beethoven or the late Haydn, with a marked tendency towards freedom in modulation.[1] In all probability the concertos were performed by the young composer with some amateur symphonic orchestra or other at Liége or Aix-la-Chapelle. The *Fantaisie* was often played by him at his concerts in Belgium and France. There is some confusion about the early trios and the three others published in 1842; one of them is undoubtedly the later *Trio de Salon*. As for the symphony, it would appear from a note in the full score that it was performed, or at least read through in rehearsal, by the Philharmonic Society of Orléans on February 16, 1841.

After a lull of fifteen months, during which his elder son was steadily working at his piano-playing with Zimmermann, Nicholas-Joseph began anew his efforts to launch him as a composer-pianist. And so we find the lad of fourteen once again appearing in public, and playing his own and others' works.

Thus on February 23, 1837, a concert was held at the Athénée Musical; several artists took part in a varied programme, according to the custom of a period when the solo recital was unknown. The public went not to hear the young prodigy, but the famous artists—Géraldy, the well-known concert singer who later joined the staff of the Brussels Conservatoire, his pupil Mlle Nau, a young Spaniard from New York who the previous year had made her debut at the Paris Opéra as the page in *Les Huguenots* and was then at the beginning of her brilliant career in France, England, and America.

César Franck was not entirely crushed under the eminence of his colleagues; his dual talent was observed. In a sympathetic notice the *Gazette musicale* wrote:

> This young person of no more than thirteen years of age [in truth he was fourteen, but his father followed the precedent of most parents of prodigies in keeping the figure to the credible minimum] is already an adroit pianist and skilful in harmony; that says much for

[1] Julien Tiersot published a study of this work in *La Revue musicale* of December 1, 1922, and even quoted two passages from it. He also made a survey of most of Franck's unpublished works at that time in the family possession. Later Pierre de Bréville catalogued numerous manuscripts which the author has also himself seen at Nemours; they had been kept by the composer's grand-daughter, Mme Chopy, and in 1947 were deposited in the Bibliothèque Nationale.

him, but there could be a great deal more to say later. And predict with no hesitation that he will become a fine artist if he is trained with caution; care must be taken that the fertile germs of music latent in his exceptionally musical temperament should not be allowed to come to nothing.

Certain reservations following this eulogistic sentence make one think that the pianist in him had too much virility, the composer too little diversity.

In conclusion I urge him not to confuse energy with power. . . . And I cannot avoid adding the advice that any musical phrase, however charming in itself, is bound to become tiring with frequent repetition unless it is given a new significance drawn from some new harmonic or instrumental treatment.

Some weeks later, on Sunday, April 30, César-Auguste is to be found appearing on a concert-platform on an equal commercial basis with three of the best-known virtuosos of the time. They were the pianist Pixis, at that moment nearly fifty years of age and a Parisian figure of a dozen years' standing, the celebrated Alkan, and the illustrious Franz Liszt. For a beginner it was an astonishing and flattering occasion, the reason for it being an evening party given by the manufacturer Pape to his clients to demonstrate the excellence of his latest pianos. Once again the older people did not wholly outshine the youngest. "Auguste Franck" won praise for the "purity and precision" with which he rendered a fantasy by Hummel. One cannot but wonder whether, at this early concert, he was noticed in the smallest degree by his later admirer and patron, Liszt?

His third public appearance, on May 14, 1837, had an equally good reception from both the public and the musical Press. Once again the scene of operations was Pape's piano *salons*, and the whole affair was arranged by Father Franck in association with the singer Mlle Drouart and two young instrumentalists of the first rank—the violinist Delphin Alard (1815–88), then on the road to becoming one of the leading players of his time, and the 'cellist Chevillard (1811–77), who later became the exponent of Beethoven string quartets; both were destined for professorships at the Paris Conservatoire.

The advance publicity was carefully handled. Tickets (the public were informed) could be obtained from M. Franck, 22

Rue Montholon, and a paragraph was issued announcing "several distinguished artists; and certain unfamiliar works will be given, like a trio by Schubert, a quartet by Weber, and another by Beethoven—all first performances." The musical Press lifted up its voice in praise the following days.

It is difficult to accept all the newspaper accounts of the concert at their face-value. There is a strong flavour of our parent-impresario's own style when we read in the *Gazette musicale* of May 21 and in the *Ménestrel* of May 28 such familiar phrases about this young pianist's "staggering the public by the contrast between his age (he has hardly left the school-room) and the maturity of his talents." One may put more faith in a second notice that appeared in the *Gazette*, which criticized points in the programme, in particular the "mutilation" of Weber's one and only string quartet (no doubt rescored as a trio), but praised the pianist himself: "Young M. Franck," it runs, "has earned special mention; he has great musical feeling, and his early advanced development foretells for him a future as one of the major pianists." The paper mentioned in addition his ease, his self-possession, his intelligence, his passionate energy, his expressiveness and musical feeling.

It was not long before the young artist, with all this praise round him, was to change his plans entirely, taking on the rôle of a plain student of piano and composition at the Paris Conservatoire.

CHAPTER III

The Paris Conservatoire
(1837–42)

THE King's mandate of naturalization reached Nicolas-Joseph Franck on September 22, 1837. He considered it rash to abandon his Belgian status at once and in public, in case it might serve some later purpose; his main anxiety was to use his new French citizenship to force a way for his sons through the portals of the Conservatoire. To this end he lost no time in presenting himself at the Secretariat in the Rue Bergère—he was, in fact, the first of the parents to be enrolled, as witness the fact that on the register of candidates for the entrance examination into the music school César-Auguste and Joseph are numbered one and two. A note was added to the effect that their father was a naturalized Frenchman and they were "proposed by M. Edmond Blanc," a Secretary of the Ministry for the Interior who was responsible under the Council of State for such requests of privilege.

César-Auguste, then some fifteen years old, was accepted for the counterpoint class of Leborne, Reicha's successor, and joined it on October 4; he also joined, on October 20, after a qualifying examination, M. Zimmermann's special piano-class. Joseph, then aged twelve, went for violin to Habeneck and for *solfège* to Le Couppey.

The elder son's instrumental lessons may be assumed to have been a formality; like so many other brilliant players, especially foreigners, who passed through the Conservatoire merely to achieve the first year's highest award (Franz Liszt himself wanted to do so), César-Auguste had such talent and such success already that his presence in the Rue Bergère was a matter of probation, a necessary preliminary to romping home with the first prize.

The archives of the Conservatoire contain various registers on which members of the teaching staff made reports on pupils from time to time, and it is not uninteresting to examine those on the elder Franck's progress with piano, counterpoint, and organ. The remarks on his piano-work are consistently commendatory. At the first private examination of Zimmermann's class, in December 1837, César-Auguste gained the highest marks of all the entrants, and Cherubini's own personal register records quite barely: "Franck I, fifteen years one month, excellent."

It soon became evident to all concerned with the class that at the end of the academic year the newcomer would win the first prize. Nevertheless, as late as the eve of the final examination, both teacher and fellow-pupils must have had moments of doubt, for, according to a story often related in after years by the candidate, that day there was a rehearsal of the prescribed pieces; César-Auguste played Hummel's *Concerto in B minor*, no doubt in a highly romantic style, so that Zimmermann called out, "Play it like that and you'll be ploughed for a certainty!"

The finals for piano were held on August 2, 1838. Cherubini presided over a panel of examiners consisting of the composer Adolphe Adam, the success of whose opera *Le Postillon de Long-jumeau* in 1836 had brought him fame overnight, Schneitzhoeffer, the choral professor at the Conservatoire, and the pianists J. Herz, Pleyel, Le Couppey, Charles Kontzki, and the veteran Alkan. Among the six entrants were Victor Massé, the future composer of *Les Noces de Jeannette*, Henri Duvernoy, later a singing professor at the Conservatoire, and the infant prodigy of eleven, Charlot, who caused the composer Berton to record after the entrance examination in June: "Astounding! Marvellous!"

Far from fulfilling his professor's gloomy prophecy of the previous day, César-Auguste played the Hummel in his most brilliant form—not a mistake, not a false step, and with a nicely judged emotional temper. But if his success was already a certainty on account of his outstanding technique and interpretation, it was made doubly certain by the second part of the examination—a sight-reading test from manuscript; so frequently this is the rock that wrecks candidates, for there are plenty of instrumentalists who can show authority, even mastery, when playing their prescribed pieces so long prepared under their teacher's careful guidance, but when confronted with a sight-reading test instantly become nervous beginners, uncertainly stumbling over tricky rhythms and falling headlong into the traps cunningly laid for them by the writer of the test.

Franck was a fluent and well-trained sight-reader. So far from blanching, he was so full of assurance as to risk a flight of fancy audacious, even perilous, enough to make any teacher faint with horror! Instead of reading the manuscript in front of him in its proper key of E flat, he transposed it down a minor third, and read it straight off without hesitation or error in the key of C.

The effect on the judges was stupefying; they were entranced. Here before them was an unique candidate—the only one of his kind in the world—capable of doubling the difficulty of a sight-reading test for a mere whim, and carrying the joke off in public! The audience was no less impressed, and we must remember that it consisted largely of specialists able to appreciate to the full this musical trope. The whole event set up flattering echoes that reached the ears of the musical Press (particularly the *Revue et Gazette musicale* of August 19) and even of the dailies, though the latter class confined their mention to a mere news-item, in all probability sent to them by Zimmermann himself.

Faced with such a situation, what could the examiners do? It was without precedent, unique in the Conservatoire's history, not allowed for in the regulations. Some administrative action must be taken, but what would be the appropriate action in so remote a case? This weighty problem could hardly be solved at one single meeting. At least two would be essential, and then none of them could be certain that they had decided the matter according to the rules laid down. The aftermath of this astonishing affair was thus described in *La France musicale* of August 5:

> First of all the jury awarded with one voice the first prize to M. Franck. But after that the jury decided to look into the matter again. After some discussion, M. Cherubini announced with his accustomed grace: "The jury has now decided that M. Franck stands so incomparably far ahead of his fellow competitors that it is impossible to nominate another to share the prize with him. Accordingly, a second first-prize will be given to those who would in ordinary circumstances have deserved the senior award."

One paper, seeking an appropriate name, called the award a "special first prize *honoris causa*"; but such a dignity, equally with the feat that earned it, was beyond the scope of the regulations laid down. The final decision may have appeared equivocal, but there it stands, even in the official but somewhat contradictory archives of the great institution. The honours list contains only these words: "First prize, M. Franck, senior (César-Auguste), aged fifteen years six months, pupil of M. Zimmermann"; but there follows a hint of the truth—"The jury decided that this was an occasion for awarding a second first-prize." The latter was shared by Duvernoy and some one of the name of Barth. Yet the fine resplendent volumes presented to the winner at the prize-giving (two-volume scores of *Don Giovanni* and *Figaro* and the score of *Alceste*) are all blocked in gold letters on the front cover with the legend: "Examination held on August 2, 1838: first prize for piano with honourable mention (Grand Prix d'honneur), unanimously awarded to M. César-Auguste Franck, aged fifteen." What in truth he had won was a special first prize, of a kind never before granted in the school's history; but so as not to upset the official rules and regulations not a trace of mention of the fact is to be found in the records.[1]

When one considers the importance of this particular musical exploit—high-light of all César-Auguste's early piano studies—one records with some surprise that in the following months and even years Father Franck was unable to obtain a morsel of publicity, not even a special paragraph. We have examined a large number of journals of all kinds without finding a word about this success at the Conservatoire. That, however, is but one of the minor problems, apart from the larger hidden mysteries of life, that beset a biographer.

The course in counterpoint and fugue turned out to be much longer and more laborious than that in piano. Here, despite his previous work with Reicha, César-Auguste made no meteoric rise; rather, for three years, he gradually climbed up the ladder, rung by rung. His own records of the work done show us his progress. The counterpoint exercises are to be found in a bound volume with the following title: "Elementary counterpoint begun at the Royal Conservatoire of Music and Rhetoric at Paris on October 4, 1837, by César-Auguste Franck, pupil of M. Leborne." Then, in the note-book on academic fugue, we may read remarks of this kind:

[1] The prize volumes were treasured first by their winner and then by his heirs, and are now in the Bibliothèque Nationale. In addition to these prizes for piano may be seen there books representing his first prize for counterpoint, 1840 (the works of Hummel), his second prize for organ (score of *William Tell*), and his two prizes from the Liége Conservatoire—the first prize for *solfège*, August 25, 1832, and the first prize for piano, February 22, 1834 (score of *Robert le Diable*).

> If I have written any hidden fifths, especially between the inner parts or between the 'cello and one of the extreme parts, it is because I wanted to make the harmony complete. . . . The passage is risky, I know, but I thought it best to retain it so as to keep closely to the chromatic character of the subject and to exend it a little in the stretto.

In one of the early trios there occurs a similar example of self-criticism, which is equal testimony to the discipline of the Conservatoire and to the independence of an usually obedient spirit. The young man gave himself wholly to these complicated exercises in counterpoint—almost gymnastic in their contortions—and seems to have derived some satisfaction therefrom. After each examination Cherubini would write in his register: "Good, . . . he is making good progress . . ." and so on.

At the first examination—July 1838, immediately before winning the piano-prize—he obtained the unanimous award of third prize for counterpoint and fugue; in 1839 the second prize; in July 1840 (he was then seventeen and a half) he was judged an undisputed first. For the following anecdote we are indebted to his later pupil, Vincent d'Indy: in 1839, it is related, on the second day of the examination, Franck wrote his fugue at great speed, and returned home some hours before the close of the session, leaving his fellow-entrants still at work. When the father reproached him for having skimped his exercise the son replied with a smile of confidence, "Oh, I think it will turn out all right!"

This examination fugue is, in fact, a work of considerable importance; far from being a pupil's set piece, it shows the hand of a master. Julien Tiersot goes so far as to call it "monumental," and wished that it were arranged for keyboard to be played in public alongside the fugues of Bach. Franck himself had some regard for its value as music, for six or seven years after writing it he made a careful copy to give as a present to his fiancée.

But for all these prizes in piano-playing and counterpoint Franck's studies were by no means at an end; he had every right to enter for the Prix de Rome, the highest target for the young composer's aim. He decided to take up the organ, in the autumn of 1840—a decision based partly upon his natural tastes and his scholarly interests, partly upon his hope of finding an organist's post. François Benoist, who won the Prix de Rome in 1815, was then the professor of organ, and had been for some twenty years, with an established reputation for the accompaniment of plain-chant and for improvising fugues on a given theme. Under him César-Auguste could acquire a thorough grounding, not only as a player of the instrument but also as an improviser. For similar reasons a good many of his fellow-students in piano passed on to Benoist's class. By unanimous verdict he was given the second prize (with no one sharing the honour) at his first examination, on July 21, 1841. Farther than this he was never to go along this particular road.

Reasonable reward, one might imagine, for a first effort; but Franck was not satisfied, the less so because he had brought off once again (no one noticed it!) another astonishing feat of musicianship on the same lines as his transposition in sight-reading. He used often to tell the story about himself, and in his turn his disciple and biographer, Vincent d'Indy, used also to tell it as he heard it from the master, though it is possible that the details as they reach us are not strictly in conformity with what happened!

Two themes were given by the examining panel of 1841 for the examinees to treat in improvisation—the one for a fugue, the other for a sonata. Between the two Franck sensed a kinship; his natural flair for counterpoint suggested to him the notion of treating them simultaneously. In his inner mind he felt he could be happy in using the two themes together as the basis for an improvisation of complex form and of a length unusual in such tests of skill. The examiners were fogged; that great contrapuntist Cherubini was not presiding, and the others understood nothing of his intentions and achievement, and therefore gave him nothing in return. Benoist was still enthusiastic about his pupil's work and tried to explain what he had done and what they had not noticed. It was useless; even thus enlightened, the panel stuck to their first view and gave Franck the second prize.

It may well be that the incident occurred exactly as Franck recounted it; but not a written word of testimony occurs either in the official documents or in the Press accounts of the examination. The *Gazette* of July 25, 1841, prints that

> the organ competition was of special interest. Three students who had all won prizes for fugue pitted their talents against each other—MM. Franck, Laurent, and Duvernoy. M. Franck, who came second on the prize-list, shows promise of becoming a fine organist and certainly does credit to his teacher M. Benoist.

La France musicale of July 28 and the *Ménestrel* of July 25 printed no more than the bare facts, presumably passed to them by the Secretary of the Conservatoire:

> Organ examination: first prize, M. Laurent, entering for the second time—four votes; M. Franck received three votes. Second prize, M. Franck—seven votes, *nem. con.*; joined the organ-class only six months ago.

The examiners expressed no further opinion, but we are in possession of the views of one Conservatoire professor, Chevalier Pastou, an elderly musician and a Napoleonic veteran, who taught ear-training and aural harmony and had invented a system of teaching then in common use, the *Lyre harmonique*, as it was called. He was without question capable of perceiving the candidate's qualifications as a contrapuntist. At the organ session he jotted down for his own use his various judgments. The following words are all that he wrote about Franck: "M. Franck, eighteen years six months; chorale—bass fair, upper parts excellent; fugue—some good points at the beginning, but often poor in the working-out." No reference to the skill or ingenuity of the dual treatment of the theme.[1] One may perhaps infer that through excess of technical facility Franck had made the error of confusing composition with improvisation. Entirely preoccupied with his self-imposed problem of counterpoint, he no doubt paid too little attention to the details of organ-technique. The same point occurred later in his life, even when his fame as an organist was at its height; time and again the criticism was expressed that in the excitement of improvising he allowed his style of playing to become too pianistic (or some similar comment). Six months of specialized study were insufficient to make of him an accomplished organist; even as long as thirty and forty years later his playing was characterized rather by fire and impetuosity than by accuracy, and he always had a tendency to treat the organ in a manner more suited to his first familiar instrument, the piano.

One can only speculate in the absence of knowledge; but some basis for speculation is to be found in the official reports on Franck's examination work during the year 1840–41—a source

---

[1] Pastou's notes are luckily preserved among his autographs at the Conservatoire library.

of information hitherto not tapped, it would seem. The Conservatoire registers contain certain comments like the following:
"M. Franck must put in some hard work. . . . Fugue still not up
to standard." The latter is Cherubini's own view on December
7, 1840. Berton, a composer of considerable age, was the adjudicator in June 1841, and wrote about Duvernoy: "Excellent, quite
exceptional on all sides"; but about Franck he left but one word
—"poor."

We may take it, I think, that the d'Indy legend foisted on
Franck was not exactly in accordance with the true story; blame
the judges as we may for incompetence and lack of perception,
the fact remains that it was the candidate's own limitations in
handling an instrument new to him, at which he was inexperienced
and only half-trained, that stood between César-Auguste and the
first prize. He may have earned his laurels as an improviser but
not as a performer.

There could be little doubt that the following year Franck
would carry off the first prize for organ with flying colours. It
is possible that he was turning over in his mind some fresh idea
for a new sensational appearance that would be on a par with his
success as a pianist. But he did not compete in 1842.

This was the year when he was due to submit a composition
for the Rome Prize. In his own mind he had no doubt at all
beforehand that he would win it, the more so because the other
entrants were of definitely inferior grade as musicians. He was
lifted off his feet, at this time, by his dual abilities and training in
organ-playing and composition. In the spring of 1842 he gave
in his notice that he was leaving the Conservatoire as a student.
There was general astonishment, and no one could imagine why
he had suddenly taken this amazing decision, which was not, of
course, his own, but his father's. His exit from the Conservatoire
is noted in the register quite simply as a "voluntary" retirement.
Chapter V will, perhaps, throw more light on his inner reasons;
but it is difficult to analyse so complex and sudden a change of
plans.

Franck had spent five years at the Royal Conservatoire under
the best available teachers. He had not wasted his time. He had
absorbed the best musical culture and background of his period,
and he had shown himself to be in many fields the superior of his
class-mates. Outside his normal work at the college and in those

many hours his ruthless father had forced him to devote to piano-practice and composition, merely for commercial ends, he had gained precious experience from the rehearsals of the Conservatoire's concerts. Into these the Conservatoire pupils were allowed to go freely, and perhaps his entry was made even more easy by the fact that Habeneck, the conductor, was his brother Joseph's professor of violin. One could hear there the symphonies of Haydn, Mozart, and Beethoven (Wagner himself records his astonishment at hearing Beethoven's later works there), overtures and arias by Méhul (well known by César-Auguste from childhood days in Liége), the best of Weber's overtures (also known to him in Belgium), a quantity of Handel, and less of Rameau. He was already familiar with many of the chamber works of these composers from his Liége experiences, and also because of the chamber-music meetings regularly given by first-rate players —among them the 'cellist Chevillard. In a more romantic vein, he had ready opportunity to hear the successful operas of the day (at the so-called French Opéra) by Meyerbeer, Halévy, and Rossini, who held the operatic field unchallenged, and also a large number of comic operas, dozens of gay tunes from which he borrowed for his popular 'fantasies' for piano solo or violin and piano.

Franck was not yet a fully educated musician; his knowledge was limited to music of the eighteenth century and the earlier years of the nineteenth. He had not come into contact with a single professor who could introduce him to music of a kind that would satisfy his contrapuntal instincts; he had not yet discovered the sixteenth-century masters. That rich harvest of the polyphonic music of the Renaissance was still lying ungarnered, known by none, not even the musical scholars of the time. This old music was to see the light again in unexpected and aristocratic surroundings—those of the Prince of Moscow—after he had left the Conservatoire. It is a curious fact, one that the imagination boggles at, that Franck was never interested in the polyphonic repertoire, not even when, fifty years after, one of his pupils, Henry Expert, decided to devote his whole life to its study.

CHAPTER IV

Teaching and Concert-giving during the Conservatoire Period
(1838–42)

WHILE he was working up for his final piano examination César-Auguste almost entirely gave up playing in public; as far as we know, he appeared only once during the scholastic year 1837–38, on April 1, 1838. He was then one of a group of artists who gave a long concert in the Salle Chantereine, one of his colleagues being no other than his young brother Joseph, who was still at the Conservatoire under Habeneck for violin and Le Couppey for *solfège*—for the latter subject he was to take the first prize at the end of the year. The others were the clarinet-player Liverini, the singers Oller and the two Mlles Cundell, the young violinist Lecointe (first prize at the Conservatoire in 1837), and the 'cellist Georges Hainl, who later became conductor first at the Grand Theatre at Lyons and then at the Paris Opéra.

The programme was typical and conformed to the fashions of the time—fashions before which even Chopin had to bow in his concerts: a septet by Moscheles (announced as "first performance in Paris"), a *Fantaisie concertante* composed by Osborne and de Bériot in collaboration, an anonymous sonata for clarinet and piano, arias and duets by Rossini and Mercadante, Thalberg's *Fantasia on "Don Giovanni,"* and a host of other items which included "the second grand *trio-concertante* in E flat," for piano, violin, and violoncello, by César-Auguste Franck—"first performance." As to the identity of this trio we know nothing, for only one Press-notice appeared, as far as we can discover—that in the *Ménestrel* of April 8, which confined itself to a line or two: "The audience at the Salle Chantereine warmly applauded the young pianist, and no less so Mlles Cundell and M. Hainl and Liverini. His compositions, too, were loudly acclaimed."

No reference is to be found in the musical Press to Franck as the brilliant prize-winner of the summer of 1838. His father seems to have neglected the chance of extracting publicity out of that spectacular event and the unique title it conferred on him. Rather he was looking, it would appear, to the possibilities of the teaching profession as a more ready source of livelihood than concert-work, and indeed, in the mid-nineteenth century, as in our own times, the financial return from concerts was slender at best, and more often showed a loss than a profit.

From the beginning of the autumn of 1838, Father Franck made efforts to have printed here and there an announcement like the following, which appeared in the *Revue et Gazette musicale* of September 23:

> M. César-Auguste Franck will inaugurate, on October 1 next, two classes for pianists, one for ladies and one for gentlemen. The course extends over nine months and will consist of three lessons a week of two hours each. Each class will be limited to five pupils. One day every week will be devoted entirely to sight-reading, analysis, and transposition, on a new method devised by M. Franck himself. Applicants should register at the professor's house, 22 Rue Montholon, on Wednesdays and Thursdays between 10.30 A.M. and noon. Should more than five students apply for each class admission will be by examination.

From this plain announcement we observe that the Conservatoire prize-winner makes no use of his academic success, but adopts certain of the procedures in use at the Conservatoire— the number and length of the lessons, for instance, and the resort to an entrance competition (was it in fact ever necessary?). There is also a subtle allusion to his recent sight-reading exploit in the new, simple, and personal method offered; of its exact nature we are ignorant.

Similar paragraphs appeared in the musical papers each subsequent year during October. In 1839 and 1840, after the second and first prizes for counterpoint and fugue, they were slightly expanded so as to cover these newly won awards. Thus in the *Ménestrel* of October 18, 1840, we read that

> M. César-Auguste Franck's courses in piano, harmony, counterpoint, and fugue, etc. will reopen for their third year on November 15. The syllabus and all particulars are available at his house, 22 Rue Montholon, on Sundays from 2 to 4 P.M.

Again on October 24, 1841, *La France musicale* announced the resumption of the classes for the fourth year on November 15, and gives the temporary address of the professor and his family at 6 Rue de Trévise, while on October 16, 1842, all three musical journals drew attention once more to the classes, but gave the new address of 43 Rue Laffitte.

In addition to these courses given in his own house, César-Auguste found it necessary (as he did all through the rest of his life) to take private pupils both in Paris itself and outside. He also took up teaching work in boarding schools, and for more than thirty years continued to teach in the most diverse institutions; the College Rollin, for example, where about 1842 the young Offenbach was teaching the 'cello; he and Franck even gave concerts together from time to time, for in those days the future composer of comic operas was a musician of no less high ideals than his pianist colleague and a fanatical enemy of that commercialism in music of which he later became one of the outstanding representatives. Then there were a young ladies' college at Auteuil, the Augustine College of the Assumption at 234 Faubourg Saint-Honoré, and the Jesuit College at Vaugirard, where some twenty-five years after he joined the staff he found among his pupils two of his future disciples—the composers Arthur Coquard and Henri Duparc; there was also the school in the Rue des Martyrs where he gave lessons in 1840 or so to a girl who later became his wife.

On an average the fees paid by such schools varied from one and a half to two francs a half-hour lesson. César-Auguste took it all in his stride; it was his profession and he loved music, even teaching it. In order to maintain his father, mother, and younger brother, he even took on without complaining all sorts of obscure jobs as an accompanist that ill accorded with his talents and successes at the Conservatoire.

It was a hard life for him, this incessant round of pupils, and not made easier by the ill-tempered and even vindictive behaviour of his father, who in his egotism continually wielded a grim and sometimes brutal authoritarianism that indelibly scarred his children's memories; family anecdotes galore about Nicolas-Joseph were handed down through César's children and grand-children, and recounted by his cousins and in particular by his future pupil Cécile Boutet de Monvel. It was forced labour indeed; the last ounce of pianistic energy was squeezed out of him daily, and in the matter of out-of-pocket expenses he was treated like a common thief. His itinerary was settled before he started, and the journeys between two lessons timed in advance with exactitude. Outside his professional calls he had no acquaintances. His day ended as early as possible after sundown so as to avoid unnecessary expenditure on candles. In his *Interviews from the Past*, Vincent d'Indy's father, who knew the family in 1840, styles Nicolas-Joseph "the Thénardier of music,"[1] and the cousins regarded him as his sons' evil genius. Many a tale has been told of the unfair threats with which he bullied his sons: "If you are disobedient, you know it is your *mother* who suffers for it. . . ."

The only advantage César-Auguste derived from his academic honours was a temporary association with the Conservatoire Concerts Society, and even that was of no financial value to him. Eight months after his successful examination, on March 24, 1839, he appeared as soloist with that famous orchestra, then conducted by Habeneck; between Beethoven's 'Pastoral' Symphony and a symphony of Mozart's he played the adagio and finale of the *E flat Fantaisie* of Hummel, whose piano-works he had often played and possessed complete in the form of his prize for counterpoint. But his performance under such select conditions seems to have awakened few repercussions, since these concerts were never reported in the ordinary way. Hector Berlioz, however, wrote in the *Revue musicale* on March 31, 1839, in high praise of "this young virtuoso's abilities, the brilliance, vigour, and precision of his playing, and the admirable qualities he displayed not only as pianist but as a musician."

He had also taken part in a remarkable concert two months previously in the Erard piano *salon*. It was not a recital; neither that title nor that type of concert yet existed, and Franz Liszt was the one man who dared to give what were at first called "solo concerts" or even "mono-concerts" in the manner that soon after became popular with pianists. César-Auguste's was the old-fashioned type of concert with a hotch-potch programme designed, not on artistic principles, but simply to show off in the most varied ways possible the artists taking part. This appalling programme is worth summarizing here as typical of the concerts of a hundred and more years ago. A long list of instrumental

[1] The reference is to the innkeeper in Victor Hugo's *Les Misérables*.

works was diversified with unspecified arias and duets sung by Annette Lebrun, whose very name is forgotten, Oller-Costello, and Ponchard, a violinist turned singer and a teacher of singing at the Paris Conservatoire. The main instrumental items included a quintet by Hummel, in which César-Auguste and Joseph Franck were joined by the 'cellist Franchomme and the double-bass player Labro (also on the Conservatoire staff); a "grand fantasy" by Doehler on melodies from Donizetti's opera *Anna Bolena*, which César played; a sonata by Hummel, played by the two brothers; a violin solo by de Bériot, played by Joseph; and three of César's own compositions—a new piano fantasy, one of the trios, and a cantata, *Notre Dame des orages* ("Our Lady of the Storms"). The cantata was in all probability written as a kind of practice-work for the Rome Prize competition. It cannot have been of much musical value since the composer—usually so careful about his manuscripts—did not keep a copy of it; but we know that the text was provided by the Count of Pastouret, a specialist in such librettos who wrote the poems for the Rome Prize cantatas in 1838, 1839, 1841, 1842, and 1843. The *Ménestrel* of January 13, 1839, considered it "a conscientious production, in which unfortunately the piano at times overwhelms the voice —no uncommon failing in pianist-composers."

An account of the concert (omitting all reference to the cantata, however) which appeared in the *Revue musicale* of January 17, 1839, is of some importance, for it mentions for the first time, and perhaps for the last, César-Auguste's recent academic successes.

> Last Thursday a concert was given by M. César-Auguste Franck at the *salons* of M. Erard. Particular interest attached to the event on account of the recent triumphs scored by the artist in the Conservatoire examinations, for a discerning public there had a chance of confirming the official opinion of the pundits. The audience applauded the young prize-winner in a manner that enhanced his academic rewards.

After a passage praising the performance of the Hummel quintet and commending the singers and Joseph, there followed an interesting discussion of the elder brother's work as a composer.

> M. Franck gave us a trio of his own, which shows that he has made good progress both in formal design and in continuity of ideas.

The part-writing exhibits skill and experience, and the melodic ideas, though one might criticize them as striking rather than original, are competently handled. In particular, the minuet deserves special mention as a happy conception carried out with great liveliness.

The trio in question was that in B flat, the second of the three trios published some three or four years later; it is known under the title of *Trio de Salon*. Ever since its publication the minuet has always been a favourite as an eighteenth-century pastiche that delights all ears.

The *Revue musicale* was no less kind to Franck as a player: "As a pianist, he won universal support, especially in Doehler's Fantasia on melodies from *Anna Bolena*, where he displayed all the ease and suppleness of his technique." An echo of these 1839 concerts even reached Germany; on May 15 the *Allgemeine Musikzeitung* hailed César Franck as the pupil of Zimmermann and as a first-class pianist, even putting him on a level with the virtuoso Anton von Kontski.

The concert, however—"too long and starting too late"— aroused no such enthusiasm in *La France musicale* (January 13); the article was signed with the initials A.M., but was actually written by Antoine Marmontel, a pianist, a year or two older than César-Auguste, who had gained the first prize for piano in 1832—not, we need hardly add, with similar honours! As the future successor at the Conservatoire of his old master, Zimmermann, he was doubtless suspicious instinctively of a possible rival, especially one with a unique academic record. Accordingly, the critic's sceptre in his hand, he looked down on his colleague from a superior level, with an almost insulting disdain.

To him the whole thing appeared less like a concert than like "a family reunion, with the two brothers—both very young— taking the stage turn by turn." César-Auguste he treated as a mere beginner:

M. C.-A. Franck may show considerable aptitude for the piano. But it is a matter of regret that he should submit his talents—as yet by no means mature—without further thought to the judgment of a critical public. Again, he shows promise of technical facility. When one day in the future, after studying some wise and carefully thought out piano method (like that of Thalberg and his school), he has gained the certainty of touch and the muscular firmness this difficult instrument demands, we have little doubt that he will take a high place in the great family of pianists.

One can well imagine with what exasperation the brilliant laureate must have read these condescending phrases and even more the rage of the impresario-father, who would take each one of them as a personal insult to himself!

Other concerts, mere family affairs, were given by the Franck brothers at the end of the season 1838–39 (May 30, 1839) and 1839–40 (May 31, 1840) at the Société d'Emulation (the Faubourg Saint-Germain group); they caused little stir; the *Ménestrel* alone printed a few complimentary lines recording their success. The programme comprised one of the forty or fifty *Duos concertants* written by Osborne and the violinist de Bériot in collaboration, an Air and Variations for Violin by the second-named, a famous *Fantaisie* of Thalberg's, and a 'Concert Solo' by César-Auguste. Such were the fashionable pieces of the time, beloved by the public whom Father Franck was determined to please.

Another 'grand concert' of the usual kind was given in the piano *salons* of Pape on February 27, 1840; here the two brothers were joined by the 'cellist Rignault and four singers; among the latter the leading light was undoubtedly the tenor Roger, of the Opéra-Comique, who sang some Schubert charmingly and an aria from Gluck's *Orpheus* less so. Four other vocal items alternated with the instrumental works, which included a violin piece of de Bériot's, played by Joseph; various studies written by the foremost pianists of the day; a salon-piece by Weber; and the 'Prayer' from Thalberg's *Moïse*, played by César, who also presented himself as a composer in one of his trios.

Apart from a few words about César's warm reception in the *Ménestrel* of March 1 and a word or two in *La France musicale* of April 5, there was a long notice from the pen of Maurice Bourges in the *Gazette*. The article merits some consideration here on account of both its importance and the status of the writer.

Maurice Bourges, not yet thirty years old but already one of the principal critics of music, was a literary man as well as a composer; he had written some chamber music as well as some theatre music for the Opéra-Comique, and had translated into French the oratorios of Bach and Mendelssohn and the operas of Weber. His opinion is clearly based on a careful observation of both the composer and the pianist, and as such its praise was worth having.

The trio which opened the concert was felt by Bourges to be "admirable in style and full of interesting points of detail." No doubt this was the *First Trio* of 1842, which later was recognized as important in the history of music, thanks to the belief and labours of Vincent d'Indy. Bourges, we notice, who may have heard it in 1840, laid no stress on its cyclic tendencies two years later. He praised it, indeed, as "the third item, which caught the general ear by its original lay-out" (he referred to the finale). The andante he found somewhat diffuse; "there are dull moments which the composer would be well advised to suppress." In his opinion, nevertheless, "this scrupulously constructed work offers to the composer yet a higher rung on the ladder that will lead him to a place among the great composers of chamber music." As for his piano-playing, Bourges admits freely that "it is a hard task for a pianist to merit any special distinction at this particular moment in the century when fine pianists are two a penny." But unreserved praise follows immediately:

> M. C.-A. Franck sweeps all difficulties out of his path as he proceeds. His fingers are extraordinarily lively; he is by turns mellow and energetic, elegant and warm-hearted, brilliant yet constructive in his style of playing. One after the other—and all with understanding—he gave us a little piece of Weber's, a group of studies by Moscheles, Chopin, Kalkbrenner, and Thalberg, in which he exhibited a sense of phrasing which is rare; after that, we heard the 'Prayer' from *Moïse*, a real test-piece, so well played that the audience could not wait till the end before applauding loudly.

An appreciative notice like this in the most important paper of the time was something of a public recognition, even a consecration of the academic judgments on him. It not only confirmed, but made public, his remarkable gifts. Unfortunately for César-Auguste, Maurice Bourges gave up his regular job as a concert critic to Henri Blanchard, though he still kept his place as one of the editorial board of the *Revue musicale*. Blanchard was no longer young—more than sixty years of age; he was a good musician, a violinist, a conductor, a composer of songs popular in the home, with some experience in theatre-music. But he had not the kindliness of his predecessor. Fétis, in his *Biographie universelle des musiciens*, characterizes him as "sarcastic, even malicious, in his epigrammatic comments." For several years the Franck family suffered under his verbal lash; not only César-Auguste and his brother Joseph, but their father too, teased Blanchard to a positively unjust frenzy of critical irritation.

After January 3 Blanchard made a first light thrust at the elder son, and then another, with a keener blade, at the impresario-father. The occasion was a concert held on December 27, 1840, in the course of which César-Auguste performed a transcription of Schubert's *Ave Maria* and the finale of *Lucia di Lammermoor*, a violin and piano sonata by Mendelssohn, his own *Premier Caprice*, a quintet by Rigel, and his own "Third Trio in F." This was not the *Third Trio* of 1842, whose finale was rewritten as the *Fourth Trio*. Another 'Third Trio,' in D minor, exists among Franck's unpublished works, bearing the opus number 22 in the first system of numbering. Blanchard poked a gentle finger of fun at César-Auguste for his familiarity with the musical fashions of the time as shown by his giving an invitation concert. Then, in the middle of commending the interpreta tion (with Joseph) of the Mendelssohn sonata, he suddenly picks up Nicolas-Joseph (whom he dubs "M. César-Auguste Franck, senior") and reproaches him for talking so loudly during his sons' performance as to provoke one of the audience to remark, "That awkward young man at the piano is making so much noise that one can't hear what that gentleman is saying!" He continues, sarcastically:

> We feel sure that in the case of M. César-Auguste Franck, senior, his paternal pride and his love of music (especially for his son's instrument, the piano) will be wounded more deeply by this remark than his pride as an orator will be flattered by this one listener's wish to hear him talk.

The *Gazette* indeed published on April 11, 1841, an article in praise of both the pianist and the composer as a sequel to the concert held on April 5 at his own house, but the note is short and has all the appearance of being based on 'information received.' On the 25th of the same month Henri Blanchard launched his main attack in full force, and a week later followed it up with strong reinforcements of irony.

About one of these two concerts Blanchard remarks that anyone may go in free, as in a bank, but that after listening to

one or two items a number of the audience went out by the
door opposite the one giving on to the Rue Valois. His cutting
notice continues:

> Like the Roman Emperors whose names he bears and who car-
> ried on their shoulders the mighty burdens of world government,
> M. César-Auguste Franck was weighed down by almost the entire
> musical responsibility of the concert. Two trios of his own com-
> posing, a solo, a quartet, and the final ensemble of the whole affair
> —César-Auguste coped manfully with them all. He came, he saw,
> he conquered: "Veni, vidi, vici." The young man unquestionably
> has talents, but his talents are mechanical. He skips about all over
> the keyboard, on and on without stopping. It is all very clean, neat,
> and dry. But as for inspiration, that is a closed book for him as
> either pianist or composer. He has knowledge, but no feeling. No
> musical phrase, no difficult passage work can alter the stereotyped
> smile on his face. . . .

And then a comparison is made with Vaucanson's famous
mechanical puppets!

One cannot help feeling that the thrower of such poisonous
darts was unfairly biassed. Was it really true that this brilliant
young hopeful from the Conservatoire, whose expressive and
even passionate playing had so recently fired his audiences, was
becoming the heartless automaton that Blanchard considered
him? It is surely more likely that the latter allowed his pen to be
carried away by the annoyance he felt against so obtrusive and
tactless a father who, in his blundering way, tried to display his
sons like goods in a shop-window, adopting the thick-skinned
methods of the commercial traveller.

As for the second concert, given on April 26, 1841, in aid of
a charity (Joseph and the singer Tagliafico assisting), the programme contained the Beethoven Quintet, a septet by Hummel,
and the usual assortment of show-pieces. In the *Gazette* of May 2
Blanchard contented himself with the sarcastic comment:

> Once again during the last few days M. César-Auguste Franck has
> given an afternoon concert at Pape's *salon*, but this time any profits
> were to be devoted to the poor in the parish of Saint-Vincent-de-
> Paul. That is certainly one way of gaining favour both with the
> angels and the critics, for what can even the most churlish critic say
> against a young man of such charitable instincts? Let us therefore
> only add that M. César-Auguste Franck, despite the pretentiousness

of his Christian names, played the music of Hummel and Beethoven with a modesty only equalled by his persuasive expressiveness.

A whole year passed by before César-Auguste—no doubt somewhat abashed by the pointedly ironic opposition of the leading musical journal—thought well to give a further concert. This next appearance of his as pianist-composer, supported by his brother Joseph and four other performers, occurred on March 11, 1842, and had for its object the demonstration of the high quality of Pape's latest production—an eight-octave piano, a marvellous instrument (according to the *Ménestrel* of March 20) which "did double honour to the manufacturer's skill and to M. César-Franck for the splendid effects he conjured from it."

Here was a new opening for Henri Blanchard's sarcasm. He entitled his article in the *Gazette* (March 20 also). "MM. César-Auguste Franck and Pape," and opened thus:

> A Roman Emperor and a Sovereign Pontiff (at least in name) joined together to give last Friday a musical evening at the rooms of the ancient chancellery of the Duke of Orleans in Rue Valois and Rue des Bon-Enfants. Pope and Emperor, Augustus Cæsar and Pope —the distinguished couple gave each other mutual support. M. César-Auguste Franck has evidently forgotten the old proverb which warns us that "if you run after two hares you will catch neither," for here he was in full cry hunting yet a third. He teaches the piano with some success, he plays the piano in the same way that he teaches it, and he hopes that he will be no less successful as a composer. Is there anyone alive who would set himself up against such a trinity of successes? We ourselves would not presume to do so.

Once again there is a palpable intention of making a fool of the young pianist-teacher-composer. The reason for this strange animosity will never be known, but it was undoubtedly personal, and no less certainly it was aimed more directly at the father, who was the impresario, than at the son, who was the musician.

We may well imagine that these incessant carpings contributed in full measure to the father's decision to renounce Paris for good and to set out in the company of César-Auguste to try his fortune in his native land.

Less than a month after this last concert came the abrupt resignation from the Conservatoire and the voyage of discovery in Belgium, under (it was hoped) the patronage of the King of the Belgians.

CHAPTER V

The Trios
(1842-43)

THE hurried flight from the Conservatoire as the scholastic year of 1841-42 was ending and a few days before the Rome-Prize competition, if not incomprehensible, is difficult to justify. Was the real reason, one wonders, the urgent need to give some concerts in Brussels so as to play immediately before the King the trios of one of his alleged subjects? To the mind of a man like Father Franck such a scheme would commend itself, for his particular game under the circumstances of the moment was to make the best of two worlds—of his double status as a Belgian born and as a French citizen. Should royal favours be granted, then his elder son would be certain to have a brilliant and publicly recognized career in his own country. The dangers of such a plan were obvious. Suppose César-Auguste should not finally give up all future hope of his future studies in composition and organ, but merely absent himself for a few weeks for a Belgian tour, even then his entry for the Rome Prize would have publicly acknowledged his French nationality, and thus the Belgian scheme would be ruined.

The family's own explanation, according to the composer's own words handed down to us through his children, was that his father desired to cut short any tendencies the young musician might develop in the direction of composing as his sole career— how he regretted this step later!—and above all to keep from him the knowledge that, thanks to his father's naturalization, he himself had been a French subject for six years past, or at least would become a full French citizen on attaining his majority.

This family tradition, based on César-Auguste's own reminiscences, has acquired a semi-official status through being recorded in Vincent d'Indy's biography. There are, in fact, certain contradictory elements in it. But maybe they are less important than the plain facts, patent for all to see; from April 22, 1842, onward César-Auguste at the age of nineteen and with high academic hopes before him ceased to be a student of organ and composition at the French national school of music, retired therefrom at his own wish (actually his father's), and was faced with the damning prospect of becoming a virtuoso-composer by profession, with the side-lines of being a church organist or a piano-teacher.

Immediately after his name was expunged from the registers at the Conservatoire he left for Belgium with his father and brother. As it turned out, the tour lasted, not, as always stated, three or four years, but no longer than the five months of the spring and summer season; it was indeed hardly more than a family holiday, with visits to Liége and the father's relations and Aix-la-Chappelle and the mother's.

One highly important event occurred during this voyage—an interview with Franz Liszt himself. The date is uncertain; it happened either about July 18, 1842, at Liége, where a festival in honour of Grétry was being held, or some days later at Brussels, where Liszt was conducting a concert and receiving various Parisian artists, in particular Mme Camille Pleyel, the one-time fiancée of Berlioz. As we shall see later, this meeting between the established pianist-composer and his beginner-colleague had important results for the latter.

By the opening of the next academic year the whole family was safely back in Paris, at 42 Rue Lafitte. The home life seems to have been normal, but rigidly ruled by paternal ambitions. César-Auguste was once more a piano-teacher who now and then, for advertising purposes, showed himself on the concert platform. As early as October he had announced the resumption of his usual classes and courses in piano, harmony, counterpoint, and fugue, as we know from the columns of the *Ménestrel*, the *Gazette*, and *La France musicale*.

One of his better-class pupils was a young man, one year older than the teacher, who had already made something of a reputation as an amateur musician, and whose family surname was destined later to come into the closest association with that of the Francks. He was Wilfrid d'Indy, uncle of the yet unborn Vincent d'Indy. Wilfrid had written some light operas, and also some sonatas, trios, and quartets, which unfortunately have made no mark on the annals of music, and was also by way of being a musical critic. A fluent pianist, he was in the habit of playing his drawing-room pieces with his violinist brother, Antonin, Vincent's father-to-be. According to *La France musicale* of June 19, 1842, the two of them won some applause for a performance of a certain *Grande Fantaisie concertante* of Wilfrid's own composition. The same fraternal team used at times to play Franck's trios, not of course in rivalry with those other two professional brothers. "We did not," one of them admits, "understand much about the scores, for we had not yet reached the level of psychological music, and believed that music should express emotion rather than philosophy or logic."[1]

The d'Indys' mother was a good musician and a capable pianist; a full account of her may be read in the author's biography of her grandson. She took a great interest in her sons' piano-master, and her name may be found in the list of subscribers to his trios.

Up to the autumn of 1842 the King of the Belgians had not shown any of the hoped-for favours to his so-called young subject. He then went to Paris, whereupon César-Auguste was instructed by his father to address to the King of what he believed to be his own country a petition for his Majesty to accept his trios as a token of homage and loyalty. The royal reply was favourable, according to information supplied by Franck senior and printed in *La France musicale* of January 8, 1843 (César-Auguste being described as a *Belgian* pianist and composer), and was certainly a promising start; no better augury for the successful launching of such a publication could be imagined than a royal dedication.

The subscription list was opened on November 1, 1842, and Father Franck applied himself to the task of gathering the names of all the musicians likely to be interested in newly published scores. To attract the main body of subscribers it was essential to gain the patronage of the famous—a heavy task involving letters and visits galore, but crowned with eventual success.

First on the list of purchasers—a precious document with autograph signatures carefully preserved among the family

[1] Coming as it does from Vincent d'Indy's father, the remark has special point: it may be found on pp. 280–281 of Antonin d'Indy's *Interviews Retrospectifs* (Paris, Ollendorf, 1894). For further information about Wilfrid d'Indy see the present author's book on Vincent d'Indy, vol. i.

papers, where it may be still seen—comes no less illustrious a name than Giacomo Meyerbeer; the second is that of Franz Liszt, followed by a brilliant catalogue of musical celebrities: Auber, successor to Cherubini as Director of the Conservatoire and composer of *La Muette de Portici* (known in England as *Masaniello*), the performance of which in 1830 in Brussels had precipitated the revolution there; Berton, professor at the Conservatoire and one-time examiner of César-Auguste, then nearing the end of his honourable career as an opera-composer; Uhran, violinist and viola-player, who had recently revived in *Les Huguenots* that long forgotten instrument the viola d'amore; Louis Adam, professor of piano at the Conservatoire, together with his son Adolphe Adam, the successful composer of *Le Chalet*, *Le Postillon de Longjumeau*, and *Si j'étais Roi;* Henri Herz, the piano-manufacturer who was also a first-rate virtuoso and taught at the Conservatoire; his elder brother, Jaques Herz, who was his assistant; another member of the Conservatoire staff, Panseron, known for his books on *solfège*, voice-training, and harmony; the Italian Donizetti and the Jewish Halévy, those two doughty champions of so-called French opera; Frédéric Chopin, who, with George Sand, was then living in the little phalanstery of the Square d'Orléans, and who, always difficult of approach, was reached through the help of Pauline Viardot; Camille Pleyel, composer and piano-manufacturer; Clapisson, the violinist whom the Institut de France was in 1854 to elect in preference to Berlioz; Onslow, a prolific composer whose works were then popular and are now totally forgotten; Ambroise Thomas, then just beginning his successful career in lyric opera; and so on and so forth.

There were seventeen patrons of the highest reputation, while the list of the 156 other subscribers includes the names of the aged Baron de Trémont, who had called on Beethoven in Vienna in 1809, the Prince de Ligne, Belgian Ambassador in Paris, and two ladies whose fame was to be perpetuated in the history of French music—the Countess Rézia d'Indy, grandmother of Vincent d'Indy and his strictest teacher, and Mme Desmousseaux, member of the Comédie Française and future mother-in-law of César-Auguste.

The subscription price was twelve francs and the total receipts were 2000 francs (£80 sterling), a considerable sum at that time and amply enough to cover the publishing costs. In the spring of 1843 appeared this collection of "Three Trios Concertants for piano, violin, and violoncello, composed by César-Auguste Franck and dedicated by permission to His Majesty the King of the Belgians." The actual marked price was eighteen francs per trio, forty-five francs for the three together; but, as was customary in the early nineteenth century, the real prices of sale were one-third of the marked price—that is to say, six francs and fifteen francs. The publisher Schlesinger, of 97 Rue de Richelieu, was responsible for the sale in France. For that country and for Belgium Franck retained all his rights, but ceded them for Germany to the Leipzig publisher Schuberth.

The publication was assured of success. Nicolas-Joseph Franck made considerable publicity in the musical Press, which published large display advertisements in their issues of the end of May and beginning of June. He saw to it that his son took the trouble to send personal presentation copies to a number of musicians in France and abroad; he also wanted César-Auguste to point to the importance of the set by forgetting his previous works and giving the new one the opus number '1.' Here he was certainly copying history, for in 1795 the young Beethoven had numbered his three trios (also published by subscription) Op. 1, though they came after a number of other youthful productions.

How were the trios received on publication—they had been already performed, and their composer continued to take part in them for another thirty or forty years? For all their grandiose patronage and the father's intensive advertising, the volumes do not seem to have attained a wide circulation in France. At that period the prevailing taste was for 'grandes fantaisies' or 'duos brillants,' for selections and arrangements from the operas, which would make such trio-sonatas look rather austere. César Franck's trios ran the risk of appearing too long, too learned, or (as one writer put it) too "scientific" to be popular. Outside the composer's own programmes they were hardly ever played. Between 1846 and 1871 Franck himself never gave them except in his family circle. Things were different in Germany, where, as we shall see, several distinguished musicians showed a lasting interest in them.

The musical Press in France seem to have attached little importance to the young composer-pianist's Opus 1; on their editorial staffs were few men sufficiently painstaking or well enough informed to be able to judge from a study of the score such seemingly difficult music; the majority of the critics spent their time merely reporting theatres and concerts. Among the principal reviews that we have been through one alone gave any account of the new trios, the *Gazette musicale;* but this one exception devoted to them a very long article of considerable merit, the author of it being Maurice Bourges, to whose ability and seriousness of purpose we have already drawn attention in connexion with a concert of 1840. His essay is worth recalling and examining in detail.

In his criticism Bourges makes a sharp distinction between the *Second Trio* (the *Trio de salon*) and the two on either side of it. For that one of the three he has nothing but the highest praise; the others arouse in him a measure of both admiration and uneasiness—a double reaction which may surprise us to-day, for we ourselves feel exactly the opposite one.

The *Trio de salon*, writes the critic of the *Gazette*, lives up to its title, for all its four movements are graceful and elegant. The first movement is always effective, distinguished in its ideas, with an attractive song-like melody of somewhat Italian style and skilfully contrived development; the andante is clear and straightforward in form, its melodies smooth and untarnished; the minuetto has something of the character of the chaconnes and passacaglias of French opera in the eighteenth century—he finds it worthy of Mouret, Rameau, and Mondonville in its charming ideas "set out and discussed with a skill unknown in our own time." The effect produced towards the end by the combining of the two subjects is original and striking. He considers the finale, however, less noteworthy, its main subject being "a somewhat commonplace sister of the modern galop," and the canonic writing too spun out.

Bourges's opinion is quite other than that held nowadays about this trio, which, if not absolutely shelved, is well-nigh forgotten. Vincent d'Indy's view in 1905 was that the work was

strongly influenced by Weber and Schubert; adorned by the composer himself with a whimsical and restrictive title, it has little of interest to offer us except some rhythmic elegances in the andante and especially in the finale.

It is still pleasant enough to listen to for those who are not bent on finding in it any of the Franckian or pre-Franckian characteristics, of which it possesses none. Those one can find in the other two trios, which are not *salon* works and in the purity of their style are closely related to classical chamber music.

Maurice Bourges treated this pair of works together as experimental music, which he adds should not however be condemned in any puritanical or Jansenistic spirit. "These indiscretions," he writes,

> offer something of a challenge to the grey-beards, and are in fact typical of a beard just beginning to grow; nothing can provide a clearer promise of developing strength than these juvenile boldnesses foretelling a future power and vitality.

César-Auguste was vindicated by Bourges, even if he annoyed the more conservative musicians by refusing to tread on the heels of his predecessors.

These two trios were a mixture of varied elements—pomposity, broad calmness, the fantastic, even the savage, he considered.

> The listener's imagination can jump at will from the austere invocation of a patriarch to the shrieks of joy of cannibals surrounding their victim, from tumultuous and bloodshot scenes of revolution to lugubrious processions of penitents under the deep shadows of their sombre veils. Here is unadulterated melodrama; it is like an English novel in the style of Ann Radcliffe.

So poetical an interpretation may seem extravagant to-day and might lead one to imagine—wrongly, however—that the writer of the article had no working knowledge of the German music of his time, saturated as it was by vigorous romanticism. The judgments of this musical critic cannot avoid astonishing us at times. He can praise the composer for his skilful writing and scoring, for his powers of development and construction, yet the harmonic style seems often to incur his censure; thus we read:

> There is an excessive desire to shock the ear without humouring it, and to make a constant display of novelty by out-of-the-way harmony and unusual combinations of sounds. . . . The acerbity and brusqueness of the dissonances are not easy to tolerate. . . . Certain passages are so hazardous that the ear refuses to accept them . . . awkward modulations foreshortened and not reasoned out.

In such respects the composer was not showing that he was what he certainly ought to be—"the humble servant of musical grammar and logic." Nevertheless, in both works he found "many excellent pages, a thoughtful idealism, a broad feeling for form, and a fine sense of general effect, which assure the composer's future." Perhaps the faults remarked by Bourges are the very qualities that to our ears, a hundred years later, recommend these trios and still give them a measure of life.

As regards the *First Trio*, "where two subjects of a pleasant and decisive character form almost the whole material of the three movements," the writer in the *Gazette* attached no importance whatever to the question of cyclic form, of which since the end of the nineteenth century we have tended to overrate the value. In all probability he had come across various essays in cyclic form in the later works of Beethoven. But it did not enter his head to think of Franck, at that time full of Beethoven and naturally inclined to follow the example of the master and his successors, as the one musician destined firmly to re-establish a musical tradition that came from sources other than Beethoven, in adopting the practice of theme-transference between the movements of a sonata. It remained for Vincent d'Indy, with his trained and untiring enthusiasm, to make that clear fifty years later.

The *Third Trio* Bourges thought "vague and indecisive in imagination," less fresh in its melodic ideas, and thus "having less chance of public favour." But he made one general remark worth repeating, so close is it to the judgment on the *Quintet* expressed forty years later by Franz Liszt:

> There are not lacking signs that the true medium for this work is the orchestra. The ideas in it are often unsuited to the medium of chamber music, and this it is, we feel sure, that gives the trio a general feeling of awkwardness, of confused thought, and of monotony.

Certainly this critic gave good advice to a young composer who scorned to follow the beaten track and was burning to open up new vistas, to make his own voyage of discovery on the sea of music, by pointing out the more dangerous aspects of originality, eccentricity, and independence of mind. He ended his advice, nevertheless, on a note of optimism: "Faith and hope must ever be the burden of the song sung by all explorers and composers."

Round the *First Trio*, in F sharp minor, Vincent d'Indy has woven a pretty and affecting legend which is still in currency: the legend of a young genius—"another like him is not to be found in any other country in the world!"—who was the first to "pick up the threads of Beethoven's discourse, so rudely cut off by Fate and lying unused and unnoticed on the ground," of the genius who, alone in his time, made use in the various movements of a work of a single directing theme, a kind of symphonic *leitmotiv*, and had by this means inaugurated the modern scheme of cyclic composition. D'Indy's *César Franck* (published in 1905) gives a full demonstration of this 'creative thought' realized by a young man only twenty years old—a demonstration (or should one call it a 'gratuitous assertion'?) which the pious disciple repeated on every available occasion, notably in his interesting memoir that was delivered before the Société Française de Musicologie on December 19, 1922, and printed in the *Revue de musicologie* of February 1923. This account of Franck, written long after the 1905 book, contains a short analysis which differs from the earlier one. The question is raised there, not of *two* cyclic themes, but of *three*, "all three expounded in the first movement, returning in the second, and coming to a climax of musical expression in the third."

In reality, the *First Trio* as a whole is little more than an imitation—one might almost call it a 'tracing'—of the sonatas, trios, and quartets of Beethoven, or even other composers, attentively studied by this gifted young musician, who early familiarized himself with the chamber music of the great German master and also with that of Schubert, Schumann, and Liszt. Through the trio there shines something of the spirit and the style of those composers, who, from the beginning of the nineteenth century, had already adopted the cyclic pattern, even if unconsciously and unsystematically. Schubert, before all, we can plainly see searching for thematic unity in his *Fantaisies*, Opp. 15 and 103, and in his E flat minor Quartet, Op. 125. Franck knew his Schubert well and loved him, and in 1844 transcribed for piano four of his songs. We can see, too, something of a 'pre-Franckist' character in Schubert's shifting tonalities.

To recognize the merits of the *First Trio*, there is no need whatever to attribute to it the imaginary virtue of having originated cyclic form, for in that matter it was no more than an adaptation of previous ideas. We can observe in the work, as in its companions, certain awkwardnesses, certain reminiscent passages, certain pianistic commonplaces in the style of the 1840's; we may notice the abuse of the unison in the scoring, the stationary tonality so surprising in one who later became the champion of continual modulation (the first two movements remain in the one key, major or minor, of F sharp without moving even to the dominant!); we may perceive, along with some delicate piano-writing, a promising tendency towards chromaticism—the result perhaps of his familiarity with the works of Liszt, his model, or at any rate the model imposed on him by his father. At the same time no one can help admiring the deep dramatic feeling, the captivating lyrical outpouring, which were almost unknown in French music at this period, and which provide a foretaste, one might say a prophecy, of the passionate tumult of soul that forty years later brought into being the impetuous *Quintet*. Far more important than the reasonably good instrumental writing and the not very striking recurrence of the themes are the fine emotional qualities of the work, its disciplined intensity of spirit, its prolific melodic invention, which won the welcome and active sympathy of Franz Liszt and, later, of Hans von Bülow and other German musicians.

For the emotional force of the *First Trio*, which touches the heart of every man, for its recurring themes, which strike practically no one, Vincent d'Indy has propounded a dramatic explanation, a kind of romantic exegesis, which is not improbable and may therefore be retained here. There is no indication that this explanation emanated from Franck himself, but it was quite possibly transmitted more or less as we have it by the Master to his disciple.

> One might say that the first theme is searching under multiple disguises and subtle transformations to entice the second theme along into its own turbulent atmosphere; but the theme resists temptation right to the end by the unaided power of its own simple and serene purity.

The *Third Trio*, in B minor, though clearly superior to the second (the *Trio de salon*), is not equal in value to the first. There is too

much filling in on the piano, as well as an abuse of runs and of
double-stopping. Yet, especially in the first movement, we find
some good themes either vigorous or charming, and the finale
has a quality only accounted for by the date of its composition,
several years subsequent to that of the other two movements.

After leaving the Paris Conservatoire in 1842, as we have seen
at the opening of this chapter, César-Auguste made the acquaintance in Belgium of Franz Liszt, already at the height of his
fame. The celebrated virtuoso read through the three trios, then
in preparation for publishing. He expressed admiration for the
set as a whole, but considered the finale of No. 3 too long; in
his opinion this movement could well constitute a complete work
on its own. He had no difficulty in persuading his newly made
friend to replace it by a shorter movement, which was written
during that same year of 1842. It is not surprising that the new
finale showed much firmer handling than the others, and also a
higher symphonic purpose. Vincent d'Indy praised its Beethoven-
like spirit and drew attention to its ingenious variations and its
curious alternating rhythms.

The finale withdrawn from the *Third Trio* became the *Fourth
Trio* (Op. 2), separately published by Schuberth for all foreign
countries and, like the others, reserved for France by the composer himself; the title-page bears a grateful dedication from
César-Auguste to his "friend Franz Liszt." The *Fourth Trio* thus
contains one movement only, which is notable for the lyrical
quality of its themes and the feverish character of certain acces-
sory chromatic figures. Vincent d'Indy points to a lack of
balance, but acknowledges the work's superiority over the *Second
Trio* and even the *Third Trio*.

Liszt liked this Opus 2 and often played it, as he did the three
others of Opus 1. It was probably the design and length of the
single movement that excluded it from French programmes. The
first performance in France—or, at least, in Paris, at the Société
Nationale—was not given until December 14, 1878, nearly forty
years after publication. On the other hand, the publisher
Schuberth made it widely known all over Germany, a proof of
which is to be found in the numerous editions of his *Musikalischer
Conversations-Lexikon*, containing this entry:

> These four piano trios rank among the best-written musical con-
> ceptions of modern times. When Franz Liszt received at his house

the pick of the musicians of the day, he would always prefer to play them the Trios by Franck.

Farther on we shall come upon other proofs of the surprising diffusion of these works in Germany.

We can guess the date of the *Fourth Trio*, not of its composition, but of its adaptation (1842). With regard to the three previous trios, it has always been accepted that they were written only shortly before the time of their subscription, in 1842; Vincent d'Indy has dated them 1841. In reality they are anterior to that date; they have undoubtedly been confused with some other pieces written several years earlier, for three instruments, or with a *Symphonie concertante* (Op. 13, according to the first numbering). The *Trio de salon* is in all probability the work performed on January 10, 1839, by the young composer with his brother Joseph Franck and the 'cellist Franchomme—a concert we have mentioned before. Perhaps it may be nothing else but the *Grand Trio concertant*, in E minor, transposed into another key, that was played on April 1, 1838, with Joseph Franck and Georges Hainl the 'cellist. An odd conjuncture of circumstances, difficult to explain otherwise, leads us to the above belief. In a review of the printed copy of Opus 1 Maurice Bourges wrote about the *Trio de salon*:

> The learned doctors will no doubt notice and condemn in the score some consecutive fifths in similar motion between the violoncello and the upper part of the left hand, bars 71, 72, and 78 of the finale.

Now would this musical critic have been likely to pay attention to such academic trifles and bothered with printing them if his attention had not been directly drawn to such minor details? One observes, however, that on the manuscript of the *Second Trio* (Op. 16 in the old numbering) the following note by César-Auguste appears: "The composer forewarns the student that he will find three consecutive fifths in this movement." May we not take it then that it was this candid statement, repeated verbally, that suggested to Maurice Bourges his little harmonic dig? A simple enough conjecture, in truth, for we have not been able to find among the family archives this *Third Trio*, which has been written about elsewhere by Julien Tiersot and Pierre de Bréville. Another trio (Op. 22, old numbering), in D minor, might even be the first version, transposed, of the *First Trio*, the famous one in F sharp minor, which, as we have seen, was played on February 21, 1840, by the brothers Franck and the 'cellist Rignault.

Thus, the famous trios of 1841, published in 1843, must come from several years earlier than the date fixed by Vicent d'Indy; Franck must have written them between his fifteenth and his eighteenth years; and long before their publication as Op. 1 and Op. 2 they had several times been put to the test of public performance in Paris and Brussels without anyone noticing their supposed cyclic connexion with a form alleged to have been abandoned since Beethoven.

CHAPTER VI

Concerts from 1842 to 1845

DURING the period of the subscribing and publishing of the trios, and for several years afterwards, the Francks were in the habit of giving a weekly concert in their own house. The important part of the programmes was César-Auguste's own compositions—the trios, of course, which had achieved the actuality of print, and numerous other pieces, mostly for piano-solo, which bore the opus numbers 3 to 15. The usual Grand Caprices and Fantasias on tunes from the fashionable operas had the greatest success; but there was also chamber music other than the trios; we may be permitted to leave on one side the piano-solo with string orchestra which the composer resuscitated in the form of a duet between Ruth and Boaz in his later Biblical eclogue *Ruth*.

These family recitals were not confined to the two sons of the house and their usual associates. Foreign artists visiting Paris were also to be heard, especially pianists; like the Bavarian Joseph Schad (1812–79), who from living in Switzerland was counted a Swiss, but from 1847 settled in Bordeaux, or the Danish Rudolf Willmers (1821–78), composer of a nocturne entitled *Sérénade érotique*. The guests (as we know from the *Gazette musicale* of February 5, 1843) played their own works. There is no question that that shrewd business-man, Nicolas-Joseph, gained a great deal of goodwill from such artists at the mere cost of his musical 'at homes.'

On the whole the Press was favourable to Franck at both his private and public appearances, but at times made reservations, some with sly touches of humour aroused less by the skill of the principal performer than by the grandiose and slightly ridiculous Christian names with which he had been saddled and by the indiscreet behaviour of the organizer (that is, of course, his father). One or two harsh comments may be found, for example, in the course of the year 1845.

The general tone of the criticisms of 1843 is more moderate, with occasional ironic flashes; for instance (*Gazette musicale* of February 5, 1843):

> M. Franck, whose ambitious Christian names we decline to remember any longer, is a young artist of skill both as a composer and as a pianist. It is not his fault if he lacks that indescribable something which carries one off one's feet; not all the criticism in the world can give it to him. Let it be said then that his piano-playing is fluent, crisp, and sparkling; his composing that of a man with his wits about him.

The same paper on March 25, dealing with a concert given the night before at the Erard piano *salons*, indulges in a mild pun:

> M. César-Auguste Franck announces in his programme that he comes from Liége; *légerdemain*, alas, he conspicuously lacks. He played firmly and produced some good effects in his *Trio in F sharp minor*, dedicated to H.R.H. the King of the Belgians. . . . César-Auguste Franck from Liége should be satisfied with France, as France is with him.

Various works by the pianist himself were played, for piano, for violin (by Joseph), for 'cello (by Chevillard), for solo voice and vocal trio and for female-voice choir; it is probable that the vocal items were extracts either from a cantata designed for the Rome Prize, or from the opera *Stradella*, a student-work written in sketch form at this time.

Of *Stradella* there remain a complete manuscript and also separate copies of a vocal trio. The score, a thick volume of 160 pages, is inscribed on the title-page: "*Stradella*, opera in three acts, text by Émile Deschamps, music by César-Auguste Franck." It consists of a series of arias, duets, trios, and choruses, all with piano accompaniment. Only towards the end does one find any orchestral indications, and they are all rather childish: "organ alone at first, later the orchestra joins in. . .muted violins. . . trombones. . .full brass. . ." This suite of detached pieces is preceded by an overture pieced together from their material. The manuscript bears no sign of place or date of composition, but on the parts for the vocal trios occurs the address "15 Rue la Bruyère," where the Francks housed themselves at the end of 1844 after leaving the Rue Laffitte. These minor problems of *Stradella* are easy enough to solve. The score was based on a libretto already set by Niedermeyer as an opera produced in Paris in 1836. It cannot therefore have been intended for theatrical representation, and was indeed no more than a long student-exercise—a supposition made even more probable in that the manuscript copy is not, like all the other works, carefully written out, but confused and careless, though the trio-parts are clear enough.

To fill any concert-hall it was essential to engage a number of artists, each with his own following, for there was at the time an enormous number of concerts being held in Paris. The celebrated Castil-Blaze claims in *La France musicale* of April 16, 1843, that he had had five hundred concerts to cover since November, and that on Sunday, April 2, alone, he was expected to listen to nine announced for the same hour. A more picturesque account of this plethora of performances is given by Chevalier Pastou, professor at the Conservatoire and subscriber to the Franck trio-edition, in a letter to be found in autograph in the library of the Conservatoire. When the singer Géraldy asked him for complimentary tickets for his benefit concert Pastou sent them at once with a note saying: "My dear friend, the public has been so over-fed with concerts this season that it is impossible to sell a single ticket—not even for the most popular singers."

The concerts given by the brothers Franck were held in inexpensive halls of no great repute, so that, frequent though they were, they seldom received as much as a mention in the papers. However, *La France musicale* of April 23, 1843, noticed the Francks' appearance "at a musical evening given by the Count of M." (the Count of Montendre, a keen music-lover, to whom César-Auguste in this same year dedicated his *Andante quietoso*, for violin and piano), where they played along with the 'cellist Lebouc two of the Beethoven trios.

At the end of the year the family impresario once again dragged them off on a short tour, which he announced in the musical papers of June 25; the plan was for them to appear in public in Northern France, at Cambrai, Valenciennes, and so on, and after that (so the announcement alleged) "in the principal towns in Belgium and Germany." As it fell out, these "principal towns in Belgium" reduced themselves to Liége, Spa, and Brussels, while those in Germany seem to have been one only—Aix-la-Chapelle, where, owing to their mother's birth there, they were

sure to collect an audience of relations, friends, and family connexions. César-Auguste and Joseph had the honour of performing
the trios at the Palace of Laeken before King Leopold I; an important event, no doubt, but one which was not followed (any more
than the royal dedication of the trios was) by the splendid results
dreamed of by the father of these two virtuosos of dual (or, at
least, uncertain) nationality.

We find a tiny echo of the two Brussels concerts in the *Gazette
musicale* of August 13—a polite line or two merely recording the
event and the success of the trios at Pape's piano *salons*. A more
important article of the 27th of the same month prints an account
of the concert given on the 10th at the Grande Harmonie Hall.
There the Francks are recognized as Belgians and, indeed,
acclaimed as such:

> A few weeks ago we had occasion to applaud the first efforts of
> M. César-Auguste Franck, still a very young man, and we made no
> doubt then that his precocious talents would develop in the most
> brilliant manner. Our expectations have not been deceived. A
> promising young pianist has become already a master, and Belgium
> may add one more great artist to her roll of great musicians. Diffi-
> culties do not exist for him; he overcomes the most formidable
> barriers without effort and also without losing one whit of his
> natural delicacy and expressive power. The pieces of his own
> composition which he played yesterday show harmonic insight;
> he is clearly of a serious turn of mind which under wise guidance
> should open up a wide outlet for his abilities. His younger brother,
> Joseph, follows worthily in his footsteps; we listened to his violin
> solo with great pleasure, for he has a pure tone and a fine expressive-
> ness—qualities that should later bring him into the first rank of
> violinists.

One programme preserved in the family archives shows that
the young Francks made good use of local musical societies; at
the Liége concert of October 27 we find, among the *Trio de salon*
and the usual pieces by Thalberg and de Bériot (a violin and
piano fantasy on *Les Huguenots*), choral items by the local Orpheus
Society. This is the concert referred to with an error of date in
the *Gazette musicale* of December 17, 1843.

Not long after his return to Paris César-Auguste received a
gold medal from the King of the Belgians (his rightful King, as
he believed). The *Gazette musicale* of December 31, 1843, tells

the glad news to the French musical public by quoting the following paragraphs from the *Journal de Liége*:

> H.M. the King of the Belgians, in a letter dated the 8th of this month, has bestowed a magnificent gold medal on M. César-Auguste Franck, already well known as a pianist. On the obverse is a portrait of the King and on the reverse the inscription: "Presented by H.M. the King of the Belgians to César-Auguste Franck." This remarkable pianist-composer recently dedicated to His Majesty three trios written by himself for piano, violin, and violoncello; the works have had considerable success already and their composer was unanimously acclaimed when he played them at his concerts in Aix-la-Chapelle, Brussels, and Liége.

The medal in question is, of course, that of 1842, about which the father issued at least three public announcements.

Great honour, little profit! It seemed as if the only result of that royal dedication, to which father had so fondly looked for financial reward, was a pretty little medal in gold! Teaching must again be resorted to, and that soon; and so we read in *La France musicale* and the *Gazette* of December 24, 1843, the familiar advertisement that, "having returned from his tour," César-Auguste would re-open his courses and classes at 43 Rue Laffitte, and all the rest of the rigmarole.

Illness disturbed the even cause of the year 1844. On two occasions the *Gazette musicale* published bulletins of César-Auguste's state of health; the first, on March 24, said that he had been laid up by a serious complaint for three months, but was so far recovered that he hoped soon to resume his teaching; the second, on November 3, that he was back in harness, in terms like these: "Our young and already famous pianist and contrapuntist M. César-Auguste Franck, of Liége, is now fully restored to health—a matter of congratulation to his many pupils and friends." This was followed, we need hardly add, by the usual announcement of his practical and theoretical classes, this time at the new address of 15 Rue Labruyère.

His indisposition did not prevent Franck from giving in the spring of 1844 his usual concerts at home, which caused a short notice in the *Gazette* of March 31, commenting on the warm welcome of the large public attending: "M. Auguste Franck is a pianist who plays and interprets all kinds of works, and also transcribes the songs of Schubert, and does it all very well; his own music he performs with no less skill."

The piano transcriptions of four Schubert songs here referred to were published by Chaillot in 1844, about the same time as Richault published three other pieces for piano or piano and violin—occasional works often played by the composer, like the fantasies on Dalayrac's *Gulistan*, which had just been produced at the Opéra-Comique along with an operatic triple-bill of Adolphe Adam's works. At this period César-Auguste also wrote a *Ballade* for piano (Op. 9) and a solo for piano with string accompaniment. These two latter compositions may be seen in the family records, the second reappearing the following year in the score of *Ruth*.

One need feel no surprise at the number of fantasies Franck wrote on the fashionable light operas like *Gulistan* if one remembers the public taste for such things under Louis-Philippe. There is a one-page advertisement to be seen in the *Gazette* of October 27, 1844, devoted entirely to the publications of Schlesinger: on that single page one finds announced four 'grand duets' by Kalkbrenner and Panofka on *La Reine de Chypre*, *La Favorita*, *La Juive*, and *Charles VI*; various selections of the same kind from *Les Huguenots*, made by Thalberg and de Bériot; others on *Beatrice di Tenda*, by Thalberg and Panofka; on *Robert Le Diable*, by Wolff and de Bériot; on *La Favorita*, *Le Reine de Chypre*, and *Guitarrero*, by Panofka; some *Fantaisies concertantes* on *Les Huguenots*, by Vieuxtemps and Grégoir, on *La Favorita* and *La Juive*, by Messemaker—but we will not continue the list. Music from the theatre, from grand opera, lyric opera, Italian opera, was spilling over the edge into the concert-halls; the public would always flock in to hear such 'fantaisies' and 'duos brillants,' but showed no interest whatever, save for an enlightened few, in serious and seemingly austere chamber music. Nicolas-Joseph's first interest was money; in exploiting his children he could hardly be expected not to force his elder son's talent for composition into the most profitable channel.

The autumn of 1844 brought to César-Auguste the pleasure of reading in the *Gazette musicale* (issue of October 13) a most complimentary notice of his variations for piano-duet on *God save the King*—his Opus 4, written in 1842 for his English pupils,

the sisters Stratton. A leading critic, Georges Kastner, wrote
about it thus:

> This is the work of an accomplished musician; we have long
> known M. Franck as such, and the duet now before us can only add
> to his reputation. It is in fact a striking piece, skilfully developed,
> well written for the instrument, and, above all, distinguished by the
> interest and variety of its formal lay-out.

These words should have been printed some time before they
actually appeared; the reason for the delay was political, explained
by the writer thus: "Our relations with a certain neighbouring
country were recently of a kind to prevent our publishing a
critical account of a work based on *God save the King*."[1]

Good auspices ushered in the birth of the new year of 1845.
Through the influence of Féréol, a veteran of the Opéra-Comique
of whom more will be written later, the Franck brothers were
engaged by the Musical Institute of Orléans to give there a
chamber-music concert. It was a great success, although their
programme was, we gather, a little stiff for a provincial public;
for among the items performed were works by Weber and by
César-Auguste himself, in particular the duet on airs from
Gulistan published in the preceding year. This was the first of a
prolonged series of concerts given in Orléans, to which we shall
have further occasion to refer.

At home, in the family centre of 15 Rue Labruyère, the
youngsters continued their recitals before an invited audience of
students and music-lovers. The centre of their programmes was
occupied by César-Auguste and his latest compositions. One
could, of course, have heard the Andantino for violin and piano
already referred to, and once again the trios, especially the *Trio
de salon*, played by the brothers with Chevillard the 'cellist. An
anonymous contributor to the *Gazette musicale* had reached the
new stage of admiring them as music "less for their technical
achievement than for their melodic inventiveness."

[1] He refers to one of the various Syrian incidents which from time to time disturbed the
friendly relations between England and France.

This autumn of 1844 a young man from Lyons, but of Hungarian origin, came to
Paris to make a first appearance; he was Charles Widor, composer, pianist, and organist.
He returned at once to Lyons, where he had a numerous following. Charles Widor was
destined to become, in the next year, the father of a son, Charles-Marie, the future
rival of César Franck as a virtuoso organist, and his successor in the professorship of organ
and improvisation at the Paris Conservatoire.

The one ambition of Nicolas-Joseph Franck just now was to attract the musical Press to his family recitals. He not only invited the critics, but, according to one of them, begged them to "make his son known, not only to the musical public in France, but to the wider public all over Europe." His shattering persistence caused nothing but sardonic laughter at first.

At that time the concert reporter of the *Gazette musicale* had taken to writing under a pseudonym; the one he chose, thinking it to be a perfect cover for his real identity, was "The Rover of Concerts."[1] His account of the March 5 concert published on the 9th of that month has a distinctly ironic flavour. He wrote:

> The Ides of March will not, we hope, be fatal to César-Auguste Franck as they were to Julius Cæsar. On the first Thursday of this inauspicious month César-Auguste performed, with his brother and M. Chevillard as companions, a trio for piano, violin, and violoncello of Marschner and another of his own composition, a sonata by Mendelssohn, a ballade for solo piano (also written by M. Auguste Franck), and (at the end) the Beethoven *Sonata in C minor* for violin and piano (Op. 30, No. 2), again with his brother. M. César-Auguste played well and untiringly; but we observe that in the manner of the true Prince-Emperor he was averse to taking all the honours unto himself, and took special pains that the proper proportion of applause should be allotted to the singer, Mlle Blanche Feyteau.

All such ironical play on his son's slightly ridiculous Christian names damped Nicolas-Joseph's ambitions about as much as water on a duck's back. He was proud of those patronymics, and he was undaunted in his assaults on those papers which had dared to underrate the manifest successes of his offspring. A concert has been planned for the 16th of March in Erard's piano *salon*. Good! We must get some advance publicity—"This young artist has not been heard in public for two whole years; yet he is beyond dispute one of our most distinguished pianists at the present moment, and one whom every one wishes to hear."

On this occasion "The Rover of Concerts" was a little more acid:

---

[1] Thus, in English, he styled himself, in the hope no doubt of a cross-Channel anonymity; he may even have hoped that readers would believe that his contributions were translated into French in the office, but his soubriquet should have been properly translated into English.

When it comes to pianists and the most famous performers in that class we must never forget M. C.-Auguste Franck, nor indeed his brother, nor even his father, M. Franck from Liége. The relations between musical critics and musicians who are out to make a successful career for themselves are always touchy. We can hardly avoid writing about these careerist violinists and pianists—so carefully nursed, so well publicized—that they play with elegance and charm; that if, by chance, they lack musical inspiration and the compelling force of genius, at least they have ease and facility. Whereupon they are up in arms and at once take steps to see that all their friends loudly proclaim the brilliance, the breadth, the general magnificence of their work; their friends of course pooh-pooh those minor virtues that one has commented on, and add that we could well do without those envious musical critics. And now for the three Francks—father, son, and Holy—but, no! We will only say "the younger son." They have some sort of a following; they have too the knack of squeezing the last drop of publicity out of their so-called reputation. They are like those authors who after publishing a new book, not only think but loudly assert that the worst fate that can befall them is to be ignored; they would rather be attacked, made fun of, torn to pieces by the critics than not be noticed at all, and so die in obscurity. And, of course, the authors are perfectly right.

Thereafter he arrives at a final judgment of the music and its interpreters, even of the impresario:

> Let us say then that the elder of the Franck sons has considerable gifts as a pianist and that he combines with them the usual self-importance of the commonplace composer. He keeps all the rules, but evidently does not know the extent of the public's powers of endurance, which, despite the proverbial politeness of the French people, wilts before the incalculable prolixity of the trios and other works of M. César-Auguste Franck. We would add that M. Joseph Franck's naïveté as a violinist is only equalled by that of M. Franck senior's admiration for his progeny; about them all there is some primitive and patriarchal quality which makes the critic hesitate to go farther or to think too seriously about M. Franck from Liége.

The imperial Christian names, the continual references to Liége, and the arrogance of the impresario-father worked together (it would seem) in depriving the musical critics of that calm impartiality essential to fair judgment. What exactly Nicolas-Joseph Franck's reactions were we can only conjecture; but it

would seem from the *Gazette musicale* that he showed his feelings
with more than his usual tactlessness, and even possibly with
some display of muscular force. For a scathing article appeared
in that paper on May 18, in which the true name of "The Rover
of Concerts" was revealed as none other than Henri Blanchard,
the epigrammatist quoted on previous pages.

The article opens in general terms, but its meaning soon
becomes both particular and transparent. In spite of the length,
parts of it must be printed here. Blanchard writes:

> The musical critic has early to learn to brave the wrath, the bitter
> spite shown by virtuosos who (as Montaigne has pointed out) can
> never have enough praise. Subscribers to the *Gazette musicale* could
> not possibly imagine how often the young students of harmony
> impose "false relations" on the poor critic. For the most part these
> cases of difficult and equivocal relations between critic and criticized
> are merely comical, but now and then they take on a more serious,
> even a dangerous, aspect; we take the liberty of drawing attention
> to one of the latter kind. One of these harmony students and his
> supporters, puffed up with an almost childish self-esteem, are fiercely
> indignant about certain articles of ours, resentful that our apprecia-
> tions have sometimes been spiced with an ironical humour and even
> with some legitimate criticism. They set themselves out, therefore,
> to call in question our competence in matters musical. But when it
> was conclusively proved to them that we were fully competent to
> criticize and qualified by knowledge to judge the causes at issue one
> of them began to show a disposition to resort to violence. The
> particular person who had guaranteed our fitness for the task
> countered this display by informing them that we were not the
> kind of person to be frightened by such threats, and that any act of
> brutal aggression would be energetically resisted. After a lapse of
> several days we received from one of these blustering artists an
> invitation to a musical evening at his own house. In spite of the
> good advice given us by certain over-cautious friends not to go near
> the place, we accepted the invitation and actually went, having taken
> the precaution to write to one of those friends to put some flowers
> on our grave should we succumb during this terrifying expedition;
> though (let us add) we privately expected to encounter nothing more
> perilous than a purely musical ambuscade, in the form of some
> never-ending sonata, fantasy, or trio which would kill us with
> boredom. What happened in fact on our arrival was that we were
> warmly welcomed and had to submit to no more lethal weapons
> than a few vain promises accompanied by compliments and thanks.

At this point in his article Henri Blanchard pins down the object at which he is aiming too firmly to allow a shadow of doubt. "And now let us come back to those virtuosos who have by no means said their last say on the concert platform—M. César-Auguste Franck, to quote one example." After praising some "interesting young ladies," who, as Franck's pupils, showed his skill as a teacher, and after a short note on a vocal trio, he continues:

> Music for the theatre does not need learned musicianship as much as freshness of melody, swiftness of movement too—that is to say, the whole business of *tempi* is indispensable to success in the lyric drama.

It is easy to imagine the embarrassment felt by César-Auguste at the centre of these polemics, and also his positive horror at this new and outlandish publicity consequent upon the clumsy audacities of his father. There must have been bitter passages between the latter and César-Auguste, who despite his age remained a mere boy, and was in any case a dutiful son. Think, too, of the atmosphere at home! Here were the mother and one son ranged against the musical manœuvrings of the father. The young man, too modest to fly into a passion, could only suffer in silence; there was no one to whom he could confide is sorrows save his mother and one girl-friend who now began to take an important place in the pattern of his life.

CHAPTER VII

"Ruth"
(1845–46)

THESE difficulties with the critics (especially the critic of the *Gazette musicale*), coupled with the financial failure of the concerts—nearly always inevitable, but most surely so at a time of such abundant musical provision—successfully deflected the business-man in Nicolas-Joseph Franck from any further notions of making a fortune, or even a livelihood, out of the exploitation of the virtuoso talents of his elder son and the lesser gifts of his younger. Too many pianists were cluttering up the streets of Paris for there to be any hope of César-Auguste's reaping a profit from the performer's life. True, Chopin was not often seen on the public platform, but that brilliant meteor Franz Liszt was constantly flashing across the Parisian skies; his rival, Thalberg, had firmly settled himself in the Horace Vernet mansion; Mme Pleyel, Berlioz's one-time fiancée, was enjoying a great success with her gifts that (so it was said) "combined the elegance of Chopin, Thalberg, and Doehler with the virility of Liszt"; quantities of foreign pianists came to the capital in search of its blessing, considered at the time indispensable to success elsewhere —on one day alone, at the end of 1844, the arrivals were announced of the Austrian Léopold de Meyer, the Bohemian Karl Evers, and the German Dreyschock!

The father devised a new and ambitious scheme for displaying his son's genius before the world. The idea was no more original this time than before; just as he had wanted César-Auguste to follow in Liszt's footsteps by adopting the career of a pianist-composer, and in those of Beethoven by starting on a new phase as a composer by the issue in 1842 of his three trios as Opus 1, so now he was taking for his new model the striking and double triumph scored in December 1844 by Félicien David with his symphonic ode *The Desert*.[1]

Oriental subjects were fashionable, and Father Franck was not one to miss the chance of profiting by the vogue when forcing his son to write music in accordance with the taste of the period. Why, then, should not César-Auguste follow the example of David, who like himself had studied the organ at the Conservatoire under Benoist? Why, indeed, should he not pick on or revive for a full-size choral and orchestral score an oriental subject, best of all a Biblical subject? César-Auguste thereupon decided to follow in the footsteps of the composer of *Joseph*, his fellow-Belgian Méhul, for whom he had entertained the liveliest admiration since his earliest days. Surely this was the very moment to produce a major score for voices and orchestra, one capable of attracting, not only the restricted few who would go to chamber concerts, but the vast general public!

It seems likely (as we shall show later) that César-Auguste made some use here of an earlier work of his childhood or, at least, his adolescence; it is possible too that the idea of a Biblical libretto was suggested to him by his close friend the Abbé Gounod. However that may be, a rhymester named Alexandre Guillemin was found willing to undertake the labour of piecing together a scenario on the Old Testament history of Ruth and Boaz, and to turn into verse (or at least rhyme) the Bible text of the story with as little alteration as possible. César-Auguste gave up writing the polite piano-pieces that he had been pouring out in 1844, in order to devote himself entirely to the new task, with the result that in a few months he composed or sketched out the music of *Ruth* in the form of some fifteen 'numbers' for soloists, chorus, and orchestra.

On September 9, 1845, the last note was added to the orchestral score, with the date written thus: "9/9 + 18/45." The next business was to find performers. A small group of singers was enrolled which included Mlles Mondutaigny (prize-winner at the Conservatoire in 1843) as Ruth, Moisson as Naomi, and Caut as

[1] The performance of *The Desert*, which had an astonishing success and was often to be repeated, had been preceded in the previous week by the first performance at the Conservatoire of another work of the same kind, *The Last King of Judah*. Maurice Bourges wrote the libretto, Georges Kastner the music, of the latter piece. Both writers had praised Franck as player and composer in their capacity as musical critics in the *Gazette musicale*. Franck's attention had certainly been attracted by this other biblical work, whose good qualities were overshadowed by the brilliant success of *The Desert*.

Orpah, with Obin as Boaz and Jourdan as a reaper. The Erard *salon* was hired for a performance of the new (or, perhaps, reconstituted) work before an invited audience—hardly a performance, since there was no chorus, and the orchestral part was played on the piano by the composer.

Nicolas-Joseph Franck was not one whit less active over this concert than he had been, four years earlier, over the subscribing of the trios, in his efforts to gain the patronage of all the leading musicians of the day. And he was highly successful. That evening there could have been seen at the Erard *salon* the illustrious Spontini, then aged seventy and living in retirement; Halévy and Meyerbeer, the Jewish princes of French opera, both at the height of their fame and in full production; Adolphe Adam, who had abandoned composition for the realization of his dream of a national lyric theatre; Moscheles, who was soon to be appointed a professor at Leipzig; Pixis, then passing through Paris; Stephen Heller, a composer considered at the time difficult and experimental; Alkan, already celebrated as both pianist and composer; Georges Kuhn, organist and professor at the Conservatoire; and, above all, Franz Liszt, a devoted admirer of our young musician. The one important name missing from this distinguished gathering is that of Hector Berlioz, who was at that moment engaged in giving concerts in Austria.

The presence of this galaxy of the great on that evening did not, however, constitute a proper 'first performance'; rather, it was an advance play-through or public rehearsal. It aroused, in fact, but little interest. The *Gazette musicale* was alone in publishing any proper account of it. Once again the writer was the arch-enemy of the Franck family, Henri Blanchard, and once again he could not resist playing his usual little games—for example, in his extended article, from which we quote passages below, he does not once mention the composer's name! With his habitual sarcasm—no less irritating as one got used to it—he is content with attributing the paternity of *Ruth* to "a young man already known in the musical world on account of his pompous classical Christian names, César-Auguste."

After a few meaningless words of introduction, Blanchard amuses himself by recalling in no sympathetic manner the young composer's instrumental music, so often heard in the form of trios: "For him melody and harmony seem to be no more than a kaleidoscope producing random geometrical patterns." The melodic style appears to Blanchard to proceed "not by conjunct intervals or motion, but by a rocky mountain-path." The new Biblical eclogue he considers an improvement on the earlier works as being "more genuinely musical and more tuneful," though it does not approach "the pure and even noble style of Méhul in his *Joseph*." Nevertheless he recognizes "the clarity and the simplicity of the conception." The rest of the notice alternates between praise and blame; thus the introduction is criticized for "the frequent leaps of a fourth in the melodies" while the Chorus of Reapers is admired for its "originality and charm."

One interesting sentence points out a resemblance between a passage in *Ruth* and a Berlioz work, the March of the Moabites recalling the Pilgrims' March in the latter's *Harold in Italy* on account of its form, its atmosphere of mystery, and its pedal-points. Another striking observation concerns the duet between Ruth and Boaz; to express the full significance of this, we are told, the composer would have needed "the poetic genius of M. de Lamartine and that precious store of melody which Rossini possessed in his prime."

This first major work showed, we must confess, little originality; there were many traces of Schubert and Berlioz, an evident influence of Méhul, and even something perhaps of Félicien David. Yet it would appear that at this first play-through on the piano all the great were attentive and afterwards complimentary, though we have no record of what they actually said.

The success was sufficiently marked, at any rate, for the decision to be made to give a further performance of *Ruth*, this time in its complete array of chorus and full orchestra. The Conservatoire itself had witnessed the first performance of *The Desert*; no other place could be considered eligible for the presentation of the new sacred eclogue. But an essential preliminary to booking the hall was to obtain the official sanction of the Minister, Montalivet, who was responsible to Louis-Philippe for his civil list. César-Auguste made this ministerial approach through the aid of Franz Liszt, who had supported his trios in 1842; the celebrated virtuoso (always so willing to help his fellow-musicians) made in turn his approach to the Comte de Montalivet through the intermediary of Ary Scheffer, the painter. To Scheffer Liszt wrote a long letter on November 12, 1845, ending with these words:

> The object of my writing you can be plainly stated: will you have the kindness to say a word or two in M. de Montalivet's ear about the special merits of M. Franck for his consideration, and if possible persuade His Excellency to grant permission for the use of the Hall of the Conservatoire during the course of the winter months for a performance of his oratorio?

One would wish to print Liszt's letter entire; here however is its essence, interesting to us, not only for its kindly picture of Franck's abilities, but also as showing the firm judgment on them expressed by a man of exceptional qualifications:

> M. César-Auguste Franck has made two mistakes. First, his Christian names are César-Auguste; second, he writes good music quite seriously. He is the bearer of this letter to you. I am sure that Meyerbeer has already confirmed to you the high opinion which I have expressed about his oratorio *Ruth*, and I have little doubt that the sincere support of that great master will carry great weight with you.

Farther on Liszt continues:

> The important thing at the moment for this young man is to find a time and a place for a full audition. If only he could benefit by some scheme for musical productions similar to that which painters enjoy with their annual or even decennial art exhibitions I have not the least doubt that the subject of my recommendation would at once distinguish himself above all other aspirants; for among all those young hopefuls who sweat blood and water to set down their musical dreams on our recalcitrant manuscript paper, I do not know three who are his equals. It is not enough to have a high value as a composer; it is imperative to make that value known to and recognized by all, and before achieving that end there are grave difficulties and many rungs of the ladder to climb.

Liszt was not unaware of certain barriers to success in young Franck himself. "He will find the road," writes Liszt,

> steeper and more rocky than others may, for, as I have told you, he made the fundamental error of being christened César-Auguste, and, in addition, I fancy he is lacking in that convenient social sense

that opens all doors before him. For these very reasons, I venture to suggest to you that men of spirit and good will should rally on his side, and the great friendship which you have for so many years shown towards me makes me hope that you will forgive any indiscretion I may have made in thus approaching you at this moment.

With Meyerbeer and Liszt behind it, the application was readily acceded to. Before long, announcements began to appear that on January 4, 1846, a formal performance of *Ruth* would take place. To the singers named above (save that this time Mlle Lavoye of the Opéra-Comique took the original singer's place in the part of Ruth) were added an orchestra of forty-eight players and a choir of seventy voices under the direction of Tilmant, at that time conductor of the Théâtre-Italien and assistant to Habeneck at the Société des Concerts du Conservatoire.

Among the crowd assembled in that historic hall the *Journal des Débats* noted the presence of Meyerbeer and Spontini (his second hearing), who "on several occasions gave active signs of their keen approval of the music."

Only the most important of the many Press notices will be referred to here—those of the *Gazette musicale* and the *Journal des Débats*.

Once more the duty of reporting the concert for the *Gazette* fell upon the inimical Henri Blanchard. Even his few words of praise had something of an ironic flavour, nor could he keep away from his gibes about the composer's names:

> In spite of the pompous and ambitious titles bestowed on him at birth, for which indeed he cannot be held responsible, M. César-Auguste Franck is naïveté itself, and this natural simplicity he has turned to good use in writing his oratorio *Ruth*.

In truth, it was a well-merited criticism!

The writer had already expressed his opinion of the score at the previous piano run-through, and therefore confined himself to commenting on the orchestration—favourably perforce: "Such restrained scoring is very rare with young composers." He pointed once more to the kinship between the Moabites' March and the Pilgrims' March from Berlioz's *Harold in Italy*, a family likeness made plainer by the orchestral treatment. He refers again to the beauties of the Reapers' song, though expressing regret that it was not further developed and even recapitulated, and also to the broad effect of the Twilight song—the latter was actually encored at the performance. And he praised the skilful distribution of the wind instruments in the Introduction, which however he found "over-long and somewhat monotonous in melodic design."

Blanchard's article concludes thus:

> We may therefore account this a success for M. Franck and his performers. On the other hand, we may be permitted to advise the young composer to turn his hand next to a more purely emotional subject if he wishes as an artist to live up to his splendid names. All through the score this Biblical and mystical love-story glows with no greater brightness than a few faint glimmers in a musical twilight. The composer seems to be always within hail of the Promised Land, but never to reach it. He tries hard enough, indeed, for he indulges in an over-fondness for orchestral tremolos. In Naomi's aria—tremolo; when Boaz sends for the Moabites—tremolo; he foretells that his progeny by Ruth shall be blessed—tremolo; and dozens of other tremolos that need not be particularized here.

The article in the *Journal des Débats* of January 20 was of more importance on account of its length and its wide circulation. It was not written by Berlioz, who was then at Prague on a concert-tour, but by a conscientious musician signing himself "E.D." Though these initials might suggest that the author of the article was Deldevez, the future conductor of the Société des Concerts du Conservatoire, in all probability they referred to one Desmarest who reported opera in Berlioz's absence. Meticulously detailed and sympathetic, his account covers two whole pages of the *Débats*.

From the start he recalls David's success with *The Desert* and refers also to Berlioz; he writes:

> M. Franck is a young pianist whose handful of compositions—all of them well written and original—have attracted the attention of serious artists, but whose name, barely a month or two ago, was as unknown to the general public perhaps as that of M. Félicien David before the first performance of *The Desert*.

The critic's intention is to copy Berlioz's fraternal gesture to David by claiming him as a welcome newcomer to France's roll of important composers; in attempting to do so, he writes thus:

To make a man great overnight is the prerogative of kings, and the task in music should be left to the kings of criticism. That is, I fear, an unhappy circumstance for M. Franck, for, if I were entitled by my position to do so, I would award him at least some of the splinters torn from that crown which a year ago, in like conditions, M. Berlioz demanded for the composer of *The Desert*—how splendidly he worded his demand, my readers will remember.

A flattering start, clearly intended to catch the reader's attention! After that Berlioz's understudy goes more deeply into the music of *Ruth* itself, largely in the most laudatory spirit. All the same, he slips in a criticism of the opening of the second part where there are introduced "certain imitations of the viols and the bagpipes and those mountain-pasture calls on the oboe which from time long past have been the property of Switzerland, the Tyrol, or the Auvergne." The special beauty of the Evening Prayer (that is, the Twilight song, the second number of the published score) is singled out for praise; about its second verse, "Glory to God," the critic writes that "it pours out an unanimous feeling of delight, and as a result had to be played twice." The article also rightly points out that in this Evening Prayer, in 8-bar phrase-rhythm, "the modulation from the minor to the major in the fifth bar, given as it is to the whole chorus, produces a most imposing effect."

The writer went so far as to see in César-Auguste "the new white hope of the modern school of music," and supported his opinion by praising the composer's individuality in avoiding the common Italian banalities and his "lucid, firm, and colourful orchestration, which never displays itself at the expense of the basic harmonic scheme."

To form a reasoned estimate of the quality of *Ruth* as it was heard in 1845–46, one has to study the full score in its original form of that date, which (along with the second version) has been carefully kept among the family papers. The version for voice and piano that Hartmann eventually published after the 1870 war contains a large number of corrections and rewritings that were added to the first version after a lapse of twenty-five years of thought or, at least, of patient writing. Vincent d'Indy unfortunately used the later Hartmann text, comparatively modern in style, as the basis for his warm appreciation of the work that appears in his book on César Franck (1906). He did not consult the original manuscript, and, indeed, was unaware of its existence. We shall deal on a later page with the remodelled 1871 version and how it was received.

It is hard to believe that the whole of the first version of *Ruth* was written in the year of 1845, especially as the composer himself admitted having made use in it of an earlier work, a piece for piano-solo with string quartet accompaniment. One does not doubt young Franck's intention, his determination, to compose a work of genuine Biblical simplicity, but one cannot forget that he was still the brilliant prize-winner in the Conservatoire classes for counterpoint and fugue, schooled in every technical musical device, and taking a great delight therein. Yet the whole of the first section (the part that has not undergone substantial revision) is so naïve as to be positively childish. Melodically, it is at best artless; the puerile harmony is both flat and meaningless, while the choral writing is no more than a string of platitudes; there is a total absence of polyphony, and the modulation is feeble, despite some sudden changes of key in the typical Franckist manner, without mention of a disregard for accent and prosody which cries out for ironic comments! All these palpable short-comings, on the other hand, are most probably the very qualities which produced in that audience of a hundred years ago the impression of an unsullied ingenuousness of soul which seems to have touched them deeply, and which no doubt was the impression that Father Franck, in his anxiety to recapture something of *The Desert's* overnight success, had urged his son to try to produce.

Simplicity is the rarest of all good qualities, according to Saint-Saëns. That composer, discussing Félicien David in an essay reproduced in his *Harmonie et Mélodie*, wrote the following words which apply equally to *Ruth* and to César Franck:

> Ingenuousness—simplicity—it was by such quality of mind that David attained his remarkable successes with *Lalla-Rookh* and *The Desert*. The public was not expecting that. The public is ready for anything else that may come along—majestic effects, delicate moments, striking melodies, sonorous orchestration, new and original harmonies, and so on—but it stands defenceless before a mind which opens its inner recesses to the world and says quite simply what it means.

Immediately after the performance of January 4, 1846, the
Duke of Montpensier summoned César-Auguste to his box to
offer his personal congratulations, informing him that his Biblical
eclogue would very soon be given a performance at Court. Here
was a hopeful piece of news! After the neglect on the part of
the King of the Belgians it now really looked as if Nicolas-Joseph
was to receive full compensation from the royal family of
France, which would provide a good opportunity for César-
Auguste and his brother to adopt officially their father's naturalization.

A suitably grand announcement was hurried off to the newspapers and reviews, but unfortunately it had none of the hoped-for
results. Instead, the *Ménestrel* gave but a couple of lines to a bare
statement of the world-shaking news, while *La France musicale*
of January 11 reproduced the father's letter in full, including the
end of it which ran: "I shall be greatly obliged if you could
kindly see your way to mentioning this official announcement,"
and added with cruel irony: "It will readily be seen that an
official announcement as important as that which M. Franck
senior has sent to us relieves us of any obligation to print an
account of his son's oratorio." The same inopportune com-
muniqué had the effect of loosening Blanchard's ironical pen; he
ends his long report by saying:

If by any chance we should appear to be a little severe on M.
Franck, the reason is that he is young, that he has been well taught,
and that he is about to be honoured by all the splendours of the
French Royal Court, and even perhaps by M. Acache, the delegate
of the Emperor of Morocco.

The concert at the Court of Louis-Phillipe never advanced
beyond the stage of a hopeful project. An attempt was made to
fill the gap by giving a further concert on March 20 at the Erard
salon, comprising certain portions of *Ruth* (with piano alone)
and four other unspecified items. Thwarted by the failure of the
royal project, Nicolas-Joseph kept up his courage and began to
turn over new ideas in his head. He suddenly remembered that
after the first triumphant success of *The Desert* Félicien David's
oratorio had been presented at the Théâtre-Italien: here was a
wonderful precedent to follow! So he instantly made it public
that his son's work was on the point of receiving the same honour:

"It is now almost certain that the new oratorio will be played in its entirety at the Théâtre-Italien in the early part of next month." The next month passed by, and the succeeding months as well, but nothing happened. The grandiose but costly scheme evaporated into thin air! After the spring of 1846 *Ruth* was destined, like the *Damnation de Faust* at the end of the same year, to sink into a long sleep of oblivion.

CHAPTER VIII

Idyll: Betrothal and Marriage
(1840–48)

DURING the early forties César-Auguste Franck had picked out from among his pupils at the boarding-school in the Rue des Martyrs a certain girl who showed unusual musical talent—Félicité Saillot. She continued learning music with him after her normal scholastic terms had ended, and went on with her piano, harmony, and even a little elementary composition.

Eugénie-Félicité-Caroline Saillot (1824–1918) made use of the theatrical name of her parents, the Desmousseaux, who played at the Comédie-Française. On the mother's side she sprang from the celebrated dynasty of the Baptistes; at one period in the history of the national theatre they had provided a major portion of its cast. Daughter, granddaughter, great-granddaughter of actors in French comedy, she was the first to break the family tradition by not herself entering the theatrical business. Her education, especially from her mother, was strict and precise, on the conventional lines of the upper middle classes.

Her father, Félicité-Auguste Saillot (1785–1854), whose stage-name was Desmousseaux, was a reasonably good actor and also a man of culture and intelligence. He had given good service to the Comédie-Française, as much on the business side as on the performer's. One of his colleagues described him as "a man naturally capable of success in any profession except, unfortunately, the one he had embraced!" The criticism is over-severe, for he was continuously on the stage for twenty-eight years; his success could not have been due, as has been suggested, solely to the influence of the actor Baptiste, whom he succeeded in the rôles of the 'heavy father' after marrying his daughter.

This daughter, Françoise-Josephine-Anselme (Baptiste) (1790–1857), had studied under her father at the Paris Conservatoire. From her twenty-fifth year onward she played the title-rôles at the Comédie-Française as a soubrette, parts that ill suited her; after 1817 she turned to playing the parts of tragic confidantes and duennas, in which she was very successful. So great was her talent that she acted at the theatre until 1852—that is, till her sixty-third year. She took her husband's stage name, and was always referred to as Madame Desmousseaux.

Sensitive and intelligent, she had a great love for music and was herself an amateur singer; her name appears on the list of subscribers in 1842 for the trios of Franck. Her daughter's education was of close interest to her, and as a result she became friendly with the young piano-teacher, whose character she admired as much as his musical gifts, even studying herself under him for a time. She would amuse herself by writing little dance-movements on themes given her by César-Auguste. Towards him she always showed a truly maternal kindness.

Félicité Saillot-Desmousseaux did not give up her music lessons when she left school; indeed she appeared at Franck's pupils' concerts, in the accounts of which her name is to be found, and during this time her mother pressed her to do some composing on her own.

A great friendship grew up between the Desmousseaux and their daughter's teacher; master and pupil were something of the same age, only two years dividing them. The friendship developed to intimacy, and our "famous master" and "young women's oracle," as he was called, soon came to look on the Desmousseaux as a new-found family. In his own family his mother's affection never quite made up for the masterful inhumanity of his father. He found great compensation in the Desmousseaux family and their house—the charm of a young girl, soon to be his betrothed, the kindly understanding of two Comédie-Française players of experience, an intellectual background, an aura of general affection towards him. He arranged matters so that he could spend more time at the house than was strictly necessary for his lessons, at least when he could avoid his father's relentless eye. And Mme Desmousseaux aided and abetted him by an underground plan of her own devising, which enabled César-Auguste to come to them to work at music, especially at composition, without having to send in an account of the time thus snatched from his proper musical duties.

The Desmousseaux family put themselves to some inconvenience to find concerts and pupils for their young friend. It is not beyond credibility that through the family Franck made himself known in the specialized circle of the Comédie-Française, and it is a matter of certainty that his engagements at Orléans were the result of his new friends' influence. As we have seen, the town of Orléans engaged the two brothers Franck for the first time to play there in 1845. César-Auguste revisited the town five times each winter for the next twenty years or so, not as a soloist, but as the accompanist of the municipal concerts held there. This regular employment may be put down to the influence of a cousin of the Desmousseaux, Louis Second (surnamed Féréol), who, after a period of study at the military college of Saint-Cyr, had suddenly achieved a brilliant career as a singer at the Opéra-Comique. He then retired, went to Orléans to live, and became Captain of the Fire Brigade—a most important figure in the town.

Claire, daughter of this second Louis, spent several months in Paris between 1845 and 1847 to study piano-playing and the theory of music with César-Auguste, with a view to becoming her father's accompanist at his singing-lessons, and during this period she lived at the Desmousseaux family home, a kind of sisterly rival of her teacher's *fiancée*. She left behind for us to read some delightful portraits and pictures of her Parisian visits. Her *Vieux Souvenirs* has never been published, but in the manuscript one can read of Félicité Desmousseaux's "doting" on her piano-teacher. "Félicité," we are told,

> had but one ambition in her musical work—to satisfy M. Franck, and she was therefore bowed down with a continual fear lest she might make the smallest finger-slip in her lessons which would make him tap his foot with impatience—a common habit of his in front of his pupils! So seldom did these lessons occur without tears as the result that Desmousseaux was in the habit of nicknaming the daughter "my musical Niobe."

A curious and important incident took place in 1846, not long after the first performance at the Conservatoire of *Ruth*, the reception of which had worn down Father Franck's ambitions to a mere shadow; it was an incident which hurried on and made inevitable the pending separation between father and son.

César-Auguste wrote a setting of the familiar poem of Reboul, *L'Ange et l'enfant* ("The Angel and the Child")—a moving little

song, full of charm and simplicity and meaning. Vincent d'Indy
calls it "a little masterpiece of expressive song." His father either
took a dislike to the song itself, or he was exasperated in a tyrannical mood by the somewhat imprudent dedication, "To Mlle
F. Desmousseaux, in pleasant memories." In any case, Father
Franck found in this manuscript the proof of his son's intention
to get married, a project to be damned on principle, since marriage would inevitably interfere with his son's future career as a
virtuoso pianist. He tore up the score. Revolted by such an
abominable act, César-Auguste hastened off to the Desmousseaux
household to write out from memory a second copy, and then to
present it instantly to young Félicité.[1] At that very moment he
made up his mind to leave his parents' home for good and all,
and to live alone; he determined to rid himself of an unbearable
paternal oppression, and to lead his own life, not as a bullied and
nomadic virtuoso, but as a quietly established professional
musician.

Before completing his new plans he had of course to continue
his teaching to the end of the academic year, so as to cause no
dislocation in his pupils' lives. At the beginning of May he took
part in a charity concert at the Salle Erard. On the 18th of the
same month he had the pleasant task of offering to his fiancée a
signed copy of his song *Combien j'ai douce souvenance* ("How
sweet my memories are"), which was before long to be published
with a dedication to Pauline Viardot. On June 1 he held a pupils'
concert, at which Félicité Desmousseaux could have been heard
playing an andante of Thalberg and, as a piano-duet with one of
her fellow-pupils, Mlle Cordier (a singer as well as a pianist), a
new piece by César-Auguste. Joseph Franck played as a violinist
and also as a pianist, joining with his brother in a duet arrangement of an air from Grétry's *Lucile* which had just been published by Pacini-Bonaldi. This particular pupils' concert was to
be the last public appearance César-Auguste made under his
father's domination: an account of it can be read in the *Gazette*
of June 7.

The conditions of this family break-up were aggravated by
the extraordinary maliciousness of the father, which showed
itself in all manner of ways: one day, as we have seen, he would

---

[1] *L'Ange et l'enfant* was not to see the light of public print for thirty-two years; in 1878
Hamelle published it with a new dedication prefixed thereto: "To Mme César Franck."

rail at César-Auguste for causing distress to his mother; the next he would forecast a disastrous future for anyone like his son, and shout at him: "Don't forget what happened to M. de Praslin!" (At this period all the talk of the town was the case of M. de Praslin, who had been poisoned by his wife.) Happily César-Auguste had once again his mother on his side; in the face of all the sorrow the separation might cause her, she remained firm in her belief in her son's level-headedness and love. On her son's suggestion the hour fixed for his departure from his family was a Sunday afternoon, at a time when the parents would be taking their weekly stroll. It was indeed a hurried flight, for the composer could carry away only a few personal possessions, and was obliged to leave behind with his tyrannical father nearly all his music as well as his fine grand piano, a precious reminder of the Grand Prix d'Honneur at the Conservatoire in 1838. So strong was his filial affection, however, that he also left behind him a written undertaking to pay off all his father's debts, which the latter alleged had been incurred solely in educating his son; they totalled 11,000 francs—the equivalent, that is, of more than a million francs in 1951.

César-Auguste was well aware that in thus leaving his father's house he had condemned himself to lead the obscure and modest life of a humble music-teacher. He voluntarily gave up all hope of his name's appearing in those newspapers and reviews which under the irksome solicitations of his father had been in the habit of writing kindly notices of his work as a pianist and composer. Gone were all the excessive publicity and its effect on the critics; the virtuoso had retired from public view to a life which would be no longer embittered by the ambition to follow in the footsteps of Liszt or to vie with the most celebrated pianists.

It was César-Auguste's intention to make a clean break with his father and to let it be known he had done so; he therefore ceased to tack on to his name the words "from Liége," which were thereafter used only by his brother Joseph; he dropped the second of his imperial Christian names that had been made such fun of; he became plain César Franck and mostly signed himself merely "C. Franck." He was determined to become a new person, as different as possible from the other.

A large part of his time outside his numerous teaching-periods he spent with the Desmousseaux family. Life with them was peaceful and even at times gay. Throughout his childhood and adolescence César had lived in complete isolation, condemned by his father to the forced labour of a virtuoso and a fashionable composer, practically without friends and with no emotional support save his mother's love for him. For the first time in his life he found himself among people who were personally sympathetic to him and even, because of his string of successes, laudatory of him. His ready acceptance in the family was comforting to his fiancée's parents—Desmousseaux, a man of experience, took a hand in managing his business affairs; Félicité was absolutely whole-hearted in her love for him; her friends were amused by the shyness, openness, and engaging candour of this exceptional young man, already famous yet no more than a boy. He presented a manuscript of his song *Robin Gray* to his fiancée's cousin, who had come from Orléans to study the piano with him and whose memoirs we have already quoted; at this particular moment this young lady was honoured by a ceremonious dedication "To Mlle Claire Féréol," but a year or two later she was to become, in his dedications of other songs, "To my Cousin Claire" and even "To my dear Cousin Claire." Franck wrote music for the girls to dance to—a polka in the latest style and a piano quadrille called *Les Délicieux*, which he signed only with the consonants of his name, "CSRGSTFRNCK"—musical trifles which have nevertheless been preserved in their original manuscripts. There was a family move to teach him to dance, so that he would not be out of the picture at the ball during the wedding ceremonies. Meantime he proceeded with the musical instruction of his fiancée, who never till her old age relaxed her interest in the art, and at one later period even taught it herself.

The Desmousseaux family had by now sized up César Franck's limitations in general culture—his artistic background and knowledge were elementary. They set themselves therefore to widen and develop his literary interests. For themselves and their children they enjoyed the privilege of free admission into the royal theatres—the Opéra, the Opéra-Comique; and to these they took César-Auguste to hear the standard operatic works, and also the plays at the Comédie-Française. At this last house he met once again his old Conservatoire friend Jacques Offenbach, now installed at the conductor's desk there. Thus was he introduced to the repertory of the time, especially the more serious plays in

which the Desmousseaux parents had so long been leading performers. We have unfortunately to record here that while the
love-histories of the heros of Corneille and Racine unfolded
themselves slowly in Alexandrines in the long speeches of classical
tragedy César slept: it all seemed to him a waste of his time.
Those few and short hours of leisure that he could snatch from
his professorial labours he wanted to devote to composition, the
branch of music in which he had some projective ideas and an
unlimited ambition.

His ambition was not without some basis of justification.
Franz Liszt was behind him with support, and had not only
patronized his trios, but took the trouble to express, in 1846, the
pleasure he would have in playing Franck's works. (Hans von
Bülow had already played No. 1 in Berlin with some success.)
There was also another basis. Mendelssohn at this time had
reached the climax of his brilliant and all-too-short career as a
leading German composer and conductor. A copy of the trios
had been sent to him in 1845. Mendelssohn acknowledged their
reception after some delay in a letter dated from Leipzig on
December 22, 1846. He wrote:

> I should much like to discuss with you in detail these works of
> yours, telling you how much in them I find excellent and also where
> they seem to me to be lacking. But that would be an impossible
> task to accomplish in writing, and one I should never succeed in
> even if I were to write in my own language.

Not long after, Mendelssohn took up the matter again with a
view to arranging a meeting with his French colleague, "to play
the music over together and to have a long talk about it."
Before that meeting could be arranged death had struck Mendelssohn down, and one may well imagine that had he lived a few
years longer Franck's future course would have been greatly
altered. *Ruth*, for example, would have become known in
Germany under the powerful enterprise of the conductor of the
principal German orchestra—an event that would have opened
all the bridges across the Rhine to the young Belgian, who had
already been taken up by a publisher there and also by some
well-known artists.[1]

---

[1] Mendelssohn's letter was addressed to 15 Rue la Bruyère—that is to say, to the house
of his parents, which César had quitted some six months before: the letter was forwarded
to 15 Rue Blanche.

While patiently awaiting his future career as a successful composer—not as a virtuoso pianist any more—César pursued his courtship with his fiancée, slowly and discreetly indeed, since Mme Desmousseaux, for all her theatrical career, was a strict mother. She would never leave the young people alone and, as the future Mme César Franck often told her children and grandchildren in later years, watched over their meetings with a severe eye, knitting all the time. Our ways have changed during a hundred years!

In such a new atmosphere of peace and comfort (a touch enervating perhaps?) the closing months of the year 1846 and the whole twelve of 1847 passed by practically without interruption. César's life, however, was not without its troubles, apart from the usual ups and downs of teaching, composing, and his love and anxiety for his own family. The times themselves were anxious politically and socially; very soon came the audible explosion of the February Revolution in Paris, a movement towards which he was by no means neutral. His mind was as much occupied just then by religious and philosophical problems as it was by artistic questions, and we shall see on a later page a somewhat curious manifestation of these wider interests. There is no doubt that he discussed current affairs with his future in-laws, and more than likely with one of his fellow-students at the Conservatoire, his senior by four years, Charles Gounod. On his return from the Italian sojourn involved by his winning the Prix de Rome Gounod underwent an interesting change of mental outlook. He accepted the post of precentor and organist at the Church for Foreign Missions where, supported by a few choristers, he attempted to improve the repertory of church music. For several months in 1847 and 1848 he was a theological student, and actually wore a cassock, and thus it was he took unto himself the title of the "Abbé" Gounod,[1] a title he saw fit to cling to for the rest of his life.

The young man, in this ecclesiastic stage of his life, had not the least suspicion in his mind that he would before very long abandon his priestly career. An opening into the world of the theatre had not yet presented itself, and he would have been the last person to foresee it. In the meantime, he occupied his mind with philosophy and the history of religion and theology: his

[1] Not 'abbot,' but 'priest'—'the Reverend,' as we say in English parlance.

ecclesiastical studies did not neglect the arts, particularly that of music in the Roman Catholic culture he had been brought up in. He was delighted to discuss all César Franck's worries and troubles about art and religion, for they were so near to his own. Gounod had for the time being directed his energies as a composer towards church music, and so the elder lent the younger various books on the subject from his library and encouraged him to come and talk about things; we find Gounod writing on September 14, 1847:

> Come as often as you can find time; my door, as you well know, is always open to you and myself no less ready to welcome you. I hope you will find me ever friendly towards any scheme you put your hand to.

It was hardly to be expected that this friendship would be lasting. The lives of the two musicians, which at first appeared to move along in parallel courses, soon changed to an extent which showed the difference between their natures. One of the two continued unceasingly in his church work and became a plain, unsophisticated family-man. The other before long embarked on his theatrical enterprises with all their moral risks, to become eventually the composer of *Faust* and a great power in the musical world. Twenty years later the Franco-Prussian War of 1870–71 found the two composer-friends following paths even more widely divergent, for Gounod, by that time a man of international reputation, betook himself to England, where his startling adventures had the effect of saddening and even alienating Franck, who by now was a patriotic Frenchman and one of the most important figures in the musical renaissance of his adopted country. The clash between the two personalities was unavoidable, and was accentuated when each of them turned to the writing of oratorios—particularly the two versions of *Rédemption*—and each became leader of a school of French composers, the one in symphonic music, the other in opera. In the good-natured César Franck the change of attitude towards his friend amounted to no more than a candid judgment of his music; he regarded the successful composer of *Faust* with indifference, even perhaps with a touch of disdain and distaste, which between the years of 1880 and 1890 showed itself in a more marked degree.

During the long period of his betrothal (1846–48) César Franck had undertaken and completed a major orchestral work based upon a poem by Victor Hugo in his *Feuilles d'automne* of 1831, *Ce qu'on entend sur la montagne*. The manuscript still exists, but Georges Franck, César's elder son, mentioned only the title to Alfred Ernst for his biographical article on Franck in the *Grande Encyclopédie*. Vincent d'Indy was not acquainted with the work and even thought it was called *La Sermon sur la montagne*.

The title, *Ce qu'on entend sur la montagne*, is familiar to musicians as that of one of the symphonic poems of Liszt which was to appear in 1857. Julien Tiersot makes this publication date the basis of an article in the *Revue musicale* of December 1, 1922, where he expresses his wonder and admiration that young Franck should have thought of the notion of writing a musical commentary on Hugo's poem no less than a dozen years or so before the Hungarian composer, and even credits the former with the idea of inventing the 'symphonic poem,' a form of programme music always acknowledged to be of Liszt's creation. But before he prostrated himself before Franck's supposed originality Tiersot did not take the trouble to verify the real chronology of Liszt's output. The truth is that Liszt had some time before conceived the idea of writing certain descriptive works, and in particular the *Bergsymphonie*. When he completed it round about 1847 he was doing no more than taking up anew an older idea that he had been turning over in his mind since about 1830 and had put into sketch-form about 1833. It would seem more than probable that at his various meetings with his Franco-Belgian colleague in Brussels and Paris, mostly in connexion with the performance of the trios, Liszt had propounded his views on music, which were no doubt listened to with enthusiastic attention. We may well suppose without any improbability that the very poem from the *Feuilles d'automne* itself had been mentioned as a subject for a symphonic poem peculiarly suitable for programmatic treatment in music, illustrating a poem that dealt so eloquently with the opposing forces of nature and humanity.

However that may be, Franck was much taken by the subject; its pantheism and social outlook were calculated to appeal deeply to a young thinker in those years of change and revolution. He too wrote his "Mountain Symphony." Unfortunately for him, the completion of Liszt's work of the same name in 1849, its first performance in 1853, and its publication in 1857 condemned the other score to complete oblivion.

A study of this score, such as Julien Tiersot made with so much admiration, reveals certain beauties, but a great deal more promise. Philosophically, in its direct opposition of good and evil, we find a parallel in *Les Béatitudes*, and here and there one has a foretaste of the later symphonic poems of 1870–80—*Éolides*, *Chasseur maudit*, *Djinns*—as well as in a general way of French music of the late nineteenth century. Above all one is struck by the large scale of the composer's conception; he had not before shown much interest in high philosophy. The *Bergsymphonie* has about it something of the monumental, the epic, and is far removed from the small-scale, even slightly childish music of the oratorio *Ruth*.

From the day he left the Conservatoire César Franck had always wanted an organist's post, a wish that led him on May 24, 1845, to dedicate to the parish priest of Notre-Dame-de-Lorette an *Ave Maria*, still preserved in manuscript. There was no opening for him as organist-in-chief, for Alphonse Gilbert was in charge of the full organ there, one of the first built by Cavaillé-Coll, and so he had to be content with post of assistant organist and accompanist, though he was sometimes called on to act as deputy in his senior's place. When he was not needed for playing, he attended worship at this church. One of the well-known singers at the Opéra, Gustave Roger, noticed him one day and wrote a note in his diary, dated April 1, 1847:

> Went to Notre-Dame-de-Lorette on Maundy Thursday and listened in devout silence to the magnificent church music. Also saw César-Auguste Franck sitting quite alone, book in hand; the sight of him seated thus in the church gave me an insight into his choice of the subject of Ruth and Boaz for his oratorio.[1]

The priest-in-charge of this rich parish at the time was an excellent musician, one de Rollot. He maintained there a small company of musicians, some of whom later made their names, like Ernest-Eugène Altès, the future conductor, and Holtzen, the future tenor, of the Opéra-Comique. One could hear there the motets and masses of Haydn, Mozart, Cherubini, Lesueur, and Dietsch (conductor at the Opéra who in 1842 set to music Richard Wagner's libretto *The Flying Dutchman*). Sometimes too one

[1] G. Roger, *Le Carnet d'un tenor* (Paris, Ollendorff, 1880), p. 17.

could hear works by the choirmaster Girac, the assistant organist Franck, and even of a chorister like Holtzem, to whom the young César gave good advice.[1] It was the parish priest's policy to help on his musical colleagues and certainly he did much to help Franck, who in addition had struck up a friendship with one of the sub-priests, Abbé Dancel.

César reached his twenty-fifth year on December 10, 1847. He made no delay in notifying his father that he had attained the full age of marital freedom: on leaving the third-floor flat he was at liberty to decide without interference about the plans for his marriage.[2]

The political revolution made menacing background noises while all these marriage plans were being proposed and formalized. At the beginning of the 1848 disturbances, on February 22, César Franck and Félicité Desmousseaux were legally married with the Church's benediction. On the journey to their Parish Church of Notre-Dame-de-Lorette the wedding procession formed by the two families found itself confronted with a road-barricade, but were enabled to make their way through by the laughing assistance of the rioters.

Mothers and fathers on both sides were present, for by this time Nicolas-Joseph Franck had become resigned to the inevitable. The witnesses of the ceremony were four performers—two actors and two singers: Louis Second, surnamed Féréol; Jean-François Anselme, of the Baptiste family; Alexandre Chevillard; and Jean-Adolphe Bouchet. Of the first named (Féréol), a singer of long repute, we have written on an earlier page; Baptiste of the Comédie-Française was brother of the bride's mother; Chevillard, an excellent 'cellist and player of chamber music, was the future father of the conductor Camille Chevillard; and Bouchet was a member of the regular company at the Comédie-Française. The theatre and music thus paid equal homage to the newly married couple.

Among the signatories of the registrar of marriage we may observe (apart from the parents and the four friends mentioned)

[1] L. A. Holtzem, *Une vie d'artiste* (Lyons, 1865), pp. 41–42.
[2] Up to 1907 French usage demanded of a young man that he should not marry without his father's consent before he reached the age of twenty-five. Then he was required to make three consecutive 'respectful notifications' ('sommations respectueuses') to his father; after the receipt of the third he was free to marry where he would. Franck, born on December 10, 1822, came to the needed age on December 10, 1847, and so was able to marry on February 22, 1848.

Félix Féréol, the singer's son, a student of medicine who later became his cousin César's doctor, and Julie Monvel, a member of a theatrical family closely associated with the Desmousseaux. Brother Joseph—still a student of organ, counterpoint, and fugue —did not honour the register with his autograph.

The marriage over César Franck disappeared from public musical life. The revolution had deprived him of most of his pupils. He kept on his job as assistant organist, though the rigours of the time had obliged his parish priest to dispense with most of his musical establishment, save a few of his choristers and his second organist.

In his new apartments César found at last the home life of which he had so long dreamed. His sense of family obligations was as strong towards his wife as towards his father and mother (there was a little account of 11,000 francs to be paid off!), and his responsibilities were not lessened by the arrival of children. Georges, his first-born, came into the world at the end of the year 1848.

His wife took the closest interest in his teaching life and composing; at first she was a proud and loving pupil married to a master of the musical art, celebrated in his youth; later her attitude towards him became sharper, more insistent, a little over-dominating. After a few years of marriage, as soon as Mme César Franck had shed some of the cares of a growing family, our young composer learnt that he had only escaped from the brutal commercialism of his father to find himself under the domination of his wife—kindly, no doubt, even tender, but rigid, often ill-advised, sometimes harsh.[1]

[1] See Chapter XVIII.

CHAPTER IX

Life in Obscurity: The Young Organist
(1848–58)

LIFE was not easy during those early months of marriage, notwithstanding the help given by the Desmousseaux and by Mme Franck. Paris was going through a continual series of revolutionary outbursts, like the 'February Days,' and the 'June Days,' and the result was a grave reduction in musical activity. The young couple were forced to live in a very meagre style, with little more coming into the family purse for some twenty-five or thirty years after.

All these political happenings had an unexpected effect upon Franck, for they made him want to create music that would suit the times—an effect, however, which will surprise those who treasure in their minds an image of Franck's high-mindedness and his preoccupation with religious activities. Franck—conscientious and sensitive—had already been overcome by the philosophical eloquence of Hugo's *Ce qu'on entend sur la montagne*, and it was not to be expected that the showy motto of "Liberté, égalité, fraternité" would not grip the heart of a young Republican such as he was—full of hopes for peace and the regeneration of the human race. In 1848 it was natural that he should find the new régime exactly suited to his frame of mind. Among the leaders of it was Lamartine, and the mouthpiece of the ultra-montane world of Catholics was the paper *L'Univers*, which openly asserted the Republicanism of the new monarchic France.

Franck was an avowed Republican; to the end of his life he never altered his political loyalties. The proof of this may be summed up in an amusing story which his future pupil Pierre de Bréville has left on record. One day in the eighteen-eighties, at the end of High Mass at Sainte-Clotilde, the choir had just sung twice the motet *Domine salvam fac rempublicam*; Franck at the organ, in a moment of inattention, was about to recapitulate the whole thing on the organ, when he saw his mistake: "I am a Republican, indeed, but twice over for the Republic is enough, I think. One doesn't want to go too far!" He must have been as disappointed as George Sand when in the 1870–71 period she announced her doubtful opinion that "the Republic will be nothing, once again, but party politics. It has no finer ideals, philosophy, or religion."

On December 10, 1848, Louis-Napoléon was elected President of the Constitutional Assembly. The tragic 'June Days' were too much for César Franck, and he gave his support whole-heartedly to the Republic, which he believed to be a brotherly system of government, as new as it was beneficent. His enthusiasm for the new President was unbounded, but he was incapable of seeing in him a new emperor, a coming avatar. He wrote and published a setting for voice and piano of a patriotic poem by Colonel Bernard Delfosse, *Les trois exilés* ("The Three Exiles"). The florid cover had lithographed on it portraits of Napoléon I, the Duke of Reischtadt, and Louis-Napoléon. The musical style may be called 'military band,' so we need not pause over it. But we know that the public bought it, for there is evidence of a second edition; the first was printed by Edmond Mayaud in Paris, in the Boulevard des Italiens (it was one of the Mayaud copies that César gave to his mother-in-law, whose library of presentation copies from him the family filed), and the second edition by Gérrard, at his office in the Grand Hôtel, which landed up in the library of the Paris Conservatoire.

The humanitarian projects of our young Republican went farther than this; he thought of a piece for three-part men's choir to be called "Freedom, the Workers' Song"; it was never written, but another, a "Patriotic Hymn," was at least in part committed to paper. It is an extended composition in the grand style for voices and orchestra, foreshadowing some of the composer's later works of the 1870's. The full score is of impressive dimensions. There are twenty-three pages completed or sketched in, which comprise a long orchestral prelude (much of it scored for strings at the unison or octave), a chorus of old men whose long first subject is not far removed from Beethoven's tune in the finale of the Ninth Symphony, a chorus of young men, a rough version of a female voice chorus, and other things. This cantata was no doubt intended for submission in a competition held by the Ministry of Public Instruction for national songs. Many parts of it are coloured by the manner of the 'Great Revolution,' recalling the more serious works of Méhul, for whom Franck always showed a strong admiration. The fact that the cantata was never finished is due mainly perhaps to the small hope of a public performance; another reason was that times were changing before their eyes. All those hopes and aspirations towards revolution and socialism so nobly expressed by the young composer were coming to nothing with every day that passed. Gradually the enthusiasms of the winter of 1848 passed farther and farther away, as the whole political and social movement of the new Republic (still-born, we fear) slipped slowly back into the reappearance of the Empire.

This was the second disillusionment Franck had met with during his new and hard existence as a family-man; the effect of it on him was an almost complete retirement from public music for a number of years. There was no outward sign of him as either solo pianist or composer, and the most he did on the platform was to act in the secondary capacity of accompanist—he who had swept all before him at the Paris Conservatoire in 1838! This modest occupation he followed at the Conservatoire at Orléans, where he was invited five times a year to accompany the concerts at the Institute—jobs he obtained thanks to his new cousin-by-marriage Féréol, once a singer at the Opéra-Comique and now an important resident there. Franck regularly worked there from 1848 to 1853. His fees were then raised to four hundred francs a year (£16 sterling)—that is eighty francs a visit. Contented with the increased money, he went to Orléans regularly right up to the season of 1863–64, for it gave him the opportunity to keep in touch with his wife's family, to accept outside Paris a number of profitable teaching-engagements, and even, on rare occasions, to perform some music of his own—for example, on February 16, 1849, when he was allowed to play a piano piece and a "Polish Air," the latter no doubt identical with his *Fantaisie* of 1845, dedicated to the wife of the Belgian Ambassador and published by the firm of Richault (at that time owned by Costallat).

During this time of withdrawal César was able to look back without excessive regret over the productions of his childhood, adolescence, and early manhood. A critical sense was never one of his strong qualities; yet he became fully aware of the banality, the conventional character, of the whole of his pianistic output written according to his father's prescription. He held by the trios, however, even to the *Trio de salon*, a pretty, elegant piece of writing in the early eighteenth-century manner. After all, these three works, and a fourth as well, had been highly praised first by the illustrious Franz Liszt and later by Hans von Bülow and Mendelssohn. And were they not frequently played in Germany if hardly ever in France? He thought well of them, but did not attach to them the importance with which Vincent d'Indy's authoritative opinion later invested them.

He was disappointed that his oratorio *Ruth* had on only one occasion won the attention of the musicians and the public. Some sort of rather painful consolation he could derive from the failure of the *Damnation de Faust*, that powerful work of a composer of genius, that indubitable masterpiece which had fallen into complete obscurity since the end of the year 1846, the very year of his one-night success with his own Biblical eclogue. He was no more than a minor pianist-composer, with nothing to help him on save his own talents, the regard of one or two successful musicians, and the outrageous publicity organized by his bungling father. Was it not inevitable therefore that he should be a failure at the moment which saw the fall from high places of Hector Berlioz, a master of incontestable brilliance and even of genius, a dictator in the musical Press, and a leader among writers on all matters of art? He had the advantage, at least, of not being utterly crushed by the incompetent critics who taxed Berlioz with impotence, with mere bravado, and asserted that he created "harmonic chaos" and "did not compose, but decomposed." Admittedly, Berlioz's failure had been simultaneous with the success of Félicien David, who, after *The Desert* of 1845, in 1847 presented for the admiration of the public his *Christopher Columbus*.

Here, then, we see César Franck in apparent retirement from the world of music, at least from the limelight of public acclaim, which he had so long endured. He seems to have become reconciled to his obscurity. Outside his absorbing work as an organist and a teacher he devoted himself to his wife and children, his family's joys and sorrows, the last not rare. Four children were born to him between the end of 1848 and 1856. Georges, the

eldest, was nicknamed the "Barricade" owing to the circumstances of his conception; two died young—a daughter of two
years of age in 1851, a third son of three in 1859. The father's
anguish was to reveal itself much later in a letter of condolence
to some friends who had just lost their child:

> The sorrow one feels on losing these little ones (whom one loves
> the better for their frailty) is so overwhelming that it runs the risk
> of becoming injustice towards those who are living. I have cer-
> tainly found it so myself. It has often seemed to me that those who
> remained with us were not so good by nature, nor so bright in
> mind as those I had just lost.[1]

His liking for this secluded way of living, in some degree made
necessary by his straitened financial circumstances, may be the
better understood if we remember that, sickened by the virtuoso's
life to which his father's iron will had but lately reduced him,
César still could not avoid each day noticing the self-advertising
methods of his younger brother Joseph, who from his twentieth
year on showed himself quite ready to submit to their father's
schemes for publicity.

Joseph Franck, by now back at the Conservatoire, but not as a
violin student, was to carry off in 1850 the first prize for counterpoint and fugue in Adolphe Adam's class, and in 1852 the first
prize for organ, which César himself had never won. That second
year, as organist of the Saint Thomas Aquinas Church, he published his Opus 1, a selection of motets for eight-part chorus with
organ accompaniment, dedicated to the King of the Belgians,
who sent him, as he had once sent to César, an imposing gold
medal. Paragraphs were issued to the Press presenting him as "a
distinguished organist especially learned in all matters of plain-
chant and church music." The following years saw the publication
of other compositions by him, in particular a Mass for three
voices, dedicated to the Empress Eugénie. Setting himself up as
a teacher of piano, violin, organ, harmony, and counterpoint, he
lost no opportunity to talk and write about his courses, about
performances of his Masses, about the future publication of a
large number of his works, and about his tours in Belgium and
Prussia (that is to say, Aix-la-Chapelle). Eight years after the

---

[1] On May 30, 1854, his father-in-law, Desmousseaux, died of cholera. Mme Desmousseaux came to live at her son-in-law's house, till her death on March 30, 1857.

appearance of his first work, by 1860, he had already reached his Opus 41—a *Second Concerto*, for piano and strings, once again dedicated to His Majesty the King of the Belgians.

From that time Joseph was better known, both in France and Belgium, than his brother César, who appeared to have taken his final leave of the secular concert-hall. With the latter he was in frequent communication since he was always short of cash, despite all his lessons and concerts and publications, and all the publicity provided for him by his friend the musicologist Théodore Nisard and his publisher, Repos. He had got into extravagant ways that landed him in the gravest difficulties. The two brothers were poles apart in their tastes and in their characters; yet they kept up some sort of relationship until the eve of their father's death, in 1871; then they separated and lived so much apart that after the Franco-Prussian War César's children and Joseph's children literally knew nothing of each other.[1]

What really were the relative achievements at the organ of the two brothers César and Joseph? No printed record exists that can tell us. It may perhaps be possible to arrive at an approximate idea by considering the average level of French organists in both Paris and the provinces, though it may be imagined that prize-winners from the Paris Conservatoire must have been above the average of the majority of their colleagues. The level was extremely low; the musical reviews frequently stated the fact and deplored it. Below are printed some typical opinions offered by the most enlightened critics of the mid-nineteenth century.

A four-hand arrangement for piano of one of J. S. Bach's preludes and fugues for organ had been issued in 1845. The comment of Jean-Bonaventure Laurens in the *Gazette musicale* of November 2, 1845, is characteristic. Laurens was a remarkable painter as well as a musician; born at Carpentras, he had frequently travelled in Germany, and had made good friends with the principal musicians there, Schumann, Mendelssohn, Joachim, and Brahms among them. We may take it from his words that *The Well-tempered Keyboard* (the "Forty-eight Preludes and Fugues") of Bach had often been reprinted in France, for "every

---

[1] Joseph Franck also published a number of varied works through Alphonse Leduc; *Tota pulchra est*, his "well-known motet" for two voices and organ (*Op.* 9); three volumes of eighty organ pieces, under the titles of *Leaves for the Organist*, *Flowers for the Organist*, and *Garlands for the Organist*; and an *Easy Mass*, for two equal voices bearing the opus number 191.

one who aspires to the rank of a recognized musician knows by
heart a major portion of its contents"; but the organ music of
Bach was still unknown, "for the simple reason," he alleges,

> that no publisher has ever found himself encouraged to engrave and
> print a single line of these organ works, since they all demand the
> use of the pedals, a technical feat that practically no one in this
> country seems at the moment to have mastered.

A similar opinion is to be found over the signature of Adrien
de la Fage in the *Gazette musicale* of September 19, 1847. "Not
one of our organists plays, or even knows, the music of that great
composer [Bach]"; all of them, in his opinion, improvise "God
knows how, and we unfortunately know too!" In the same
review on January 26, 1851, the elder Fétis attributes the decline
of the organ in France to the long-standing custom, since the
days of Louis XIV, of always improvising, and thus he was not
in the least surprised that organists were quite content to lap up
the public's enjoyment of a pretty registration of stops while the
music improvised was but the poorest commonplace. The critic
Henri Blanchard (old opponent of the Franck family) drew
attention as well, in the *Gazette* of July 22, 1844, to the extreme
poverty of the organ-playing in the Parisian churches. He wrote:

> There is no trace of any serious study of the art, based on
> classical and well-founded traditions. Except for M. Benoist, who
> has not played in public for some time, and M. Boëly, who either
> through modesty or misanthropy confines himself to the support of
> a very restricted musical circle, the larger number of our organists
> have not paid proper attention to fugue, and thus fall grievously
> behind our great masters of the past, like the Couperins, the Miroirs,
> the Séjans, the Becks of Bordeaux, and so on.

This distressing state of affairs in the organ world may be put
down to the meagre training of the organists, the abysmal taste
of the public, and the complete insensitiveness towards musical
beauty of the clergy, who regarded cheap and taking music as a
means of keeping their flock together. It remained (to speak
generally) for the German Adolphe Hesse, a pupil of Bach's
biographer Forkel, and after that Hesse's Belgian pupil Lemmens,
to reveal to Paris what the organist's art should truly be.

It was late spring in 1844 when Hesse, already famous for his
expounding of the great Forkel tradition, left Breslau for his first

appearances in Paris, an event which started a revolution in French organ-playing. He was heard first on an instrument that Daublaine-Callinet had built in one of the galleries of the Industrial Exhibition. A fortnight after, there took place the inauguration at the Church of Saint-Eustache of the former organ of the Abbey of Saint-Germain-des-Près, reconstructed by the same organ-builder. It was a great occasion which caused wide and lasting repercussions. Four French organists were heard to begin with: Benoist, Boëly, Fessy, and Lefébure-Wély. The two former were representative of the art of organ-playing at its highest and most skilful, Benoist having taught César at the Conservatoire and the other being an exceptionally fine player who was often to be heard at Saint-Germain-l'Auxerrois. Then followed the eye-opening performance by Hesse.

The effect he produced was extraordinary, especially in the toccatas and fugues of Bach, which he played at a comparatively slow speed and with the utmost precision of technique. One point was particularly admired—the wide range of expression that he obtained from the new arrangement of shutters in the swell-box, opening and closing at command. Every one was astounded at the virtuosity of his pedalling, then thought in France an unimportant accomplishment, and the *Gazette* of June 9, 1844, praised "his pedal-work, for, let us inform all organists, he controls his feet with the most wonderful skill."

Was César-Auguste Franck present at this remarkable occasion, we wonder? He had much to learn. During his time in Benoist's class at the Conservatoire he had made a much greater mark as an improviser than as an organist proper. Then he seems practically to have given up the organ until he was appointed assistant at Notre-Dame-de-Lorette. In any event, before many years he found himself forced to pay serious attention to the art of organ-playing, its demands, its technical limitations, and its proper style, for he was not long to remain a mere subordinate at his church.

In 1851 one of the sub-priests of Notre-Dame-de-Lorette, the Abbé Dancel, was inducted as priest-in-charge at Saint-Jean-Saint-François-au-Marais. This church possessed a new and large instrument completed in December 1846 by Cavaillé-Coll, an organ-builder of genius who had taken the place of Daublaine and Callinet. The new priest-in-charge offered César Franck the position of organist, which he enthusiastically accepted. "My new organ," he said, "is like an orchestra." He was not exaggerating. Cavaillé, through his improvements and changes, artistic as well as mechanical, was offering to church musicians the infinite tonal possibilities of the symphony orchestra. Even the cynical Blanchard (*Gazette musicale* of July 30, 1834) found this new kind of organ "spectacular, dramatic, almost too theatrical, too voluptuous!"

There is no information whatever to what extent César Franck, now thirty years of age, took advantage of the untold resources open before him at the organ-stool of Saint-Jean-Saint-François. We cannot tell. We may reasonably assume that he set himself to acquire all the new technical methods as well as the normal repertory then in use, even that of his former principal at Notre-Dame-de-Lorette. Did he, perhaps, discuss with his brother Joseph the ideas and mechanical possibilities opened up by Cavaillé-Coll's newest instruments? Without any intention of niggling, we can guess that he was at first absorbed by the thousand and one combinations of sound and varieties of tonal colouring that he found at his command; then, that he applied his mind to acquiring a solid technique, especially on the pedals, which were so often sniffed at by organists of his time. He did not give up but continued to develop his capacity for improvisation, an art in which thirty years later he became an unrivalled leader. The temptation must have been overwhelming to say good-bye to all his symphonic aspirations and to set out to rival the former masters of the organ, whose achievements his continual church duties had prevented him hitherto from studying carefully.

His nomination as principal organist of the Marais church was of considerable value to him. One result was that he was accounted one of the "artistic representatives" of this particular firm of organ-builders; another was that he was called upon to take part in the services of installation or perhaps of inauguration of other organs by the same maker. Cavaillé-Coll took pains to publicize his instruments and their players in all the musical papers. At the same time there was still a steep ladder to climb before once again the fame of the too-long-forgotten César Franck could be rebuilt.

His name is seen anew, however, with both his Christian names, in an article in the *Journal des Débats* at the end of January

1852—an article, not by Hector Berlioz, who had just then left for London to launch his latest orchestral project, the "New Philharmonic Society," but by his deputy, Joseph d'Ortigue. The essay, which was reprinted in its author's book *La Musique à l'église* ("Church Music"), dealt principally with the visits to Paris of the famous Belgian organist Lemmens, a pupil of Hesse. Lemmens was in process of reforming the whole system of organ-teaching in Belgium; and when he opened the new Cavaillé-Coll organ at the church of Saint-Vincent-de-Paul with a splendid display of virtuoso but dignified playing the *Débats* included Franck without hesitation in a list of living Parisian musicians whom that paper's critic picked out as of the first rank: among these leading musical names are found the following: Adam, Alkan, Baptiste, Batton, Beaulieu, Blanchard, Boëly, Maurice Bourges, Bousquet, Castil-Blaze, Dietsch, César-Auguste Franck, Gounod, Halévy, Trouillon-Lacombe, de la Fage, Panseron, Scudo, Simon, Stamaty, Thomas, Tulou, Mme Viardot, and Zimmermann.

The small world of music was, of course, for a long time dumbfounded by the unbelievable virtuosity of this Belgian organist on the pedal keyboard. One paper said:

> This is sheer gymnastics; toe-and-heel work, leaps and slides, double octaves, repeated chords and arpeggios, rapid scale-passages, arpeggios and trills—all executed with an attack and a certainty of touch that many an organist here would like to achieve with his hands.

It is possible, however, that what appealed to the listeners, as apart from the specialists—even the least attentive listeners—was the *legato* style of pedalling, so characteristic of Lemmens's playing and almost unknown among his Parisian colleagues.

An equally vivid and deep impression was made when, two years later, Lemmens returned to open a new organ at Saint-Eustache, the previous one, which Hesse had opened ten years before, having been set fire to after the restoration of the instrument. For the inauguration, in 1854, of this new instrument, the organ-builders called on four organists, Lemmens and three Parisians associated with their firm: Cavallo from Saint-Vincent-de-Paul, Bazille from Sainte-Elizabeth, César Franck from Saint-Jean-Saint-François, "the last-named having played" (according to the *Gazette musicale*) "a fantaisie written with great skill and performed with much vitality."

Lemmens, advertised as "organist-in-chief to His Majesty the King of the Belgians," had for five years been teaching the organ at the Royal Brussels Conservatoire; his magazine, the *Journal d'orgue*, was gaining some circulation in France and thus making his ideas known to the musical world. He played a dozen pieces, mostly of his own composition, but including the *E minor Prelude and Fugue* of Bach. After his first appearances in Paris, it was widely reported that he had brought about a revolution in organ-playing, not only by his development of pedal technique but also by introducing finger substitution, a technical accomplishment indispensable to *legato* playing, but at that time unknown to organists in Belgium and for the most part in France as well. The general opinion was that he was the direct lineal descendant of the great German organist, and astonishment, if not always admiration, was expressed at the vigour and austerity of his style, which made no concession whatsoever to the popular taste of the time.

The conscientious Franck followed the eminent Belgian's performances with the closest attention. There was so much for him to admire; not only the classic interpretation of the works of Bach, which he had often heard played by Boëly at Saint-Germain-l'Auxerrois, but also a number of points in technique, like the rapidity and evenness of the pedal-work ("His feet are everywhere at once," wrote the *Gazette*. "His feet have turned themselves into hands, with an agility that extends beyond his ankles") and the *legato* playing on the manuals; that was something Franck had never been taught at the Paris Conservatoire. A pianist as well as an organist, he never wholly acquired the *legato* style himself and in later years, being more interested in the music than in its execution, he was unable to instil it into his pupils. It was a lesson of the highest value that he learnt from the Belgian virtuoso, whom he thought of as his compatriot.

About the time of his appointment to a chief-organist's post another ambition seized upon César Franck, and he embarked upon a very different kind of musical enterprise. Fond of a quiet life, scornful of outward show, he was nevertheless unable to escape from the influence of his wife's family, under which he had come even before the wedding. His mother-in-law was a woman of the theatre; his cousin Féréol of Orléans had had a brilliant operatic career; his wife, though she had not followed in the family footsteps, had much of the actress's lively sense of the theatre in her inner soul, to the family's delight. As a great lover of both *opera seria* and *opera buffa*, it was only natural that she should want her husband to write something for the great public—music that would pay!

Franck was not unwilling to follow her advice; he would do anything to supplement his meagre income as a teacher, and was even more anxious to be rid of the crippling debt to his father. So he decided to acquire a libretto for a grand opera. He went to Alphonse Royer and Gustave Vaëz, both successful writers experienced in the theatre who, apart from translations of other librettos, had written those of *La Favorita* and *Lucia di Lammermoor* for Donizetti and *Otello* for Rossini.

The poem produced by these two touched a depth of imbecility rare even for this period: *Le Valet de ferme* ("The Farm Labourer"), the scene being Ireland at the end of the eighteenth century. It was 'grand opera,' without spoken words, and its abysmal literary quality may be gauged from this quatrain alone:

> C'est Dieu, qui m'éclaire,
> Betty, ton vieux père,
> Sera, je l'espère,
> Sauvé du trépas.

which may be translated thus into an equivalently pompous nonsense:

> From God who's above,
> Dear Betty, my love,
> Your father I learn
> Will be in his turn
> Acquitted of trespass.

César Franck devoted much time and trouble to writing the music for this absurd play, to such an extent indeed that after taking from December 1851 to the early months of 1853, his health broke down through overwork. So, at least, we are informed by Vincent d'Indy. He certainly took a holiday, partly with his cousins Brissaud at Besançon, and partly in Switzerland, where, rucksack on backs, he and his wife and his son Georges went on a short walking-tour. At Fribourg he tried out the famous organ at the Cathedral and thought it overrated.

The artistic result of his labours was certainly not brilliant. The music, which may still be read in score, is a worse than mediocre example of the poor operatic music of the period, a mere string of arias, duets, quartets, and ensembles.

Having finished the opera, he naturally hoped for a performance, and equally naturally looked for help from the influence of his librettists, who were well in with the directors of the Opéra. He wanted it brought to the notice of the Théâtre Lyrique, where Reyer's *Maître Wolfram* was about to come on and where they had just played a piece by Weckerlin with (for César) the somewhat ironic title of *L'organiste dans l'embarras* ("The Organist out of His Depth"). To this end he once again had recourse to the boundless friendship of Franz Liszt, from whom he received by return of post, on January 28, 1854, a personal note enclosing a letter of introduction to one of the brothers Escudier, directors of *La France musicale*.

In his reply to Franck Liszt protested that his opinion would have but little influence with "any of the bigwigs who have the say in operatic production." His letter to Escudier recalled the trios and *Ruth* in words like these:

> For a number of years now I have held a very high opinion of M. Franck's abilities as a composer, from a knowledge of his trios which I find most remarkable and much superior to other works of the same kind published these latter years. His oratorio *Ruth* has much of beauty in it, and has the merit of a pure and sustained style. If the opera that he wishes to have produced at the Théâtre Lyrique keeps up to the standard of these other works and is what I expect from M. Franck the Théâtre Lyrique may congratulate itself upon a lucky choice, and the best chances of success will be assured. I cannot of course judge from this distance and have not yet seen the score of the opera; I confine myself therefore to drawing your attention to M. Franck's very real talents and recommend him with affection to your kindness.

Liszt's letter drew a complete blank, and the opera never left its author's desk.

Eighteen months of silence passed, and then Franck saw a new faint glimmer of hope. He had some ground for his will-o'-the-wisp. The Emperor Napoléon III made a new appointment to the direction of the Opéra, on July 1, 1856—no other than Alphonse Royer with Vaëz as his second-in-command. Thus

Franck found his own librettists in charge of the Imperial Academy of Music, and thus too he felt certain that they would immediately launch his opera, to which they had contributed the text. There seemed to him to be no doubt about it, and so from July 13 onward the musical reviews announced that the new management would "present an unheard opera in four acts by M. César-Auguste Franck, an organist who is also well known for his fugues and piano-pieces." There are odd points about this announcement—for example, the reappearance of the two Christian names, banned for ten years, and the description of the composer's writings. It is inconceivable that it was not issued by Father Franck, fired at this change of high operatic policy by the old family ambition. Be it so or not, the announcement was premature.

Royer's first step on taking his new chair was—not to call in his collaborator Franck, oh no!—but to send his friend Vaëz in Berlin to commission an opera from Meyerbeer; he had good reasons, including the idiocy of the libretto, for not putting on his own opera. The *Gazette musicale* of July 20 retires a step or two from its previous pronouncement: "It would appear that we were somewhat hasty in forecasting the names of certain operas scheduled for production under the new direction." *Le Valet de ferme* lay on the shelf, unpublished, unknown. Franck himself was not slow in realizing the mistake he had made in plunging into a medium so alien to his character and his experience. His one grand opera, as he was often to confess to his pupils and friends, was condemned to complete neglect and silence—but not to destruction; he was too conservative by nature for that![1]

Other disappointments were to follow. The trios, as we have said, continued to interest various musicians in Germany, notably Hans von Bülow who, in a letter to his mother dated Leipzig, January 3, 1853, asked her to send them to him and even mentioned the price (four marks). Franck therefore made an effort, with the help of Franz Liszt, to find a German publisher for his

---

[1] Arthur Pougin notes in his supplement to the *Biographie universelle des musiciens*, by Fétis, that *Le Valet de ferme* was actually put into production by the National Opera scheme of Adolphe Adam in 1848, and that only the failure of that grandiose project prevented the work's being publicly played. This statement, reprinted by Georges Servières in his book *La Musique française moderne*, seems to be based on a confusion. It is not, however, impossible that Franck had conceived the idea of writing a work for Adam's theatre, which was opened on November 15, 1847, with a score written to a text by Royer and Vaëz.

chamber music. Liszt, in his letter of October 25, 1853, made it clear that it was no less difficult in Germany than in France for a publisher to make a profit out of issuing works of this specialized and austere class. "Perseverance," he wrote, "and a conviction worthy of the dignity of our art are what one needs." He expressed himself very willing to act as Franck's intermediary with German publishers, but considered it useless to write to them; rather, he would wait for an opportunity—certain to occur during the winter, for he was going to Leipzig later in the year—to speak in person to M. Härtel, "whom, unless I am mistaken, you have already approached."

The letter ends with some curious information. While waiting to see the publisher Härtel, Liszt wanted to get to know the works sent him by his friend, so he decided that he would play them through with two members of his Weimar orchestra, the violinist Laub and the 'cellist Cossman, the latter having already mentioned Franck's music to Liszt. The works sent to Liszt to try through were a sonata and a trio.[1]

What exactly did this sonata and this trio consist of? They would seem to have been intended for the German publisher Liszt was going to find. Of neither is anything known; they have left no traces save in Liszt's letter. Is it possible that they existed in one copy only which was lost in the course of Liszt's frequent tours and nomadic way of life? The question has never been asked, much less answered, and it is an interesting question. One wonders—did César, contrary to all belief, really continue during those ten or fifteen years after the trios to write large-scale chamber works for two and three players? It may be so; it may be, perhaps, that the music thus written—if it ever was, and its very existence has been unsuspected up to this day—provided material towards the compositions of César's later years. So full are the archives of the Franck family that one can only think the problem insoluble, like many others. We may venture to guess

---

[1] The violinist Laub (1832–75), born and educated in Prague, had in 1833 succeeded Joachim in the Grand Ducal Orchestra at Weimar. Cossman (1822–1910), of Jewish origin, had lived for some time in Paris and there met Franck; he was three years with the Italian opera, then back in Germany, and in Paris again in January 1850 with Joachim. In an undated letter to Franck, Liszt writes that he "simply cannot find the spare hour or two to play over his compositions." "You know how sincere my interest is. Perhaps before long it might be possible for you to spend a fortnight or so at Weimar, which would greatly delight me." An American musician, William Mason, prints the following note in his *Memories of a Musical Life* (p. 122): "Sunday, April 23, 1853, at Altenberg, 11 A.M., Liszt played two trios by Franck with Laub and Cossman."

that the sonata and trio sent out in 1853 were nothing else but old works, contemporary with the trios of 1842, or even earlier —original works, or perhaps transcriptions, that Franck passed to Liszt because the latter had already shown his interest in his compositions of this character; and this is the more likely since, as we shall see, nearly twenty years later, in 1871, the composer was to appear in public at the first concert of the Société Nationale, himself playing the least considerable of his trios—the one known as the *Trio de salon*.

Apart from the usual ups and downs of personal troubles and hope, life pursued its dull and even way. Only an occasional fact of greater or lesser significance marks the passage of the years. We have already recorded his appointment in 1851 to the organist-ship at a Parisian church, and the two occasions, in 1852 and 1854, when he appeared in public as a solo organist. On March 24, 1855, Franck played at a concert in Orléans, where he gave the andante of Haydn's *Symphony No. 36*, a song of Schubert's (under the title of *Sois toujours mes amours*), and a Chopin mazurka; that brought him in an extra sixty francs (140 francs in all). At a similar concert the following year (March 8) he played two of Mendelssohn's *Songs without Words*, the ballade from *Preciosa* arranged by Mendelssohn and Thalberg, and a nocturne by his friend Alkan. His name appears at a concert given at the Salle Pleyel by the tenor Paulin with the 'cellist Lebouc, the pro-gramme containing songs by Weckerlin, Mme de Grandval, and Franck himself, which (according to the *Revue musicale*) "gave great pleasure."

Opportunity occurred during the summer of that same year 1856 for Franck to be heard as an organist outside the walls of his church of Marais. Cavaillé-Coll was on the point of deliver-ing to the Bishop of Carcassonne the instrument he had built for the cathedral there. He begged Franck to demonstrate its new excellences to a group of interested people. The account of the performance in the *Gazette musicale* suggests that it was supplied in part by the organ-builder himself.

> M. César Franck, an excellent organist, was showing off the instru-ment's paces, and therefore threw into relief all its harmonic and tonal possibilities, at first in an austere kind of music written with great skill by himself, and later by a series of brilliant improvis-ations.

Another of his usual concerts at Orléans, on March 15, 1857, afforded him the pleasure (perhaps tinged with pain) of accompanying the now celebrated singer, Pauline Viardot, whom he had met twenty-five years earlier when she and he together were classed as infant prodigies, both pianists then. His Orléans visits went on regularly up to the end of the season of 1862–63, when he gave up the accompanying work there in favour of Van der Heuvel from the staff of the Opéra.

Some five years before his withdrawal from the regular pianist's stool at the Orléans concerts one of the programmes there, on January 22, 1858, announced Franck for the first time in this manner: "At the piano will be M. César Franck, precentor and organist-in-chief at the Parish Church of Sainte-Clotilde, in Paris." This new appointment, only recently confirmed, marked an important milestone in the composer's humble path.

The only composition that César Franck seems to have written between the years of 1848 and 1858 is his grand opera, *Le Valet de ferme*, save for a few minor pieces that were never even completed in manuscript. Two of these latter are dated 1849—on February 28 a song for voice and piano entitled *Aimer*, intended perhaps as a present for the anniversary of his marriage, and on June 15 a short cantata for two voices, *Sub tuum*, no doubt sung at a service in Notre-Dame-de-Lorette. Another little work bears the dedication date of September 1857; it is one version among many that Franck wrote of one of the *Chants du crépuscule* of Victor Hugo: "S'il est un charmant gazon . . ." The sum total of these little efforts amounts to no more than occasional music for church or home.

This astonishing musical silence, which one might well have thought to be the end of the chapter, is difficult to understand. Why, one asks, should this startling young virtuoso on the piano and the organ allow himself to be confined to his parish organ-loft and his twopenny-halfpenny pupils? Why should this ebullient young composer, this precocious mind that had produced *Ruth*, so much admired by Spontini, Meyerbeer, Liszt— why should he suddenly throw overboard all his creative hopes and ambitions?

Possibly one simple clue will elucidate the whole mystery. Here was a young artist faced with the inescapable procession of each day's material demands; he was bowed down under the burdens and labours that they incessantly heaped on his back. He had a family of four children to provide for, he was saddled with his imprudent promise to repay his father's debts, he still wanted to be helpful to his brother Joseph, and to a brother of his wife's, who was described by the family as "given over to extravagance" and as a "sponger" in any possibly remunerative quarter.

CHAPTER X

The Organist at Sainte-Clotilde
(1858–70)

WHEN, on January 22, 1858, the shy accompanist at the Orléans concerts was first faced with his new position at the Church of Sainte-Clotilde he had not the least idea that one day it would bring him into very wide fame.

His duties during the first year were of no outward importance; the organ at his disposal was only a small affair, at first in the temporary chapel of Sainte-Valère, in the Rue de Bourgogne and later in the new building, which was opened on November 30, 1857. The important thing was that he was master of the choristers; each Sunday the congregation at the two churches could see him in his precentor's robes beating time to his choir. The actual baton-work was given over, in 1859, to his young colleague Théodore Dubois, who won that year at the Conservatoire the first prize for organ and came second in the Prix de Rome; Franck at that moment mounted the organ-stool before the magnificent three-manual organ that Cavaillé-Coll had just built and installed in the church. The specification of this new instrument was so original as to cause endless discussion among the experts; nor was it without considerable influence on the future works of our newly appointed parish organist.[1]

The organ was formally opened on December 19, 1859; for whatever reason of friendship or musical politics, it had been decided that Franck should be supported by Lefébure-Wély,

[1] The Sainte-Clotilde organ had three manuals of fifty-six notes, a pedal-board of thirty notes, forty-six stops, and fifteen combination pedals. A full description of it may be found in *L'Esthétique de l'orgue*, by Jean Huré. One of the stops opened pipes of new and original quality: the trumpet, with a fine, clear sonority not far removed from that of the orchestral oboe. A specialist on the history of organs, Norbert Dufourcq, has thus described the Sainte-Clotilde instrument in his book, *La Musique d'orgue française*: "It is unquestionably the constructor's masterpiece up to this time, on account of the beauty of its foundation stops, the mysterious remoteness of the swell organ, the poetic quality of the clarinet stop on the choir organ, the limpidity of the trumpet stop that is not to be met with elsewhere, the clarity, lightness, and precision of the full organ."

"the most popular of living organists," who played some attractive improvisations. Franck's own choice of programme was of an entirely different character, as we learn from an interesting notice in the *Gazette musicale*. The editor of that paper then was a learned musician, with a special knowledge of the organ and of church music, Adrien de la Fage (1805–62); he wrote:

> The elder of the two Francks, organist of the church, began with a piece of his own written in a broad and forceful style which made a deep impression on his hearers, no less so because M. Franck then turned away from his own compositions to draw on those conceived by the genius of John Sebastian Bach.

La Fage made much of the technical and interpretative difficulties of the German Master's music, and ended his article in these words:

> M. Franck can only have attained such skill through long study and perseverance; and it has won him, from this moment onward, a firm place among organists of the very first rank. He showed himself perhaps at his best when, resuming the rôle of composer, he played an end-piece on the full organ. In this work one was confronted with the mind and the muscles of a true master-musician.

We see César Franck, then, at the age of thirty-seven, in command for the rest of his life of a magnificent organ, one of the greatest achievements of the great French organ-builder. The time had arrived in his career for him to be no longer satisfied with the ordinary organist's repertoire and those improvisations which, along with accompanying the plain-chant, seem to have been the limit of his liturgical duties; he now had the opportunity to write serious original works really worthy of publication.

Franck held his organist's profession in too high honour to allow him to descend into the easy-going habits of so many of his colleagues. A sincere Christian, but no devotee, no regular observer of his religious duties, he believed the organist's function to be to assist the priest in worship. His ambition was to devote his artistic abilities to the service of the Church, and to raise the souls of the congregation to a higher plane of religious meditation. To this end he had no need to pursue virtuosity for its own sake, no desire to tickle the ears of the congregation with banal but seductive commonplaces. In future every note he wrote down with such care and calligraphic precision was to be passed through the close-woven sieve of his weekly improvisations, which he systematically, but spontaneously, poured out in his usual in-going voluntaries, offertories, versicles, and anthems. He could not be expected to eradicate all at once from himself the pianistic habits that by now had become second nature to him, but all the same he kept continually in mind the practical lessons he had learnt from his older colleagues or from visiting organists whom he had had a chance, at long or short intervals, of hearing in Paris—from the veteran Boëly, for example, who died at the moment of Franck's accession to Sainte-Valère, but to whom he had often listened when not occupied with his own Sunday services, and from whom he probably acquired his taste for the more severe forms favoured by Bach; from Hesse of Breslau, too, whom he no doubt heard at Saint-Eustache in 1844, and Lemmens of Malines, heard with enthusiasm at Saint-Vincent-de-Paul in 1852 and at Saint-Eustache in 1854. From the last named he seems to have learned more about musical design than about the true *legato* style of organ-playing, of which the Belgian organist was the champion, and the upholder of the tradition of Bach's German successors.

It is a matter of certainty that from the very start of his work at Sainte-Clotilde he was regularly playing the major works of the Leipzig Cantor. But one may well wonder how, before his installation there, he had found time and opportunity to bring his pedal-playing up to a proper standard of technique; for he cannot have failed to realize his own shortcomings at this moment, his lack of full technical training, and the necessity to put in a great deal more donkey-work. Our view of him is supported by the knowledge that on February 28, 1858, the firm of Pleyel delivered to "M. Auguste Franck" an "upright pedal-board (No. 25,655)," obviously for practice purposes. The fact may appear astonishing to-day, for the fame of the organist of Sainte-Clotilde has spread into every part of the musical world. Conditions were different a hundred years ago. And we are aware to-day, from a variety of evidence, that that charming improviser Franck did not always show himself to be technically faultless or above criticism. All through his career, it is clear, he never acquired a first-class pedal-technique, for all his practising at home at his new pedal-board.

It is not unamusing to observe that at the very moment of Franck's appointment at Sainte-Clotilde his brother Joseph (still retaining the additional denomination "of Liége") was publishing "Six preludes and fugues for organ with obbligato pedal parts, designed for use as offertories and out-going voluntaries." The volume was dedicated to Benoist, who had taught both the brothers; it was announced by the publisher as being the work of one of those rare organists "who are seeking to attain the technical level of achievement that has commonly been reached in Germany." Some sort of fraternal rivalry was afoot, the younger brother wanting to be more up-to-date than his elder brother.

César began to publish some works. In 1858 there appeared an andantino for organ which has, if no other virtue, a certain melodic interest, already approaching the Franckist style. The following year the publisher Hartmann (now absorbed by Heugel) issued three anthems and three motets. He also wrote about fifty pieces for harmonium which as a collection later came in for considerable discussion. It was a modest start, leading on to the *Six Pieces for Organ* (1860–62), which he dedicated to six of his fellow-organists and friends.

During this period his duties as precentor and choirmaster led him to write a handful of works for voices and organ. Little need be said here about his organ accompaniments and choral arrangements of Gregorian chant according to the system, now entirely superseded, of R. P. Lambillote. Lambillote was a Jesuit who had lived at the College of Vaugirard, where Franck taught the piano; he died in 1855. The meeting of priest and musician had been a prime cause of the publication of a practical manual of Gregorian chant which was issued in a series of fascicles by the publisher A. Leclère (1858). We can possibly trace some influence in this direction from brother Joseph, who, in league with the prolific Abbé Nisard and his energetic publisher, Repos, had industrialized (or should one only say 'commercialized'?) French church music. Little attention need be paid to an *Ave Maria*, for soprano, tenor, and bass, nor to a *Solemn Mass*, for bass solo and organ, published in 1858 by Régnier-Canaux: neither has earned the honour of a reprint.

The *Mass*, for three voices, is of far greater interest; it is laid out for soprano, tenor, and bass soloists, with accompaniment for organ, harp, 'cello, and double bass. The piece is unequal, for the various sections were written at different times: the *Kyrie*, *Gloria*, and *Sanctus* were early productions and, indeed, as some other early works do, remind us of the melodic and harmonic style of Schubert; the *Agnus Dei* (a well-written piece) takes the place of another, torn up by the composer. The *Credo* seems to have been the latest in order of composition, probably 1859. Near the date of publication (1872) the work was enriched by the addition of the famous *Panis angelicus*, which at once became popular, and has remained so. It appears certain that this movement demanded the use of trumpets and trombones, for the family records show a manuscript of it "arranged for organ from wind instruments."

Opinions of this important *Mass* have differed greatly. Saint-Saëns, anything but an enthusiast usually, especially where his colleague's works were concerned, declared, "This is truly cathedralesque music!" One of Franck's pupils, Camille Benoît, published in the *Gazette musicale* of July 27, 1879, a long essay that can only be described as dithyrambic. Another pupil, Charles Bordes, in the *Courrier musicale* of November 1, 1904, reserved his admiration for certain sections only: the *Kyrie* he considered "an exquisite prayer," the *Agnus* "a pearl of musical imagination," the *Quae est ista* "an unmatched preface to the offertory," worthy (he suggested) of John Sebastian Bach. On the other hand, the *Quoniam tu solus* from the *Gloria* he considered "boisterous" and "less worthy of a soloist than of a songster on the spree." Bordes was deeply impregnated with the dogmas then recently imposed by the *Motu proprio* of Pope Pius IX; as a result, though he was devoted to his master, his valuation of the music was that it was unfitted for liturgical use. Even Vincent d'Indy, in the biography, makes no doubt of his view that "certain passages in the *Gloria* are so vulgar as to be unworthy of the hand that wrote the *Béatitudes*." The earliest section, the *Credo*, is couched in a manner more symphonic than is suitable for its purpose; it is, in fact, written in sonata form and, at least according to d'Indy, is overweighted with expressive intentions and philosophical ideas which complicate and hamper the thematic treatment. The other sections are certainly more straightforward and concise.

When he first went to work at Sainte-Clotilde Franck had not yet undergone the process of refinement, of purification in music, to which some of his disciples later subjected him by indirect means. His religious feelings were strong and his artistic ideals high; for all that he remained a working organist and choir-master. For his own church he would write good sound music in the conventional style of his period, from which a whole century divides us. Despite his unflagging inventive power in this medium of church music, as in others, he showed that he had within himself a poor sense of objective criticism, in that he was willing to follow the likes and dislikes of his contemporaries, particularly those of his wife, whose taste was none of the best. Certain deficiencies in musical culture are only too evident in this *Mass*, for all its good qualities. He had been musically biassed in the 'thirties at the Conservatoire; he had had no time to catch up with lost time during the period when he was an itinerant teacher and a busy family man. Franck himself admitted to the end of his life an almost complete ignorance of the music of Palestrina and the 'Golden Age,' which, by some extraordinary concatenation of elements, contained nothing to interest him. He turned his mind quite willingly towards the deplorable style of Père Lambillote and his versions of Gregorian canticles, and indeed composed and at times made public some works comparable to them—*Tendre Marie* ("Gentle Mary") (unpublished), and *Le Garde d'honneur* (published in 1859).

The first performance of the *Mass*, for three voices, was given at Sainte-Clotilde under the composer's direction on Easter Tuesday, April 2, 1861. The accompanying organist, Théodore Dubois, took Franck's place at the main organ. Though announced as a composition by "the senior Franck, organist and choirmaster at Sainte-Clotilde," the new *Mass* seems to have attracted little attention. The *Gazette musicale* printed no more than the bare news that "the *Mass* was excellently performed by the singers MM. Chapron and Leter, as well as by the choir and orchestra. The performers did honour to the talent of the elder of the two Francks."

In the same style as this *Mass*, and written about the same date, are a number of Franck's manuscripts, many of them incomplete. Their musical value gives us no ground for questioning Charles Bordes's judgment that the works composed by Franck for church use were of little liturgical value and unequal in their artistic worth. Had they been published they would have added but small glamour to the rising fame of the organist of Sainte-Clotilde.

After his association with Cavaillé-Coll Franck wrote a series of *Six Pieces for Organ*, published at first by Maeyens-Couvreur and later taken over by Durand. It is an excellent set of short works, one that shows (or should show) to the musical world the talents (perhaps the genius, especially in the ecclesiastical realm) of our young organist. We may take it that they are the outcome of his first serious thoughts at the organ-stool, his first laboratory experiments at the console of Sainte-Clotilde. Franck was always making experiments in his free style as he improvised for High Mass, Vespers, and Benedictions; he would pursue his course in music until he was unanswerably interrupted by the bell announcing the end of the office.

There was a period (as we have seen) when the larger number of organists were entirely without thought for the art of music in its symphonic guise or even as a medium of classical culture. They were quite content with pandering to public taste by alternating excessively brilliant registration with crawling tunes made more sentimentally appealing by the use of the *vox humana*. In improvising they were forced to cling to some kind of skeleton form; apart from flimsy musical structure (well-built, no doubt, according to the ears of the congregation) they had little understanding of music, but their improvisations probably pleased their musical friends as well as the public. César Franck had to follow suit, even in his published works; and he wanted to please his musical friends (so-called)—Chauvet, Saint-Saëns, Lefébure-Wély, his old teacher Benoist of the Conservatoire, the organ-builder Cavaillé-Coll, and the pianist Alkan (his dedicatees for the pieces).

Of the musicians mentioned above some are to-day unknown, or rather forgotten: Charles-Alexis Chauvet (1837–71). He studied at the Paris Conservatoire first piano, then organ, for which he won the senior prize in 1860. He became organist at the Church of Saint-Thomas-d'Aquin, then at Saint-Bernard, then at Saint-Merry, until he reached the height of the Trinité when it was completed as a building, in 1869. He was remarkable both as a composer and as an improviser, and was the dedicatee of the first of the *Six Pieces*, a confraternal offering by Franck to the musician who succeeded Joseph Franck at Saint-Thomas. Chauvet had a reputation for an austerity in manner and performance that was held to be Protestant; he was, in fact, one of the rare church musicians of his time to play the larger works of Bach.

On the opposite side of the musical fence stood Lefébure-Wély (1817–69), also now quite forgotten. He was the most worldly of organists, one who was quite content with 'the outside of the cup and of the platter.' He enjoyed a widespread reputation among ignorant lovers of music owing to the superficial (not to say, puerile) style of his compositions, which for six or seven years after 1869 were the joy and delight of regular attendants at the Church of Saint-Sulpice. Charles-Valentin Alkan (1813–88), known as "Alkan Senior," was an accomplished pianist and a composer of some standing; we have already observed that he had a high opinion of Franck's musical abilities, and in the author's book *Vincent d'Indy* (vol. i, p. 163) it has been recorded that the two musicians met round about 1875.

At last the real Franck appears; the *Six Pieces* may at moments throw us fleeting reminders of the style of the period, but they present the veritable Franck, the Franck-to-be, on every page of their varied contents; they are solidly mortised and mitred like the best works of Bach, and at times they follow the lead of Beethoven in his sonatas.

The *Fantaisie* (Op. 16) justifies its title by the freedom and independence of its three differing sections; these are two andantes enclosing an allegretto, and each can be detached from the others for playing as a separate piece. It is in the first section, in the course of a canon, that there appears the tune often quoted as resembling the 'Sleep' motif from *Die Walküre*—a plain coincidence, since at the time of writing down the work Franck could not possibly have known Wagner's score, though it had been published in 1856.

A more characteristic work is the *Grande Pièce symphonique*, a work of some splendour, indeed, which inspired the following euphemistic phrases from Alfred Bruneau (*Figaro*, April 29, 1898):

> It is a vast monument of song, cyclopean in architectural design, and yet decorated with the most delicately carved friezes; a huge cathedral standing before us serene and strong, a scene for human action and for triumph.

To justify Bruneau's high-flown imagery, we would add that the work is laid out in sonata form—is, indeed, a large-scale (perhaps too large-scale) symphonic design of the cyclic type, with a Beethovenesque recapitulation before the final recalling of all the themes. One cannot help noticing certain foreshadowings of the *Symphony* to come in 1888, particularly in the main subject, which seems to set us an analogous problem to solve. The musical style is by now firmly Franckist, and the intensity of emotion in the work opens up a vision of certain future works of the later period—the *Quintet* in particular.

The *Prelude, Fugue, and Variations* (Op. 18), the third piece in the set, is the best known of them thanks to the transcriptions for piano and for harmonium which Franck brought forward, in 1873, as a present for his pupils Louise and Geneviève Deslignières, who were the daughters of the headmistress of a boarding-school where he first taught piano and later became supervisor of music.

There is an obvious something in it that recalls Bach's "Forty-eight," and a listener of to-day cannot help thinking too of the later Franck work, the *Prelude, Choral, and Fugue*, another triptych for piano-solo. Moreover, in more than a detail here and there one can pre-envisage the *Symphonic Variations*, for piano and orchestra. It would be easy to point out in the organ works those passages (arpeggios, for example) which speak of pianistic training. Nevertheless, the easiness of the writing and the apparent spontaneity are striking.

An almost bucolic simplicity is to be found in the *Pastorale* (Op. 19); here, as in certain earlier pieces, one can pick up an echo of Mendelssohn. Two melodic themes are used in contrast with each other: one a singing tune, the other lively and rhythmic. *Prière* (Op. 20) is complex and difficult, but (underneath all that) emotional and touching: again two main themes are opposed, this time of more similar character and feeling; against them there is a third voice, or melody, designed expressly for the trumpet stop at Sainte-Clotilde. Entirely different in style is the *Finale*, where one finds a fanfare in a conventional military style set against a memorable tune of a type not unlike that in the *Prière*.

The whole set of the *Six Pieces* is remarkable, one would say, for the originality of its melodic invention. The organ-writing is novel, one may agree, and there is a personal character in the changing harmonies; rhythmically, the work is lacking, and the registration for the instrument quiet and unelaborate. The essential element of melody, however, is always present; it was the melody, too, that first caught the attention of those listeners in the last thirty years of the nineteenth century. The aptness of the melodies and their melismas, all so easy to follow with the ear alone, brought to Franck a general success comparable only to the local success accorded to those other pieces which for so long were never played outside the walls of the Church of Sainte-Clotilde or by other fingers than the composer's. Musicians capable of assessing the true worth of a famous organist's compositions were rare birds in 1872; and, as a result, a mere official position was of little value in attracting the attention of the larger public. To judge in our own day these *Six Pieces* at their proper level of musical value we must remember that they are nearly a hundred years old, and that they were written during a period when the worst possible taste was dominant in the Church, a petty universe in which the most popular star among all the planets and constellations was Lefébure-Wély.

Contemporary with the *Six Pieces for Organ* come some works laid out for harmonium which Franck wrote for liturgical use at Sainte-Clotilde: a *Quasi Marcia* for harmonium (Op. 22), and *Five Pieces* for harmonium (without opus number). All of them are of small size, but are interesting for their melodic intention, their flowing technique, and their gentleness of mood.

During his first weeks at Sainte-Clotilde, and even before he reached there from the temporary chapel of Sainte-Valère, Franck was filled with a great happiness and an upspringing hope. He had had word from Berlin of the performance of his *Third Trio* by Hans von Bülow. There is a mention of this event in Bülow's letters to Liszt. On February 28, 1858, Bülow writes: "On Thursday, my last 'musical evening,' Franck's *Trio in B minor*." On March 12th he gave Liszt an account of the Berlin critics' reception of the concert:

> The *Kreuzzeitung* says that after César Franck's Trio (No. 3 in B minor) your own *Conzertstück* came as a positive relief! Yet other papers, the *Nationalzeitung* and the *Spener'sche*, possibly revenge, puffed up Franck to the skies. Behold, the modern Babylon!

During the ensuing year Hans von Bülow greatly exercised himself to make Franck's works known in Germany; we find him writing to Liszt on May 24, 1859: "As far as trios are concerned, we have had no chance yet to play either the Franck or the Volkmann at Leipzig."

A mere French organist, Franck could hardly be unaffected by the possibilities of success promised him in Germany by artists of the first order, like Liszt and Bülow. To the latter he wrote a long letter which bears no date, but must have been posted during the month of March 1858. The text of it is full of interesting points.

Hans von Bülow is treated as a real friend, "the only suitable name," in Franck's opinion, "for one who has shown such interest in me of recent years, and in a sense has fought a battle for my music." For himself, Franck says, he is "handicapped by innumerable jobs of work and also tied by the composition of a Mass," which he was then scoring for orchestra. The Mass referred to must be that for three voices mentioned above, which was to appear in print in 1860. First of all, Bülow is thanked

> a thousand, thousand times for the persistence and courage with which you have constantly performed works that are anything but popular in style. Thank you once more for the success your great abilities have won for me.

Franck was worried by the reception, according to reports, of the *Third Trio* at the concert of the 9th of March. He asks Bülow if he knows the *Fourth Trio*, in B minor. "It is in one movement only. Though its public appeal is less general than that of the *First* and *Third*, I fancy you would like it; I think rather well of it myself."

Another point to observe is the inclusion of certain revealing details about two projects for the future. Franck says:

> I am proposing to write this summer a sonata for piano and violin; it is to be dedicated to Madame von Bülow, who has done for me in Berlin all you yourself have done for me in Dresden. Will you do me the honour to follow her lead and allow me to dedicate to you the next piece of instrumental music I write after the sonata?

Franck, so long silent, had thus in mind certain major essays in chamber music; as far as we know, he never actually wrote a note of them. In the preceding chapter we wrote of a sonata and a trio which were sent to Liszt, but of which no vestige remains. One wonders what manuscripts may have lain hidden in the

shelves of the German publishers, nearly all destroyed in the
bombing of 1940–45.

The other project is rather different. "It has taken my fancy,
and I find it very tempting." Bülow had considered arranging
a performance of *Ruth* at Dresden; the composer was overjoyed,
and describes his Biblical eclogue in these terms:

> It is not a very large work, lasting only about an hour and a half,
> cheap to put on, and easy for the performers. The one thing neces-
> sary is to find three artists of ability to sing the rôles of Ruth
> (soprano), Naomi (mezzo-soprano, rather low in range), and Boaz
> (bass). The other two solo parts are unimportant; Orpah is a man
> of the people, and there are plenty of singers who could undertake
> his music.

Franck's own opinion (of great importance to us) of his work of
1846 is then only expressed:

> I think you will be impressed by *Ruth*. You will find in it no
> trace of the hand that wrote the trios, for it is extremely simple;
> yet I have some affection for it myself, both for the ideas it contains
> and for the individual atmosphere of the whole work. The choral
> and orchestral writing is designed for performance under the most
> ordinary conditions.

Franck recognizes that the oratorio "needs a certain amount of
revision," and says that he will touch it up during the coming
year; he will also have a German translation made in Paris, and
if Bülow's project should come to anything will send on the
orchestral parts at the beginning of the winter. A rosy outlook!
Splendid schemes for both composition and performance! But
none of them was achieved.

The Bülow family remained staunch to César Franck. Hans
von Bülow wrote in 1860 to tell him that the publisher Schuberth
was coming to Paris to hear Franck play his *First Trio* at a concert;
we do not know if either the visit or the concert took place.
Bülow himself was in Paris in February to give some piano
concerts, and we may take it as certain that he made personal
contact with Franck. The following year, 1861, Cosima von
Bülow wrote to the composer a letter of thanks for sending her,
not a sonata, but some songs which she found "most original,
and full of charm."[1]

---

[1] Was Franck present at Wagner's concerts in Paris in 1860? It is highly probable, but
he does not appear to have had an opportunity of meeting Wagner.

Another German musician who was to devote himself to the task of making known César Franck's works was the pianist Ludwig Hermann. His long letter from Dresden dated April 11, 1861, deals with the trios, which he had recently played in that town, and gives some news of their reception:

> Your inspired *Trio No. 1* made a tremendous impression on the audience, especially the first time I played in it, and the performance was greeted with prolonged applause. The only adverse comment was about the first subject's being rather monotonous. On the other hand, the second subject, in F sharp major, was considered by every one to be wonderfully effective.

The *Third Trio* had been given a private performance before an invited audience of professional musicians; the adagio delighted the hearers, while the finale surprised them; but (we are told) those who heard it then for the second time—it had already been performed by Hermann in February—"liked it even more on this hearing than on the first." The German pianist added that he was now studying the *Fourth Trio*, and had great hopes that his playing of it would help the public to appreciate *Ruth* at Dresden.

The success of Franck's trios seems to have been fairly widespread at this period, in Germany if not elsewhere, thanks to the good offices of a group of such artists as Liszt, Bülow, and Hermann. Up to the time of the Franco-Prussian War of 1870–71 they were highly thought of and retained some hold on the public. Thenceforward they were forgotten for more than thirty years, although they were revived in France at one of the first concerts given by the Société Nationale.[1]

Considered one of the leading exponents of the organs built by Cavaillé-Coll, César Franck at times took part in the formal opening of instruments by this maker, to whom in company with Saint-Saëns and Widor he stood or acted as a professional adviser. In 1862 he gave an organ recital at the Church of Saint-Sulpice, where, three days before, the new instrument had been inaugurated by Alexandre Guilmant, at that time organist of Saint-Nicolas at Boulogne-sur-mer; this young player, one of the

---

[1] The *Trio in F sharp major* was disinterred in Munich in 1909, where it was announced as "first performance." The critic Rudolf Louis devoted an article to it in the *Münchner Neueste Nachrichten*, in the course of which he recalled that the trio had enchanted Peter Cornelius half a century before. Cornelius lived at Weimar with Liszt from 1853 onward, and no doubt thus came to know Franck's works.

future founders of the *Schola cantorum*, was some years later (March 8, 1868) to open the organ at Notre-Dame in company with Saint-Saëns, Chauvet, Loret, and Widor, and later still (1871) to be appointed Chauvet's successor at the Trinité Church. At the recital of May 2 Guilmant was supported by Camille Saint-Saëns, from the Madeleine, and "Franck, senior," from Sainte-Clotilde. The *Gazette musicale* classed Franck as "austere, but in no way pedantic." A group of organists also took part in the inauguration, on April 26, 1863, of the organ at Saint-Étienne-du-Mont, rebuilt by Cavaillé-Coll: "The elder M. Franck, from Sainte-Clotilde," writes the *Gazette* of May 3, "makes masterly use of his light-foot foundation stops and his sixteen-foot pedal stops." Another such ceremony took place on April 29 at Saint-Sulpice with Saint-Saëns, Guilmant, Bazille, and Georges Schmitt, and yet another on October 10, 1867 at Saint-Denis-du-Saint-Sacrement.

Next came an invitation to play on the new organ at the Church of the Trinité, where the young Chauvet was principal organist, on March 16, 1869, some days after the funeral of Berlioz. With him were Saint-Saëns, Widor, and other well-known players. Franck's improvisations stirred Widor to such enthusiasm that he declared that "the themes, the development, the formal completeness are all equally to be admired; in fact, he has never written down any better music than he played to-day." The *Gazette* of March 21 praised "his lively improvisations, so well carried through, in which his aim was to make contrasting play with the greatest possible number of sonorities." The critic of *La France musicale* of the same date made a point of opposing the classical type of organ-playing with that of a specialist in the more alluring type of church music.

> In the richly varied programme of this organ concert, with which the most academic-minded could not be offended, the honours went, not to Saint-Saëns, the master of strict counterpoint, nor to M. C. Franck, among whose restrained improvisations were to be heard some pleasing episodes worthy of a better proportioned and more harmonious setting.

According to this critic, the successful soloist of the party was Auguste Durand, organist, critic, and publisher-to-be, who swept the audience off its feet with his representation of a 'storm.'

> The religious style of music has no need to be plainly dull, as
> some musicians would have us think who hide their creative sterility
> under a top layer of pretentious harmony.

Two months later, in May, Franck himself was dazzled by hearing
at Notre-Dame, not the above-mentioned exponent of the picturesque style of organ-playing, but the Austrian Anton Bruckner,
who gave, among other items, a superb improvisation on a theme
by his fellow-organist Chauvet, in the form of a "Prelude, Fugue,
and Variations."

From time to time Franck was in the habit of giving 'organ-
concerts' (they were not yet given the name of 'recital') at his
own parish church. At one of these, on November 17, 1864, he
played an entire programme of his own compositions. The
accounts of it printed in the *Gazette* and *La France musicale* are
so similar that one may guess that they originated from the house
of Cavaillé-Coll.

> M. Franck played his own pieces, which are written with a
> masterly hand. One noticed in the first his happy use of chords on
> the *vox humana*, and then in the *Pièce symphonique* a distinguished
> melody played first on the clarinet and later recalled on the *voix
> celeste*. At this concert M. Franck showed himself to be a composer
> of learning as well as a skilful executant, and thus fully proved to us
> once again that the standards of organ-playing are being steadily
> raised day by day in France.

His programme on that occasion lists the following works:
Fantaisie in C, the *Grande Pièce symphonique*, the *Pastorale*, an
Andante in C sharp minor, and a Finale for full organ. Under
these somewhat vague titles we recognize the entire set of the
Six Pieces for Organ of 1860–62.

Another outstanding concert—exceptional in that it gave
Franck's compositions a very fine showing—was held on April
13, 1866. It was organized by one of the organist's friends and
supporters, the most important of them all—Franz Liszt himself.
That great musician, according to the story related by Franck to
his pupils, one day attended Mass at Sainte-Clotilde; he sat in
the choir and heard the organ improvisations; the service over,
the two old friends met, and Liszt said, "How could I ever forget
the man who wrote those trios?" Franck was slightly abashed,
and whispered a little sadly, "I fancy I have done rather better

things since them." As a result of their talk a meeting was arranged at his console between Franck, Liszt, and Théodore Dubois to plan out a special concert to be given in Sainte-Clotilde where all could hear the latest works by the composer of the trios that were so often played at Weimar.

On April 9, 1866, Liszt wrote from his Paris address to J. L. d'Ortigue, a critic of some age, the friend and deputy of Berlioz, and very knowledgeable about church music.

> It will give me great pleasure to see you once again, my dear friend, on Thursday next at 2 P.M., at the organ concert to be given at Sainte-Clotilde by Franck, a musician who greatly interests me.

According to the *Gazette musicale* of April 22, Liszt was surrounded in the church by a most distinguished company, all assembled

> to hear the regular organist of the parish, M. Franck, senior. The diverse compositions of his own that M. Franck played are all written in a strict, not to say severe, style, but one that does not exclude variety; they certainly make the fullest use of the very wide resources of the Sainte-Clotilde organ, one of M. Cavaillé-Coll's finest constructions. The composer was much congratulated by those present, a large and distinguished company. Franz Liszt, in whose honour the concert was held, warmly complimented M. Franck on the high idealism of his music and on his authoritative performances.

Liszt himself came to the concert dressed in clerical clothes—a cassock, knee-breeches, silver-buckled shoes; he was the centre of a crowd of ladies and musicians among whom was the Princess Metternich, the central figure of the audience at the first performance of *Tannhäuser* at the Opéra, in 1861. The enthusiasm shown by Liszt was unbounded; on Franck's works he pronounced: "These poetic pieces have a clearly marked place alongside the masterpieces of John Sebastian Bach"—than which no musician could wish for a more splendid consecration!

At this period, no doubt with the idea of supplementing the usual choral repertory, Franck wrote certain short oratorios, which have never been published, like *The Tower of Babel*, dated April 1865, and *The Complaint of the Israelites*, the second chorus of which, the "Canticle of Moses," we know to have been performed, since the family archives contain twenty-three parts for

four mixed voices with piano. These minor works are fore-
runners of the *Béatitudes*, *Rédemption*, and *Psalm CL*.

In 1865 César Franck took up a new abode with his wife and
his two sons (now seventeen and twelve years old respectively) in
the quarter they had desired for several years to live in—the Rue
de Rennes, later to be called the Boulevard du Montparnasse.
The address was No. 95 Rue de Rennes, off the Boulevard Saint-
Michel, a ground-floor apartment with a small garden adjoin-
ing other gardens. In this neighbourhood the composer found
peace and quiet, hardly troubled by the bells of the neighbouring
convents. Here, in 1869, he began work on one of his principal
works, *Les Béatitudes*; here too he wrote all his major orchestral
works that were to give him a lasting title to fame; and here he
continued to live and work to the end of his earthly days.[1]

[1] On the outer wall of the building where the composer lived a commemorative tablet
was put up, on December 18, 1922. The occasion was one of official ceremony followed
by a visit to César Franck's former apartment.

CHAPTER XI

The War (1870-71): The Société Nationale

FROM the day of his marriage in 1848—from two years before, indeed; from the day of his break with his father—César Franck seemed to have nothing to look forward to but the most humdrum career. His position was no better than this—he was a teacher of the piano, working for the most part in colleges and boarding schools; he was a minor organist whose chances of fame were restricted by the cultural limitations of his instrument; as a pianist he had sunk almost entirely to the modest functions of an accompanist; as a composer he was responsible for some church music which would hardly reach any ears but those of regular church-goers, and for some comparatively juvenile chamber music which had been wholly forgotten in the country of his adoption.

A sudden and fundamental change came about in Franck's life when he was reaching his fiftieth birthday. This change was entirely unforeseen and was caused by an astonishing concatenation of events which quite upset all preconceived notions of his future career. For, step by step, our modest organist, so little known, so unwilling to thrust himself before the public, was beginning to develop into one of the principal personalities of his day—a musician honoured by musicians, a prolific composer, a leader in the new musical movement.

The Franco-Prussian War put plenty of rocks in his path, especially at the time of the Siege of Paris and the Commune. After the first setback in 1870, he lost a great number of his private pupils, as he had in 1848, most of them having escaped from the much beleaguered capital before its actual capitulation.

He did not bestir himself to get them back later under his wing. And while his pupils were leaving him, so was the extra money he earned in his position as organist. He found himself with time on his hands for the first time since the Revolution of

1848, and for the same reasons. He had to undergo all the priva-
tions, first of war conditions, and then of the actual process of
siege. He played his part in the disasters with a smiling courage,
the greater because (like so many of the French people) he
cherished at first the warmest hopes of victory. A later page will
show the effect which musically and patriotically the whole affair
exercised upon him.

His sons were anxious to join in the fray, and Franck himself
made it clear that he only wished he were a Frenchman. He still
believed, owing to his father's wrong-headedness and misplaced
politics, that he was a Belgian citizen, as indeed he in fact was,
since at the age of twenty-one he had not opted for France,
which he most probably would have done had he known that
his father had been naturalized. Learning on the death of his
father (1871) that the latter had become a Frenchman César
then thought that he himself had automatically become French
too. This he declared himself to be when appointed professor at
the Conservatoire, but actually he was not French. He was not
properly naturalized until 1873, and it was necessary for him to
regularize his illegal nomination at the Conservatoire.

Out of the kindness of his heart he housed the family of some
friends of his in his apartment in the Boulevard Saint-Michel,
but he was hard put to it to overcome the difficulties of victualling
and heating. Henri Duparc, his one-time pupil at the College of
Stanislas, told some stories about these difficult times in the *Revue
musicale* of December 1922. Daily conditions of life during the
fighting were strained to an almost picturesque point. Franck
and his eldest son found themselves under the necessity of carting
or carrying the requisite coal for the family needs from one end
of Paris to the other. The family and the guests they harboured
were reduced to feeding, over a period of weeks, almost entirely
on the hot chocolate abundantly provided by Mme César Franck.
Surrounded by this general turmoil César found time to devote
himself peacefully to the writing of a major work for chorus and
orchestra. It may have been begun or merely sketched or no
more than planned in 1868, but it occupied his thoughts for a
dozen more years. The work was, of course, *Les Béatitudes*.

Meanwhile, his love for France showed itself musically on two
occasions in the composing, or at the least improvising, of music
for a set purpose. The first of them was in 1870. On November

9 of that year Paris was cheered by the news—exaggerated, alas!
—of the victory at Coulmiers. *Le Figaro* published an ode to
Paris:

> I am Paris, queen of all cities. The wind blows pitilessly, but I
> do not bend before its blast. I am covered by armour of bronze,
> and I bellow out my battle-cries. Before my heart is dried of blood,
> before I am exhausted by hunger, you will feel the strength of my
> limbs, and you will run for safety to the Rhine. On that day, I
> shall take up my harp anew, and I shall sing a great pæan of triumph.[1]

Franck was completely carried away by the patriotic enthusiasm of this poem. His pupils Arthur Coquard and Henri
Duparc, bringing with them Vincent d'Indy (all three in the
National Guard), came to visit him in the Boulevard Saint-
Michel. He read the ode aloud to them in passionate tones and
cried, "I am fired with the idea of setting it to music." The next
day Coquard and Duparc returned to see their master in between
two skirmishes with the advanced troops; Franck played and
sang to them, in a fever of excitement, the score he had been
writing since they last saw him. Unfortunately, the apparent
victory was followed by the too real defeat; the triumphal song
of Paris was no longer suited to the moment, and was, in fact,
never finished. At least, it was certainly never sung in the city
that it apostrophised until forty-five years later, in the course of
a different war, that of 1914-18.

During the Commune, in 1871, Franck was once more moved
by sentiments similar to those that had inspired his Paris ode;
he undertook an analogous project, also for voice and piano or
voice and orchestra, to be called *Patria* and based on certain
verses by Victor Hugo taken from his poem *Les Châtiments*.
The truth is that he wrote the music at the express request of
Henri Duparc. This was the first but by no means the last
time that Franck allowed a pupil of his to influence the trend of
his inspiration.

Like its precursor, the new 'patriotic ode' was heard only once,
at the time of the centenary of Franck's birth (1922). The piece

---

[1] The French text reads, in part, thus: "Je suis Paris, la reine des cités. Le vent d'orage
souffle sans pitié, mais je ne m'inclinerai pas. Je me suis revêtue d'airain et j'ai poussé de
grands cris. Avant que mon sein se tarisse et que la faim hideuse m'épuise, vous sentirez
mon bras et vous fuirez au Rhin. Je reprendrai ma harpe et je chanterai un long chant de
triomphe."

was published by Roudanez, but went out of circulation and was
never reprinted, as a result of which it is practically unknown.
Franck's heirs and assigns were always reluctant to give permission
for it to be performed and published. The vocal scores of both
Patria and *Paris* were given to Henri Duparc, who kept the
manuscripts in one of his own folders.

Some of his leisure time Franck also gave to the composition
of some offertories designed for his services at Sainte-Clotilde.
Three of them were dedicated to his parish priest, the Abbé
Hamelin. They were issued by Repos, who published most of
the works of his brother Joseph and also issued from 70 Rue
Bonaparte a review and a whole catalogue of sacred music. Of
these pieces two were later heard (as we shall see) about the year
1871, not only in the church for which they were written, but
also in a newly formed concert society.

During the winter of 1870–71, Franck received news of the
death of his father, who died on January 22, 1871, at Aix-la-
Chapelle, his mother's family home. In company with his
brother, César took steps to ensure passage through the lines of
the assailant German army and so to reach Belgium and, if possible, Germany, in the hope that they could put into proper order
the question of legacies and the family succession.[1]

His own position immediately after the war, though it still
afforded him time for composition, was one of uncertainty. It
is possible that he may have considered the possibility of establishing himself firmly outside Paris. Soubre, the Director of the
Liége Conservatoire, died on September 8, 1871, and Franck perhaps applied for his post, though there is no record of his doing
so in the archives at Liége. At any rate, the appointment was
given to a younger man, a Liégeois of long standing, Théodore
Radoux; he was an accomplished composer and had also the
advantage of being on the spot and of having taught the bassoon
in the school itself for some fifteen years. Even if César Franck
actually approached the authorities in his native town, which is
more than doubtful, he would not for long have regretted being
passed over; his future lay in Paris, and was to be very much more
brilliant than he could possibly have hoped. Even the season of

---

[1] The grandson Robert Franck is responsible for this statement. On the other hand,
there was an unbreakable tradition in the family of Sanches, of whom we shall have more
to say in connexion with *Les Éolides*, that Franck spent a part of the war-period at Azille
in the department of Aude.

1871-72 was to show him that success could arrive swiftly and unexpectedly.

Franck came forward as both composer and conductor at a charity concert on October 15, 1871; he directed long extracts from the oratorio *Ruth* (now twenty-five years old and completely forgotten), having made some important modifications and improvements in the score. The public made much of the composer, and the criticisms were numerous and favourable. Among them the *Gazette musicale* of October 22 gave its opinion that "*Ruth* has fixed the tendencies of the French neo-archaic school of composers"—whatever that may mean! By far the most interesting to the student of Franck was the essay in the *Journal des Débats* of October 24, in which Ernest Reyer, whose judgment was worth listening to, hailed both the work and the composer. He wrote:

> I keep the score of *Ruth* on my piano. I have read it and reread it, and I greatly admire it. Call it what you will—Biblical eclogue or oratorio—it is a work full of simplicity and charm, of the subtle colouring and poetic splendour of a fresco by Luini.

As the concert was given in aid of those who had been burnt out in the fire at Saint-Cloud, Reyer continues that the sufferers

> were no doubt unaware that their misfortunes had provided an opportunity for a great composer to reveal himself in public. This great composer, of such high inspiration and with so masterly a command of the orchestra, is called César Franck: mark the name carefully, for you will encounter it again this winter in a programme of the Société des Concerts du Conservatoire. So fine a musician deserves such an honour.

The essay was indeed a magnificent tribute, and its equivalent may be found in shorter form in the other specialized reviews like the *Gazette* or *L'Art musical*. Seven months later Ernest Reyer repeated and developed his views in another issue of the *Débats*, writing this time about a complete performance of the work that was given under Franck's direction in the *salons* of the Grand Hotel. Part of his second essay runs thus:

> For the first time a complete performance has been given of that excellent Biblical eclogue known as *Ruth and Boaz*. This second time of hearing it, I am no less charmed than I was at the first by the touching simplicity of its melodies and the delicate restraint of its

orchestration, as well as the sonority of the masses of sound which the composer has so skilfully built up.

Reyer then raises the whole problem of César Franck's life and presents a dramatic picture of his destiny.

It has taken a full quarter of a century for this remarkable and poetic work to come into the sunlight of performance; even then, it has needed the disastrous plight of a group of unfortunates to obtain for it a hearing at a concert arranged, not for the delectation of the musical public, but for charitable purposes. If only M. César Franck had won with *Ruth*, twenty-five years ago, the success it has had to-day how many works might he not have completed which have no doubt been stifled by discouragement, self-mistrust, and the dire necessity to provide for his daily needs? Nor must we for a moment imagine that the acclamations showered on him recently, the emotions of his audience, the thousand and one hands stretched out to have the honour of grasping his—nothing in this warm reception can in one evening compensate him for his long years spent in musical solitude, silence, and neglect. Out of this triumph there will remain to-morrow no more than the memory of one evening's success, the fugitive dream of a single occasion.

Six weeks after the first of the two performances of *Ruth* Franck encountered a new success, less striking and less widespread, with another of his adolescent works—this time one of the thirty-year-old trios. He played it himself at the first concert of the Société Nationale de Musique on November 25, 1871, his collaborators being Jules Garcin and Léon Jacquard (all three performers were later to become professors at the Conservatoire).

This new concert-giving society had been founded as early as February 25 of that year, but the political events of the Commune had so far caused a delay in the public performances. The President was Romain Bussine, soon to be appointed professor of singing at the Conservatoire, his principal coadjutor being Camille Saint-Saëns; these two gathered together a group of musicians, most of them young. The junior member of the group was Henri Duparc, then twenty-three years of age; three others had not yet reached their thirtieth year—Gabriel Fauré, who held the minor post of assistant organist at Saint-Sulpice, Jules Massenet, already well known, and Taffanel, at that time flautist at the Opéra and the Société des Concerts du Conservatoire, and the future conductor of both these orchestras. Those in their thirties were Ernest Guiraud, later professor of composition at the Conservatoire, Théodore Dubois, the future director of that institution and at that moment choirmaster at Sainte-Clotilde, and Saint-Saëns himself; of the elder members, Jules Salomon (known as Garcin) the flautist, and Bussine, the founder, had passed the age of forty, while César Franck was the senior of them all, being on the point of entering his fiftieth year. It would seem probable that Franck—ever retiring by instinct—was brought to the committee's attention through his pupil Henri Duparc, at whose house the society was set on its way, by Saint-Saëns, who held him in high esteem, and by Théodore Dubois, who, having to listen week by week to his magnificent improvisations at the organ of Sainte-Clotilde, was in a better position than anyone in Paris to appreciate Franck at his true worth.

According to statements by Saint-Saëns, this little group of musicians—some of them classical-minded and reactionary, others of them advanced Wagnereans—agreed to form themselves into a musical brotherhood, but in no sense a coterie. We need not inquire how they differed among themselves in their musical outlooks; they were determined to unite in their efforts to spread the gospel of French music and to make known the works of living French composers. Their motto was *Ars Gallica*. Their united services were made imperative by an immediate necessity to give a new lease of life to French national music after the disaster of the war. According to their statutes, published by the committee's first secretary, Alexis de Castillon, their intention was to act "in brotherly unity, with an absolute forgetfulness of self." This rule was long adhered to.[1]

It was perhaps deference to the years of their oldest member that prompted the committee to set down at the head of the programme of their opening concert one of Franck's trios, reviving it after thirty years and more, and inviting the composer himself to undertake the piano part. So it was, however, and so, too, César Franck became the first composer ever to appear under the auspices of the new society. Which of the trios was the one chosen for this performance? Not, as Vincent d'Indy wanted us to believe, the *First*, in F sharp, a prophetic work in

[1] Camille Saint-Saëns, *La Société Nationale*. The essay first appeared in the *Revue et Gazette Musicale*, and was reprinted in his book *Harmonie et mélodie* (1885).

cyclic form and the most important of the youthful compositions. It was, in fact, the old, the almost jaded, *Trio de salon*, that pretty pastiche of an early style, which could at least offend no one, not even the most conservative listener. The choice was made by the composer himself, whose critical sense was quite incapable of foreseeing the judgments of the future. On this matter, the verbatim reports of meetings preserved in the Bibliothèque du Conservatoire (reserve F.994) leave us in no possible doubt. It was unquestionably the B flat trio which opened the long series of concerts of the Société Nationale. When Vincent d'Indy some years later began to give currency to his César Franck legend no doubt he was troubled by this odd and meaningless choice; so he gathered together a collection of printed programmes, put on one side that of the opening concert, and replaced it by a copy made in his own handwriting, which reads, indefinitely, "Trio by César Franck." It would be excusable to infer from this that the work played on that evening was the *First Trio*, in F sharp.

To discover how this youthful work, so palpably reactionary, was received is difficult, though Saint-Saëns has told us that the whole concert made an astonishing success. Some of the musical reviews had suspended publication during the war; other papers were content with enumerating without comment the works played there, or merely the composers' names. The *Gazette musicale*, for example, includes Franck's name among the younger people who "without having been through the academic mill, have nevertheless the knack of touching the ears and the hearts of the public."

One may well be surprised nowadays that Franck should have thought fit to play this youthful and quite unremarkable trio as a send-off for the Société Nationale, and later on to present at its sessions other quite minor works of mediocre value. But in the early 1870's that, we must remember, would have seemed quite natural, for the *Ars Gallica* society was in those early days considerably less severe in its standards than it was to become later under the influence of Franck's own followers. Those other days, when *Le Mariage des Roses* delighted the audience at its first hearing, were they not also the days when Henri Duparc wrote a "Suite of Valses," played in piano-duet form by Gabriel Fauré and Vincent d'Indy?

CHAPTER XII

Professor of Organ at the Conservatoire (1872): "Rédemption" (1873)

THE organist François Benoist retired from active life at the opening of the year 1872. Doyen of the professorial staff at the Conservatoire, at the age of seventy-eight he had spent fifty-three years in the organ professorship, a post founded for him in 1819. On February 1 César Franck took his place.

His nomination thereto was irregular, for though Franck had imagined himself a Frenchman ever since the death of his father, he remained in fact a Belgian. He had to regularize his position with the Conservatoire in 1873. His appointment also caused some surprise and chatter in the world of music.

Other eligible candidates were named, themselves prize-winners, and among them his brother Joseph, who won in 1852 the final award which César himself failed to obtain. But the incident caused no great stir, and the newspapers fell back on the usual formula that "no better choice could have been made." Possibly there was a flutter in the small circles of the organists and the hundreds of amateurs who flocked round the Société Nationale. Franck was little known to the public, but, then, his predecessor, Benoist, was hardly less ignored despite his compositions and his length of service. It could not have been foreseen that this minor detail should later arouse so many incidents in the school and have such important results on the future development of French music.

How César Franck came to be chosen it is difficult to discover. At least two versions of the story exist. The less familiar and the less reliable is that given by Saint-Saëns in a letter of November 23, 1915, to the effect that the organ-post was to have been offered to himself; the composer of *Samson et Dalila* had refused it and recommended that it should be given to César Franck, his colleague at the Société National. But statements by Saint-Saëns, as we have had occasion to show, must be accepted with some reserve.[1]

A more credible version is that of Théodore Dubois, who worked with Franck at Sainte-Clotilde, first as assistant organist and then as precentor. It was given to the public officially by Dubois himself when, thirty-two years later, he was the speaker at the unveiling of the monument to his former colleague.

> When the professorship of organ fell vacant through the death of Benoist [actually by his retirement, for Benoist lived till 1878] I at once sought out my principal, Ambroise Thomas, and said to him, "There is at the moment one man only who is fit for the post, and that is César Franck." Thomas replied that he fully agreed and would appoint him.

One wonders if the composer of *Mignon* remembered at the time that thirty years previously he himself had figured among the subscribers to Franck's three trios.

In thus taking the initiative Théodore Dubois was able to pay a debt of recognition to his elder friend for the warm welcome the latter had accorded him fourteen years earlier, on his appointment as assistant organist at Sainte-Clotilde, and at the same time to offer him some sort of compensation; for in the previous year Franck had been a candidate for Saint-Saëns's place as organist of the Madeleine, a remunerative post which Dubois succeeded in obtaining. From another point of view, by following Dubois's advice, Ambroise Thomas—the dominating success of the French lyric theatre—was giving something of consolation to a musician who, for all his value, remained in a mediocre obscurity.

In any case, contrary to the expectation of Saint-Saëns, the new appointment did little to improve the material circumstances of the organist of Sainte-Clotilde; however much it enhanced his reputation, the stipend was only a few hundred francs a year! At the most he could give up some of his school-work so as to give more interesting and better-paid lessons in organ-playing, and particularly in composition: new pupils were likely to come after a man connected with both the Conservatoire and the Société Nationale. Some of his former piano pupils, now

---

[1] One passage in this letter runs: "Franck had great ability, and it was I who took steps (in nominating him) to find room for it to spread, and so gave him the chance to stop wasting his time in mere teaching and to devote himself to composition. Genius needs more than mere talent to develop."

known as composers, became active canvassers on his behalf: at first Arthur Coquard and Henri Duparc, and later Vincent d'Indy, who from 1872 to 1873 advised his fellow-students to put themselves under Franck, and indeed became his most persistent publicity agent.[1]

The life of obscurity ceased for Franck from the winter of 1871–72. He was surrounded by pupils who treated him with the most affectionate deference, and saw in him, not merely a brilliant player in an official teaching position, but also the most reliable adviser of the younger French school, and, indeed, one of its leaders. At last he could live to some extent in the environment of the Société Nationale. He was a regular attendant of its Sunday afternoon committee meetings. The scores submitted to the Société he studied with care and also with indulgence, though he kept strictly to the rules laid down. And these rules indeed he humbly obeyed himself, submitting his own works to the judgment and vote of his younger colleagues, several of them his pupils. His numerous lessons prevented him from attending the regular meetings of the younger members, and he was seldom to be seen at Pasdeloup's Thursday morning rehearsals, when the orchestra read through the new works. But at least he was free to go to Camille Saint-Saëns's house on Monday evenings for those friendly gatherings of the Société's members, at which they showed each other their latest scores for mutual discussion and criticism. They were gay and enthusiastic evenings, and Franck nearly always found that he was the oldest member present and so treated with respect; up to that time his public success was not sufficient to be inconvenient to his fellow-musicians—not even to the master of the house, though later Saint-Saëns came to regard him with a surly jealousy. At his own house, 65 Boulevard Saint-Michel, Franck delighted in entertaining the more artistic members of his personal circle.

Three days after his appointment—that is, on February 4, 1872 —the Société des Concerts gave a performance of the more important parts of the cantata *Ruth*. The scene was that ancient and historical hall in the Rue Bergère which had witnessed the first performance of *Ruth*, in 1846; the singers were Mmes Marie

---

[1] It was in the month of October 1872 that d'Indy became a composition pupil of Franck's under circumstances that have often been described. See on this subject the author's book, *Vincent d'Indy*, vol. i, p. 126 *et seq.*

Battu and Fursch-Madier, MM. Bouhy and Bosquin. The Press notices were kindly; thus *L'Art musical* wrote that the work "shows the hand of a master who, if he has not entirely escaped the influence of Félicien David, yet possesses in himself both style and talent." Some months later Franck was to make a personal appearance in the same hall, where at the Société's concert at the end of December 1872 he played on the organ a prelude and a fugue in E minor.

The end of this happy year, which had seen the rise to eminence of a musician too often overlooked, was marked by the performance of *Ruth* (mentioned earlier) at the Grand Hotel concerts under the composer's direction. As a result of it Ernest Reyer, musical critic of the *Journal des Débats*, wrote the second of the enthusiastic articles already referred to, which seemed to fix once for all the position of a composer hitherto ignored and now starting life afresh.

One might well have imagined, remembering those earlier trios, that this new musical blossoming would be seen in the field of chamber music. That did not come till six or seven years later, and in the meantime it was choral and orchestral music that absorbed Franck's attention and brought him such warm satisfaction and such painful disappointment.

From its earliest foundation the Société Nationale had proposed to give symphonic concerts confined to the works of its own members—an idea instigated by Saint-Saëns, but stifled at birth by the financial prudence of his co-founder, Bussine. The project of full-scale concerts at less frequent intervals than those of chamber music still remained in the air, and it was with a view to their happening in the future that César Franck decided to write a major work; his decision was strengthened by the success of his earlier oratorio, *Ruth*, revived in 1871 after thirty-six years of oblivion. He set himself to compose a work partly for singing, partly for declamation—*Rédemption*—and according to his son wrote the work "in a single breath" in 1871–72, thus interrupting the completion of the *Béatitudes*. The final page is dated November 7.

The text of *Rédemption*, which is entitled not "oratorio" but "symphonic poem for mezzo-soprano, mixed choir, and orchestra," was by the librettist Édouard Blau. Massenet had considered setting it to music but had given up the idea. The subject and scheme were grandiose, not to say overwhelming, and may be briefly summarized thus. In Part I humanity, swamped by the dark waters of paganism, hears from the angels the announcing of Christ's coming; all men unite their voices in a Christmas hymn. Part II is a purely symphonic commentary on the following brief argument: "The centuries pass. The joy of a world transformed and gladdened by Christ's word." In Part III the angels lament the Fall of man, and an archangel pronounces a new redemption to come through prayer; mankind, repentant, sings a hymn to charity.

It is not difficult to understand why such a subject did not attract Massenet, why he had preferred the amiable libretto of *Marie-Madeleine* as more in keeping with his vague and sensual religiosity. On the other hand, *Rédemption*, so full of the inspiration of the Christian faith, was exactly the right subject for César Franck. "I firmly believe," he used to say, "all that I find therein." He felt a profound conviction, as well as the power that he could accomplish the task. Were such personal things in fact enough to enable the composer to realize his musical ambitions?

A minute analysis of the score—or, rather, of the first of its two versions, that played in 1873—is printed in Vincent d'Indy's *César Franck*. The analysis suggests that Franck's musical foundation was tonality, and that in the oratorio he applied for the first time his previously established principles of tonal architecture, "which later formed the basis of all his teaching": tonal architecture that is closely related to the poet's meaning—with music in the first and third parts which proceeds from obscure to luminous tonalities, the second veering from warm keys to cold and dull keys. This mobile tonal colour-scheme is rated as essential to Franck's music by his ardent disciple, who was to exploit the method systematically in his own compositions.

Unfortunately, on the one occasion when the first version of the work was given in public the symphonic movement was omitted and the orchestral playing abominable, so that the public had little chance of appreciating the purely Franckian tonal methods.

Some notes on the differences between the first and second versions of *Rédemption* may be read below; the first, we may here observe, gave sub-titles to the first and third movements of

"Once upon a time" and "To-day," and included the declamation of poems; for a long time both features of the work have been expunged.

The first performance of *Rédemption* had been reserved in advance for the second half of a sacred concert to be held on Maundy Thursday, April 10, 1873, the first half being devoted to vocal music by Rossini, Saint-Saëns, Lalo, and Mme de Granval. The next day, a second concert was to give a performance of Massenet's *Marie-Madeleine*. The occasion marked the first appearance of a new institution, the Concert National, later to develop into the Concerts Colonne. The newly formed orchestra was conducted by a newcomer, previously one of Pasdeloup's violinists and a man remarkable for his insight, his initiative, and his commercial abilities. From the very start things began to go wrong—with the choir-rehearsals, taken partly by Vincent d'Indy, who found difficulty in controlling the chorus from the Opéra, and especially with the orchestral rehearsals.[1]

At the first orchestral run-through badly copied and hopelessly incorrect parts upset the players, with the result that Vincent d'Indy, Henri Duparc, and Camille Benoît had to spend two nights and a day making minute revisions and corrections. At the full rehearsal the orchestra protested against playing the close of the first part, on the grounds that it was written in the rarely used key of F sharp major and was therefore unplayable. Both players and conductor disdained to try to settle the difficulties, the former because they had never heard of any composer outside the world of the theatre, the latter because for his own reputation he counted less on Franck's work than on next day's *Marie-Madeleine*. The rehearsals indeed were so badly directed that it was decided at the last moment to omit the orchestral section linking the two other parts, thus removing the essential element which would have revealed the composer's gifts as a symphonist. In such manner was smashed to the ground the shapely edifice César Franck had erected in his imagination.

It was the same with the soloists, who did not take kindly to the new score—with the reciters, especially the famous Mounet-Sully, whose inflated solemnity was a bad introduction for the listener to so devout a work, with Mme de Caters, whose vanity was not satisfied with the archangel's fine aria and who de-

[1] For a full account of these rehearsals see the author's *Vincent d'Indy*, vol. i, pp. 140–142.

manded, as compensation, to sing some Rossini. Vincent d'Indy wrote an account of the concert in a long letter to one of his cousins:

> The orchestra was execrable; it was only with difficulty that one could pick up the accompaniment in the vocal parts—if, indeed, one could get as far as that! But that was the fault of the conductor, who is totally inexperienced.

All these circumstances were enough to ensure the failure of the work—a failure clearly marked by the attitude of the audience; one by one they went out and left the rest of the work to be performed in a practically empty hall! Mme César Franck, foreseeing disaster with so ill-prepared a concert, had refused to attend, and sat at home awaiting her husband's return. When he came in, pale and terribly upset, his first words were: "Of one thing I am quite certain—it's a beautiful work."

This resounding failure was not lessened by the extremely reserved welcome afforded by the critics. The musical Press had little to say. A couple of lines in the *Ménestrel* merely announced "a new production of M. Franck's, remarkable in respect of both style and orchestration." A somewhat longer notice in the *Gazette musicale* praised the work as being

> in the grand manner, with an appeal both noble and severe. M. Franck handles the academic forms with great skill, but can find room as well for inspiration and emotion. There is nothing outstanding about *Rédemption*, to tell the truth, but the general style of the music is maintained at a high level, and it leaves behind an impression of both strength and serenity.

The daily Press hardly mentioned the work. One young critic, Adolphe Jullien (later to become of great importance), wrote in *Français* in praise of "an exceptional musician of equal talent and modesty, who has so long endured the frowns of fortune, consoling himself for his disappointment as a composer by his success as an organist." He commended the score for its construction, for its distinctive form, for its musicianship and its high-mindedness; but he made clear his view that

> inspiration is lacking, as well as a sense of grandeur, of the sublime. To attack a superhuman poem of this kind something more is needed than the pure and polished talent which created *Ruth—*

something like the thundering genius of Beethoven or the extravagant imagination of Berlioz.

Ernest Reyer, the distinguished critic on the *Journal des Débats*, wrote a similar notice which disappointed and deeply hurt Franck. He too compared *Ruth* with *Rédemption*, but could find in the new work none of "that delightful grace and charm and generous colouring" of the earlier. Franck, he alleged, had plainly made a mistake in judgment, and "not all the ability and resource of a master can cover up his error." The article was the more cutting in that it appeared several months after a long eulogy of the earlier work, and equally in that the same issue of the *Débats* contained ten or twelve columns in praise of Massenet and his *Marie-Madeleine*.

The failure of *Rédemption*, though it did not deter the Minister of Education from ordering a certain number of the scores for the libraries, prompted two of Franck's pupils to take a most delicate step. Henri Duparc and Vincent d'Indy took upon themselves to point out to their master the paramount need to remodel his score. It is possible that Mme Franck had already suggested the same idea to her husband. At first the composer received their suggestions with a bad grace, though they were offered with great respect and a lively devotion, but little by little he gave way to their entreaties and to acknowledge their timeliness. With many regrets, he modified the whole tonal scheme, he threw out those excessively sharpened keys that had fogged Colonne's players, and, after various attempts at remodelling the symphony of religious elation, he decided to rewrite it completely on new thematic material.

The original *Morceau symphonique* of 1872 has not disappeared; it occurs in a reduction for four hands in the edition of 1874 published by Hartmann, the joint-founder of the Concert National. The first orchestral score was preserved by the composer and can be read to-day at the Bibliothèque Nationale in an unbound pamphlet of 63 pages, separate from the rest of the manuscript. Its suppression is no matter for regret; the thematic development is overdone, and, as even d'Indy himself admits, the melodic invention is not up to that of the final version, often to be heard at concerts.

Conscientious and disinterested as always, Franck did not hesi-

TITLE-PAGE OF "THE THREE EXILES"

PART OF THE SKETCH-MANUSCRIPT OF "LES ÉOLIDES"

tate to buy back from Hartmann the entire first printing of what he now considered an imperfect work, and destroyed all the copies, leaving the field clear for the second version, rewritten in accordance with the critical suggestions of his best pupils. He admitted in all simplicity his faith in their judgment, especially in that of the somewhat censorious d'Indy. Indeed, on one occasion he spoke of the symphonic interlude to another of his pupils, Augusta Holmès, saying:

"I finished the scoring, but I then shewed the piece to a pupil in whom I have great faith and who pointed out a number of other changes I ought to make. So I have rewritten it, and now I fancy it is not too bad."

The second version was issued in 1874 by the same publisher, who later disposed of the rights to the publishing house of Heugel.[1]

Further disappointments over *Rédemption* were in store for César Franck from the summer of 1873 onward. It was then, as his biography records, that Vincent d'Indy made his first extended tour in Germany, taking with him two copies of the score to present on his master's behalf to Liszt and to Brahms. The former immediately received the work and its bearer with an equally warm welcome, praising the *Morceau symphonique* highly after playing through the duet version with d'Indy. A few days later, however, he ran through *Rédemption* with one of his American pupils, skipping various pages and scanning the rest with a rapidity that showed he was but little interested.[2] On the other hand, Brahms, as we know from d'Indy's often-quoted reports, refused the gift of the score which the young Frenchman sent on to him at Tützing.

The later version of the Interlude was played on the piano by Franck himself at the Société Nationale on February 13, 1874; the title was even more brief than in the revised version: "Centuries pass by, the world begins to blossom under the teaching of Christ." On May 16 following, the same society gave another concert, presenting Gabriel Fauré's Symphony, under Colonne;

[1] In an unpublished letter of March 8, 1876, to his friend Langrand, Vincent d'Indy remarks on the publisher's neglect of his composer: "Once again Franck has recently been made a fool of by Hartmann. Pasdeloup had given him a time for rehearsing the symphonic interlude from *Rédemption*; on the Thursday morning, every one present, it was found that Hartmann (whose job it is to do so) has failed to send over the orchestral parts; so up goes the rehearsal!"

[2] See Amy Fay, *Music Study in Germany.*

Saint-Saëns's *Phaëton*, under the composer; and the first part of
Rédemption, with Franck directing the orchestra and the Bourgault-Ducoudray chorus. This new presentation was the same
as that given at a charity concert at the Théâtre Ventadour, the
choir by now having become "M. César Franck's Choral
Society." About these performances under the composer's baton
we quote one or two Press opinions.

The *Chronique musicale* wrote in some scorn:

> It is difficult to analyse this work, for the poem is as vaguely
> mystical as the music. One's first task is to hold the score in one's
> hand and to follow with the eyes, over the continuous orchestral
> texture, the interminable recitatives of 'Man,' which are printed,
> but neither sung nor even declaimed as in *The Desert* and other
> symphonic poems. One's second task involves listening to choruses
> of men and angels, and even the *melopœïas* of archangels. We use
> the word advisedly, for of plain rhythmic motifs, of true melody,
> not a trace is to be found in any part of *Rédemption*. Wagner adepts
> and the anti-melodists should be fully satisfied with their evening's
> listening. There is never any exuberance of tune or rhythm to dis-
> turb their enjoyment.

For the *Gazette*, *Rédemption* had considerable merit, but the
general background was "somewhat grey and austere, lacking
those luminous touches of colour which catch the public's
attention and so make for popularity."

In *Les Débats* Ernest Reyer mixed praise and blame in almost
equal quantities. As a writer of operas himself, he considered
that Franck "too openly betrayed himself as an organist, a fervent
admirer and disciple of the great Sebastian Bach," and that he
indulged too much in that scholastic device of canon. The harmonic richness, the skilful orchestration, and "certain moments
of real inspiration" he commended. He reproduced his article of
1873, referred without appreciation to the *Morceau symphonique*,
and assured his readers of his "admiration and sympathy for so
able a composer."

Success remained elusive till twenty-two years later, some
time, alas, after Franck's death! On December 20 and 27, 1896,
Rédemption was revived at the Concerts Colonne, arousing
general enthusiasm, not only among musicians, but also among
literary men. Thus, Octave Mirbeau in *Le Journal* compared
the composers of the two *Rédemptions*, Franck and Gounod, to

the latter's disadvantage; and Georges Rodenbach wrote a similar essay in *Figaro*. These new recruits to a Franckism now at last triumphant were taken to task by André Hallays in *Les Débats*; he wrote:

> Whose fault was it if fame and success delayed so long in reaching this great musician? The real culprits are the writers who did nothing to stir up the apathy of conductors and to stimulate the interest of the public.

In 1896 they were too late on the scene: their no doubt praiseworthy action should properly have come at the time when the concert promoters were giving Franck the cold shoulder and when no one would play his works except the Société Nationale —a society (he continued) "considered to be a somewhat ridiculous shrine dedicated to the cult of boredom, laughed at in musical circles, and unable to inspire a line from the littérateurs."

The definitive score of *Rédemption* consists of two parts of equal length, separated by the symphonic interlude, each part divided into three. Space does not permit any description here of the hundred or so lines of poetry declaimed without music, which have for a long time been omitted from performances.

A short prelude of some fifty bars opens the first part; it is founded on a delightful theme (to be sung later by the angels) which the horn announces through violin arpeggios and the clarinet continues. The theme is treated in continuous canon with Franck's habitual dexterity when using strict academic devices. There is a vigorous terrestrial chorus written in the ordinary choral style of the nineteenth century, in which pagan sensualism is proclaimed in a manner more rowdy and brutal than powerful. Then follows a chorus of angels, in which the theme foreshadowed in the orchestral introduction is sung with a touching calm in canon with the orchestra: "We are messengers from heaven." In a brief transition passage a male chorus —questioning, restless, dark-toned—is posed against the short responses of the angels' chorus; the men's choir restates in striking terms the opening celestial theme and shapes it into a ritornello that suitably introduces the archangel's song. Here the annunciation of the Saviour's birth in the stable at Bethlehem is unfolded above a development of the angels' music. Then comes the hymn of gladness, with the choir reaching the key of E major, in place of the F sharp major which the Odéon musicians ana-thematized in 1873. To end this first part the whole choir sings a Christmas hymn.

The interlude, now called 'Symphony,' is built on two main ideas—an admirable tune expressing gladness and hope, which Emmanuel Chabrier described as "the very soul of music," and an energetic appeal from the trombones, discussed in continued modulations with the horns and trumpets. These two main ideas are developed, contrasted, and combined with the arch-angel's theme and a reminiscence of the Christmas hymn. It is a finely wrought piece of counterpoint, and has won some popularity, but it is a pity that so often it is played at a slow and dragging tempo, quite contrary to its true character of joyful faith.[1]

The opening chorus of the third part is based upon an expres-sive figure in the accompaniment, first given out by the violas. Mankind, although redeemed by the birth of Christ, is still assailed by doubt among the overwhelming evils of the world. The angels return after a short time, and, in undefined harmonies, weep for humanity's plight, and restate, in canon with the orchestra, their earlier poignant phrases. "We are messengers from heaven, from a distant realm. . . ." In another aria the archangel tells mankind that if they repent God will pardon them. The final chorus opens on men's voices, and reaches a great height when the voices of the human beings are united with those of the angels; the ending of the work is a superb achieve-ment.

There is much to admire in this large work for chorus and orchestra, the first of Franck's that the public had heard since *Ruth* was produced in 1846; the fine choral writing with its clever spacing, the occasionally startling harmonies (so difficult to sing!). At the same time, one must point a critical finger at the inexperienced orchestration—a fault excusable in a composer who had heard his own scoring only once, and that twenty-six years previously. This is an oft-heard criticism, but it has found a challenger in Guy Ropartz, himself a pupil of Franck's, a com-poser, and a conductor with experience at both Nancy and

---

[1] Franck himself wanted both the interlude and the archangel's air to move along at a good speed, provided the final chorus was not 'galloped'; so Franck's pupils testify in *Lettres de l'ouvreuse* of December 28, 1896 (*Accords perdus*, pp. 64–65).

Strasbourg. For him, his master's orchestration is as solid as a rock, and he quotes in proof the enthusiasm of the orchestra at Nancy when the strings alone ran through the whole of *Rédemption*. Their enthusiasm was justified, for the string-writing was throughout good and in a contrapuntal style that suited Franck. On the other hand, in the view of the critic Jean d'Udine, "the guide-rope of the earth-bound double-basses was continually holding back the flight of the too-captive balloon." In other words, the 'cellos, doubled almost incessantly by the basses and often by the bassoons and the fourth horn, give out a kind of humming purr that weighs heavily on the ear.

A good deal less happy is the writing for wood-wind and brass. The former are handled rather as if they were the strings, which makes them sound unsatisfactory; for example, the long fourths given to the oboes, E flat–B flat or E–B, immediately before the first main chorus, are unpleasing to the ear, and again the duet in the overture between the clarinet and the open notes of the horn introducing the angels' chorus is ineffective. The brass-writing is no better; the trumpets are limited to calls or fanfares, and are never used quietly in the background; the trombones are confined to solemn outbursts; the horns are employed after the manner of the choir organ which the composer suddenly adds to his other manuals. In general—if so obvious a comment may be permitted—the genial organist's scoring is based upon his registration at the console at Sainte-Clotilde, a fault which was never quite absent from the later works, but is naturally more apparent in the first big achievement of his resuscitation as a composer.

As it stands before us to-day *Rédemption* excites admiration for its profusion of melody, richness of harmony, solidity of construction, and inventiveness in development. It is a transitional work, marking the start of a new period, and as such bears traces of several influences, good and bad—of Meyerbeer, Berlioz, Gounod, and, above all, Wagner. At the opening one finds something of the calm of the *Lohengrin* Prelude, a reminiscence of *Tannhäuser* intervenes, even in the Symphonic Interlude one perceives a fleeting allusion to *Tristan*. There is no hint of *The Ring*—Franck did not then know the scores; he was not to read that of *Walküre* until the holiday months of 1873, and then, much to Henri Duparc's indignation, he declared he had no taste for the work!

Over and above all these influences—as a whole unimportant
—one admires on every page Franck's own personal style.
Rédemption takes its place among the best French oratorios of the
second half of the nineteenth century; the score is unquestionably
superior to that other *Rédemption*, composed by Gounod some
ten years later, and also to the frigid works of Théodore Dubois;
indeed it stands up firmly in comparison with the serious works
of Saint-Saëns or the voluptuous pieces of Massenet.[1]

To arrive at a balanced judgment of the oratorio it is necessary
to view it in the right historical perspective, as Vincent d'Indy
so often pleaded. *Rédemption* was conceived and completed
round about the period of Meyerbeer and his rivals, whose
musical ideals were low and even vulgar—at a period, too, when
the best works of the great masters were unknown even to the
leading musicians of the day, at least as far as performance was
concerned. If *Rédemption* seems to us to-day an imperfect work
and somewhat dated, it remains a considerable achievement,
thanks to its idealism, its musicianship, its power, and its striking
sincerity.

[1] Franck suffered considerably from the semi-obscurity in which his score was allowed
to remain when the oratorio of the same name by his old friend Gounod won triumphant
successes in Birmingham, New York, and Paris in 1882–84. One day, at the organ in
Sainte-Clotilde, he asked his pupil Tournemire, "Do you know *Rédemption*?" "What,
Gounod's work?" was the reply. "No," said Franck, "mine. Have a look at it, and
you will see that it is a better work altogether than the one you mentioned."

CHAPTER XIII

The Conservatoire:
"Les Éolides": "Les Béatitudes"
(1872–80)

FIRMLY established in the world of music by his new post
at the Conservatoire, and by his success as an organist and as
a composer of symphonic works and chamber music, Franck
was often to be seen in public. He could be heard when new
organs were installed, he could be seen conducting various choral
societies, especially that founded by his colleague Bourgault-
Ducoudray, which before long became "M. César Franck's
Singers." He was present as a member of the adjudicating panel
at the Conservatoire, having as companions at the examinations
of 1872 Ambroise Thomas, Georges Bizet, his own predecessor
and former teacher Benoist, Jules Cohen, and Saint-Saëns, and
at the examinations of 1873 Thomas again, Victor Massé,
Massenet, Widor, and Paladilhe. Later he was also a regular
adjudicator at the examinations in counterpoint and fugue. His
name once more began to appear in the Press in association with
those of his pupils who won prizes for organ-playing and
improvisation.

A rumour soon began to spread—bandied about in some cases
with a certain amount of ill-feeling—that the newly appointed
professor (he was sometimes spoken of as the son of a Prussian)
spent more time and pains in his organ-lessons over teaching
improvisation than over the technique of the instrument. Those
of his colleagues who taught the advanced pupils preparing for
the Rome Prize were frequently heard to complain that they
were subjected to a kind of rivalry on Franck's part, which
annoyed them, and was to annoy them a great deal more some
years later when there had grown up on all sides a new spirit in
music, called "Franckist."

The regular custom at the Conservatoire during the practical examinations was to lay stress on this or that candidate's previous failures. Thus, if in 1872 Franck's pupil carried off the first prize for organ, his success was attributed to his previous teacher, but if in 1874 he was not awarded the prize, then the responsibility for this failure was fathered on the new teacher. In 1875 Vincent d'Indy, who had studied the organ with Franck for eighteen months, had great hopes of coming out top of the list of candidates, but, instead, he was only *proxime accessit*. If we may accept the word of the disappointed pupil, Franck was absolutely astounded at the decision. Ambroise Thomas expressed his personal regrets to Franck; but the story went round in well-informed musical circles that one of the examiners, Jules Cohen, had refused to give d'Indy the first prize in order to satisfy his own animosity against the professor, the candidate, and the candidate's uncle, Wilfrid d'Indy, the amateur composer.

Bickerings and rivalries of this sort were common enough at the Conservatoire examinations; but Franck with his simple and trusting nature was incapable of such things, incapable too of understanding how much back-chat of the nastier kind there could be even in a Conservatoire whose atmosphere he himself always found kindly disposed towards him and filled with the boundless and over-devoted admiration of his keener pupils; among these the chief was Vincent d'Indy, who under circumstances often related became his pupil for composition.

One of the ex-pupils of the Conservatoire—the most brilliant of his time—showed anything but a patronizing attitude towards the professor of organ; that was Georges Bizet. The winter of 1874–75 was remarkable for the first performance of *Carmen* at the Opéra-Comique, and during these months Bizet frequently attended Franck's courses of lessons. When he was seventeen years of age, in 1855, he had won the first prize for organ in Benoist's class, and twenty years later he thought it would be useful and instructive to listen now and then to the teaching methods of the new professor. The result of these visits[1] was that three of the pupils in the organ-class had the excitement of attending the first performance of *Carmen*, and one of the three, Vincent d'Indy, the chance of actually assisting behind the scenes in all the performances of 1875.

[1] See Léon Vallas, *Vincent d'Indy* (vol. i, pp. 200–202).

Franck himself often appeared in the programmes of the Société Nationale; some thirty times in the first ten years, but mostly with minor works. The Société gave his Offertory, *Quae est ista, Dextera Domini*, written in 1871, for soloists, choir, and organ; some other religious pieces[1]; his *Andantino quietoso*, for violin and piano; some portions of *Ruth*; some songs raked up from the past of thirty years before, like *Le Sylphe, L'Ange et l'enfant*, and *Souvenance*, and some new songs like *Passez toujours*, the *Lied*, and *Le Mariage des Roses*. On February 7, 1874, he played on the harmonium, with Vincent d'Indy at the piano, an arrangement of his *Prelude, Fugue, and Variations*, and on the 13th of the same month he himself gave at the piano a rewritten version of the interlude from *Rédemption*. He also conducted the first part of this fine oratorio on May 16 of the same year, with chorus and orchestra. The third of the trios was played in 1872, the first of them in 1873, 1874, 1877, and 1878, up to that time held in high respect and never spoken or written about without praise. At all these performances Camille Saint-Saëns was the pianist.

Massenet, who always thought well of César Franck and his work, has told in his book *Mes Souvenirs* how the publishing office of Hartmann, organizer of the Concert National, founded in 1873,

> was the regular meeting-place for all of us young musicians, among them César Franck, whose sublime music had not at this time reached a wide enough public. That little shop at 17 Boulevard de la Madeleine became the hub of the musical world. Bizet, Saint-Saëns, Lalo, Franck, Holmès were all part and parcel of our little brotherhood. Every one chattered away gaily and in the warmest enthusiasm about their faith in our great art, which was to light up all their lives.

From the regular round of duties as teacher, organist, and composer one minor event stands out as important and memorable; on November 15, 1874, at the Pasdeloup Concerts Franck was lucky enough to hear the Prelude to *Tristan und Isolde* on the first performance after Wagner's own Paris concerts of 1860.

---

[1] The Conservatoire Library contains the manuscripts of two other motets: *Domine, Domine*, for three voices and organ, and *Domine non secundum, Veni Creator*, and *Quare tremuerant* for three voices, organ, and double bass, composed for the feast of Sainte-Clotilde

His memory retained a deep impression of this music, so much so that one finds fugitive reminders of it in the forthcoming works for organ and for orchestra, most of all in *Les Éolides*, the symphonic poem composed during the coming year.

The symphonic poem as a form of musical expression had by now become fashionable in France. Saint-Saëns in 1871 had started the ball rolling with some admirably descriptive pieces— *Le Rouet d'Omphale*, *Phaëton*, and the *Danse macabre*, and had yet to write *La Jeunesse d'Hercule*, dedicated to Henri Duparc, who had just finished his score of *Lénore* after a ballad by Bürger. Franck's next work was inspired by a poem of Leconte de Lisle, and was intended to be a commentary on that poem: certain lines at least will come back to the mind out of these verses addressed to the daughters of Æolus—"Brises flottantes des cieux . . . qui de baisers capricieux caressent les monts et les plaines."[1] Before turning his hand to this particular subject for music Franck had long sought a starting-point for his inspiration, and had found nothing that sufficiently attracted him. The summer of 1875 took him on a long journey through France, to Azille in the Aude, where Auguste Sanches, his friend and wine-merchant, lived. Wine-grower by trade, Sanches was also a great lover of music and played the harmonium, and he had given Franck the liberty of his house in Languedoc. The trip involved a tedious route down the valley of the Rhône, with a break planned ahead at Valence. He arrived there in the middle of the *mistral*, that cutting north wind of the South of France, and was buffeted about by its violence. "But," said he, "these are the Æolids!" He conceived the idea that, without unduly stretching the lines of Leconte de Lisle's poem, he was entitled to add thereto something a little more violent than their poetic breathings and to make a more complete and more vivid picture of the winds as he knew them than the poet's sighs and kisses. "The Æolids," he confided to his pupil Louis de Serres, ten years later, "sometimes get out of temper!" Inspiration soon came to him; he first improvised and then wrote down some fifty bars or so. Once in Sanches's house he had no trouble in completing the work, or at least a fully detailed sketch of his musical interpretation of the poem. He jotted it down to begin with on three

[1] "Floating breezes in the skies . . . which greet hills and plains alike with a whimsical kiss."

staves, and at the end of his holiday he was able to sign and date the manuscript "Azille, September 28, 1875."

How hard Franck worked during those summer weeks of 1875 we can discover from various manuscripts still in the possession of the Sanches family. There we can find the following: two copies, one for piano, the other for orchestra, of portions of Beethoven's *Mass in C*, probably intended as a gift for the Sanches; a copy of a chorus out of Rossini's *Comte Ory*; a little piece for piano or harmonium, written on a half-page in pencil and signed, but not dated; a copy of a *Quasi Marcia*, for harmonium, "presented to Mademoiselle Alice Sanches"; a short chorus with piano accompaniment called *Le Philistin mordra la poussière* ("The Philistines biting the Dust"), written for a *comédie de salon* dated August 29, the day before the completion of the fifth 'Béatitude'; a copy of one of the versions of the song to Victor Hugo's words, *S'il est un charmant gazon*, inscribed "To my very dear friends, a little reminder of my stay at Azille, September 29, 1875."

Les Éolides was performed in Paris in 1876; the full score bears the finishing date of June 7. It was to wait long months before its first appearance under the Société Nationale, which seldom performed works involving an orchestra. During that interval the Société gave a hearing to (among other works) two motets by Franck: *Veni Creator*, for tenor and bass, and *Panis angelicus*, for tenor (Vergnet), organ, 'cello, and harp, recently added to the *Mass*, for three voices. One can imagine what must have been the impatience of the Franckist party, always anxious to hear anything whatever by their master except an early trio of 1840 or a motet written for church use.

The Société Nationale eventually produced *Les Éolides* at its seventieth concert, on Sunday May 13, 1877, held in the Salle Erard with Colonne as conductor. The specialized public of the *Ars Gallica* gave it the warmest of welcomes, as was to be expected, for this was the first time that Franck had come forward with a major work of purely symphonic design. The musical reviews put on record the importance of the event and of the work itself: thus we read in the *Gazette musicale* of May 20th:

> M. César Franck's new orchestral work is a genuine little master-piece. The style is chromatic in the extreme, but that is suited to the programme the author has followed—"*O brises changeantes des cieux,*

vierges filles d'Éole"[1]—a programme carried out, moreover, without any excessive attempt at realism. We can commend unreservedly this truly poetic piece, except perhaps for a certain monotony engendered by the too frequent use of the same phrase-shapes.

Absolute in design as it was, a translation into musical terms of a delicate poetic imagery, this symphonic poem was scored, not for full orchestra, but for double wood-wind, two horns, one cornet, one trumpet, harp, percussion, and strings. The texture was largely canonic. The form was solidly built up on a sound basis of key-relationships (so characteristic of the mature Franck), the whole work being developed out of two continually opposed and unconnected keys. D'Indy, who was very much more strict in his views on tonality than his master, tells us that we can find in the work certain deviations from proper practice which (in the opinion of the pupil) would never have been sanctioned in a purely symphonic work with no descriptive background; but, then, d'Indy, who spent his life damning programme music without ceasing for one moment to write it himself, also expressed the opinion that nothing in the score had been left to chance or momentary whim, and that the work as a whole showed no trace of that spirit of improvisation often apparent in similar works by Berlioz and Liszt—an opinion that could easily be disputed! He is struck with wonder that in the last section of *Les Éolides*, with its combination of three melodies in counterpoint, Franck's artistic genius has succeeded in creating the symphonic counterpart of Leconte de Lisle's final verse: "*Le repos et l'amour, la grâce et l'harmonie.*"

The supreme value of the score lies principally in its basic thematic ideas. The first theme, which sets off the second and third, is languid in character and is obviously indebted to the chromaticisms of *Tristan*, here to be observed for the first time in Franck. The two other themes are broader in style and have a typical Franckist smoothness, but they too seem to be imbued with Wagnerism, and develop an atmosphere which in more than one passage recalls the Venusberg of *Tannhäuser*. Its direct appeal comes partly also from a certain delicate picturesqueness in the music: at the opening a limpid stream of melody, broadening out into a dialogue between strings and wind—subtle, almost quivering, harmonies—the whole work orchestrated with a light

---

[1] "O veering winds of the sky, virgin daughters of Æolus."

touch and an enchanting variety of colouring that were hardly to
be expected of the composer.

Les Éolides was played at Brussels at the Popular Concerts of
Joseph Dupont on January 19, 1879, and reappeared at the
Société Nationale, in Paris, on April 4, 1881, where it had a
renewed success. The *Ménestrel* of April 10 recognizes the harmonic richness and the poetic colouring of the instrumentation, but deplores "the absence of a single melodic phrase that is
coherent and clearly stated"—a strange view to take! An entirely
different reception awaited the work at the Concerts Lamoureux
on February 26, 1882: the public did not take to the work at all.
Franck took his setback in good part, saying quite simply,
"Well, there we are—at least nobody hooted!" He perhaps did
not hear certain deprecatory sounds from unsympathetic quarters
of the hall! But he was disappointed and hurt when Lamoureux,
whose programmes were always played at two concerts and were
only altered once a fortnight, did not announce the repeat performance of *Les Éolides*; indeed, the conductor refused for a
dozen years or so to include the work in the repertoire of his
society. One of the *Ménestrel* critics wrote, with an observation
of the Provençal climate that was not so out of place as it seemed
at the time:

> Instead of the spring-like breezes we had expected, M. Franck
> takes us away and exposes us to the full blast of the *mistral*. It augurs
> ill for the future. Too much musical knowledge sometimes pro-
> duces odd anomalies, and *Les Éolides* of M. Franck is a long way
> away from the least important pages of his oratorio *Ruth and Boaz*,
> which remains his best work up to now.

So once again a new work was pushed aside by the critics in
favour of an old one of thirty years before. Franck's pupils
urged their master to take his proper place in the advance guard
of music; they fought manfully against the totally opposed ideals
of the musician's sons and especially of his wife, who remained
always faithful to her youthful likes and dislikes, and expected
him still to write popular and profitable music. Before long,
on the performance of another new work, the Quintet, we get
some idea of the sharpness of the fight of which Franck was the
subject—a fight in the background between his family circle
and the artistic circle of his friends and supporters, which grew

to quite big proportions—the stakes being his whole future as a composer.

One of the longest of Franck's own letters that has survived—it bears no date, but was written in August 1876—gives us some precise information about the composer's artistic life at this period. He first of all deals with the Conservatoire:

> I have been very busy at the Conservatoire this year, much more so than usual. To begin with, I had to take on a considerable number of pupils, all of whom—both girls and boys, seven in all—had been thought fit to sit for the examination. In addition, I was asked to set the papers for the harmony examination and fugue, and naturally I had to take part in the adjudicating of that examination. I was also called upon to perform the same function in the examination in counterpoint and fugue, quite apart from that of my own class, which was of exceptionally high standard this year. I am finding, however, that my pupils are treated with an unusual severity, and I have the feeling that there is a certain opposition against me among the members of the panel, which makes me rather sad since I am quite certain that it comes from people whom I had thought to be my friends. Despite all that, my little group carried off one second prize by unanimous vote (Samuel Rousseau), one *proxime accessit*, also unanimous, and two honourable mentions. These last three awards were all won by girls [Mlles Renaud, Genty, and Papot].

The professor was evidently less astonished at the fact that among the jury were one or two members, like Jules Cohen, hostile to him, than that these judges were specialists in organ-playing and yet after hearing his pupils did not consider them to show a high enough standard of technique, a branch of the organist's equipment which Franck was inclined to neglect in his teaching.

The same letter also tells us much about Franck's activities as a composer.

> I am back again in the thick of composing this week. I play the piano; I read; I have just completed the score of an orchestral work called *Les Éolides*, after a poem by Leconte de Lisle. I have also all but finished the reduction of it for piano duet, which we shall be playing together, I hope, this coming winter.

The Universal Exhibition, held in Paris in 1878, focused the limelight of publicity on the organist-composer side of Franck's art. A series of organ concerts was given at the Trocadéro, in that strange oriental palace that had just been erected. Guilmant, Gigout, and Saint-Saëns were all invited to play there before César Franck's appearance on October 1. The *Gazette musicale* wrote:

> The organ-concert given by M. C. Franck was (so to speak) a kind of epitome of a single musical personality: composer, improviser, executant—in all three characters, the musician proved himself able to provide unaided a complete programme, and to do so with the authority of a master.

Improvisations in the free style were played on airs by Félicien David (the opening chorus of *The Desert*), by Berlioz (two motifs from *The Childhood of Christ*), and by Bizet (two from *L'Arlésienne*), together with Russian, Swedish, and English tunes, "treated at first separately and then superimposed on each other." The whole performance showed "musical gifts far more advanced and more complete than we know of in any other musician." The programme of more formal works played was of outstanding interest; the scores had been revised or written expressly for this concert, and the registration was specially undertaken to suit the new Cavaillé-Coll organ. The works in question were a *Fantaisie in A*, a *Cantabile in B*, and *Pièce héroique*.

The first of them, whose somewhat tentative construction justifies its title of *Fantaisie*, is the least satisfactory of the set, just as it is undoubtedly the earliest to be written. It is characterized by an excess of full stops, pauses, silences; there are dull passages, and too many pianistic effects like repeated chords and arpeggios. In the *Cantabile* there shyly peep out some slight memories of *Tristan und Isolde*, which would seem to date the piece about 1875; one admires in it a long and serene melody which in its final development is treated in canon. The *Pièce héroique* is built on two opposing themes, the one rhythmic, the other melodic; this latter, transformed into a chorale, forms the climax of the work: repeated chords are one of its noticeable features. Interesting as they are, these three sizeable pieces remain the product of the transition period, which resulted in the full-scale oratorio about to be discussed below.

For more than ten years César Franck had been devoting a part of his leisure time to the composition of *Les Béatitudes*, which he had only put aside, with some reluctance, to write a few minor pieces and that other oratorio *Rédemption*. The subject of *Les Béatitudes* was of absorbing interest to him. He had all his life been drawn towards the Sermon on the Mount, as recounted in the Gospel according to Saint Matthew; he was profoundly moved in his inmost being by this divine yet human utterance, in which Jesus Christ gave promise of happiness to men of true faith. He asked the wife of a schoolmaster friend, a Mme Colomb, to put together for him a libretto in verse, commenting on Christ's words, paraphrasing them, even dramatizing them by the introduction of various characters. The text as delivered was, in truth, rather flat and earth-bound; but Franck turned to it at once, and as soon as he could embarked upon his long-drawn-out task of setting it to music, about which we know certain details.

Serious work began in 1869; the prologue and the first 'Béatitude' had been set down on paper just before the outbreak of the Franco-Prussian War of 1870. He hurried off to Clamart for a meeting at his friend Henri Duparc's house, so as to show him how the new major work was intended to open; for Franck always liked most of all to have the approval, and indeed the critical suggestions, of his best pupils on any work he had in hand. Soon after, he invited to his house Duparc and Alexis de Castillon to show them the same opening numbers.

Castillon was visibly affected when he left the house in the Boulevard Saint-Michel, and said to his companion:

"It's always the same with that man—I always feel that he has something in him quite beyond the mere qualities of a great musician. He makes me think of Fra Angelico—people have said that Fra Angelico painted with his inner soul, and the same words might be applied to Franck: he has the soul of a seraph."[1]

Neither the Franco-Prussian War nor the Commune dammed the slow-flowing stream of the composer's persistent work; on the contrary, the whole series of disasters gave him time for composing, as had the similar circumstances of 1848. Throughout the siege and bombardment of Paris Franck pursued an uninterrupted course of putting down on paper the notes that were, ten years later, to become the prologue of the work. He also

[1] Letter to Bréville, May 31, 1923.

CÉSAR FRANCK IN 1889

CÉSAR FRANCK IN 1848

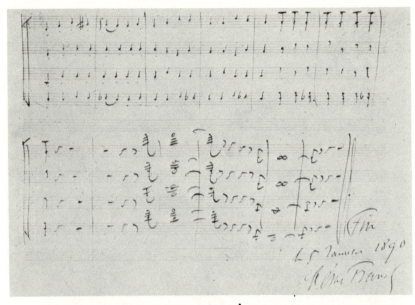

CONCLUDING LINES OF FRANCK'S MANUSCRIPT OF THE
STRING QUARTET

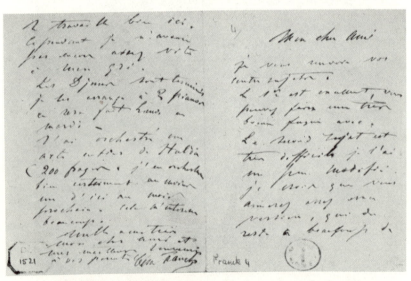

PART OF A LETTER WRITTEN BY FRANCK IN 1884
TO PIERRE DE BRÉVILLE

orchestrated the three first sections of *Les Béatitudes* during the siege of Paris. Some of the sections show actual dates on the scores: No. 4, September 3, 1870, the day of the fall of Sedan; No. 5, August 28, 1875; and the concluding date is given as July 10, 1879. Each separate part of *Les Béatitudes* was played over to the composer's friends and pupils as soon as it was ready to be heard.

The literary text offered to Franck suffered from the disadvantage of a rigid uniformity. Each of the eight cantos was cast in exactly the same mould. Each sets before us two contrasted pictures of human types—the strong and the weak, the just and the unjust, the cruel and the charitable; the antithesis is eight times repeated. Towards the end of each canto is heard the voice of Christ, propounding the message of each Beatitude. The monotony of the text imposes itself relentlessly upon the music: even the repeated entries of the voice of Christ do not vary the sameness of the general plan, for though the music given to Christ's voice is solemn, beautiful in itself, and serenely emotional, the main theme of it is subjected to but little variation.

No one has ever properly discussed the really great qualities of this oratorio. So many pages of its score compel from us the warmest admiration; so often one is confronted with high sentiment and its proper expression in music that can be here grandiose, there touching in equal measure. One thinks at random of certain memorable passages—the delightful song of the comforting angels in the prologue, the celestial chorus that so happily rounds off the first 'Béatitude,' the vocal quintet of heavenly voices in the second, the moving chorus of sorrowers in the third, the whole of the fourth with its tenor solo, the celestial choir in the fifth, the cantilena *Mater dolorosa* and the ever moving key-changes of 'O eternal justice' in the eighth.

Particularly striking is the melodic unity, achieved by the return in each section of the theme of Jesus Christ—sometimes syncopated and once, in the third 'Béatitude,' in inversion; and this unity is the more noticeable in that the beautiful Christ-theme recurs frequently in the main text of the work. Another excellent quality is the skilful progression of keys and modes; yet another the carefully managed variety of sonorities, with solos for various voices, equal-voice choruses for men or women, choral quintets accompanied or unaccompanied, and the like.

On the other side of the argument, everybody, including Franck's most consistent eulogist, Vincent d'Indy, seems to be aware of its manifest weaknesses. All the music dealing with the true spirit of religion reveals the hand of a master, but whenever the subject of the music is Satan, or its intention is to paint a picture of the evil human passions, to personify injustice, tyranny, cruelty, revolt, then the composer has resorted to the conventional musical language of his time, to the manner of Meyerbeer or even that of the local choral society. It is easy, too, to point to an absence of stylistic unity, though this may well be excused in a score written piecemeal, as this was, over a period of ten years, at a period when the composer was in an evolutionary stage and was havering between his own characteristic idiom and those other so different idioms of Mendelssohn, the Schumann of *Faust*, the Berlioz of *The Childhood of Christ*, and Gounod.

Only one complete performance of the oratorio was heard by Franck in his lifetime: that was given at his own apartment on the Boulevard Saint-Michel on February 20, 1879, and even then the orchestral part was played on the piano and the choruses sung by amateurs. The enthusiasm it aroused was not the less lively on that account, but though it was more or less whole-hearted it was not general, especially among certain parts of the audience. A small choir had been formed of friends and pupils of the organ-class; the soloists included professional singers like Mouliérat, Quirot, and Seguin, and also pupils or ex-pupils of the Conservatoire like the composer Camille Benoît: to Franck's ear they all sang "like angels." The piano part was taken by Vincent d'Indy since Franck had sprained his wrist the day before. As for the audience, one might have noticed the absence of certain important people who had been invited; the Minister of Fine Arts, the Directors of the Conservatoire and of the Opéra, certain influential critics—all of them were unavoidably prevented by previous engagements, and so on; at the same time one would have recognized the composers Édouard Lalo and Victorin de Joncières, the publisher Brandus, Charles Bannelier, editor-in-chief of the *Gazette musicale*, and Édouard Colonne, who waited till three years after Franck's death before presenting this major oratorio at his concerts at the Châtelet. Musically, the performance was unsatisfactory; Franck's abrupt modulations more than once sent the choir completely awry, especially in the eighth

'Béatitude.' But Franck himself was highly delighted with it all and afterwards embraced his performers!

The impression of monotony, inseparable from a work laid out in eight pictures all of the same design and style, was heightened by the substitution of piano for orchestra. In the face of every one's anxiety to admire the work and its composer, the total effect aroused disappointment strong enough and general enough to cause even the pupils and friends taking part to question whether the work would have been successful had it been played in its entirety at a public concert. Franck himself was quite resigned to the adverse opinion and was not at all hurt, for he had never for a moment imagined that his *Béatitudes* could properly be given complete at a single sitting. He was quite content to perform each of the eight parts of his monumental work on different occasions—or, at least, the most important of them—and, thus separated, they met with general approval and favour. But Franck himself never heard either the second or the seventh.[1]

The first complete performance, given in Paris three years after Franck's death, provides us with a survey of critical opinion on the work as a whole. One section of the Press, thanks to the Franckists, was wholly or almost wholly enthusiastic in its favour. The other section was full of reservations and even of severe criticisms. Of these latter, we will quote two, both written by responsible critics. The first is that of Adolphe Jullien in the *Journal des Débats*. Jullien admits that the work has merits, but he points to a certain opinion that had been expressed by another and confesses that he cannot imagine anyone seriously writing about it in terms like these:

> The most powerful work produced for at least thirty years . . .
> sufficient harmonic novelty to nourish music for the next century
> . . . indeed, one of the most important creations in all music. On a
> level with Sebastian Bach's *B minor Mass* and Wagner's *Parsifal*!

[1] The dates of the performances were as follows: June 27, 1878, Prologue and No. 1 'Béatitude,' by the Société des Concerts du Conservatoire, at the Trocadéro; April 20, 1879, *Mater Dolorosa*, at the Société Nationale; . . . 1880, No. 4, at the Châtelet; May 28, 1880, No. 6, in the chapel at Versailles; January 8 and 15, 1882, No. 6, at the Conservatoire concerts; February 18, 1882, No. 3, at the Société Nationale; January 30, 1887, Prologue, No. 3, and No. 8, at the Franck Festival, in the Cirque d'Hiver; January 21, 1888, No. 5, at the Société Nationale; June 6, 1889, No. 8, at the concerts at the Exhibition, under Édouard Colonne; May 17, 1890, No. 6, at the Société Nationale, under Vincent d'Indy. The first complete performances took place one year and three years after Franck's death—at Dijon, on June 15, 16, and 18, 1891, under the direction of the Abbé Maître; in Paris, on March 19, 1893, at the Colonne Concerts.

Exaggerated praise of this kind Jullien considered to be most damaging form of flattery by friends.

The article of Camille Bellaigue in the *Revue des Deux-Mondes* is excessively harsh; opponent of Franckism, future opponent of D'Indyism and Debussyism, this reactionary critic opens with these words:

> God in Heaven! It is possible that César Franck had a vision of Him in writing this work, but never for one moment does he reveal that vision to us in his music. What a miserable fate, to have to listen to all these eight 'Béatitudes' one after another without a moment of happy relief!

Then he sets out to damn the music in general and each of its constituent elements. The musical ideas he finds indifferent and even valueless, not heavy indeed, but merely wearisome; the melodic line in his view lacks colour and variety, the harmony always strained and only rarely original and striking, the orchestration thick and opaque; and so on.

Counter to these opinions may be set up that of Vincent d'Indy printed in his book on César Franck; it is a magnificent eulogy, with but few reservations, and may be roughly summarized thus: in its full dimensions *Les Béatitudes* appears to d'Indy to be a musical epic, the greatest work that had occurred in musical history for a very long time.

Such adoring appreciation of his master by a disciple is equally excessive with Bellaigue's censure. After seventy years we can arrive at a more balanced judgment, more moderate and with more thought for details.

A week after the run-through of *Les Béatitudes*, on February 27, 1879, Franck took part in the inauguration of the full organ at Saint-François-Xavier, and on March 21 at that of the organ in Saint-Eustache, which Merklin had just rebuilt; on this second occasion, according to the *Gazette musicale*, he played "his *Fantaisie in A*, entitled *Cantabile*"—which means, of course, his *Fantaisie in A* as well as his *Cantabile*. On May 23, 1880, he conducted his *Mass*, for three voices, at the Church of the Trinité. A discriminating audience, the *Gazette musicale* of May 30 tells us, was much impressed, especially by the *Gloria*, the opening of the *Credo*, the *Agnus Dei*, and "the beautiful *Panis angelicus*, a section of the work often sung separately at concerts and greatly applauded, even encored at times." The 28th of the same month, in the chapel at Versailles, the first performance of the sixth 'Béatitude' was given, in aid of the benevolent fund for artists and musicians.

César Franck had at that time scored a considerable success at the Société Nationale, which was several times repeated. On December 14, 1878, on January 25, 1879, and on January 3, 1880, he had heard performances of his *Fourth Trio*, the one written for Liszt, which seems to have waited forty years for its first hearing in France, though its dedicatee had occasionally played it in Germany. The piano part was played by Saint-Saëns, and afterwards by Delaborde. At the concert of January 3, 1880, Franck, loudly hailed as a composer, joined his colleague at the piano and with him played some duets by Paul Lacombe, thereby winning for himself (it is reported in the Press) "a real success as an elegant and expressive pianist." The trio was warmly received: "a work of very original shape, absorbing despite its length," wrote the *Gazette musicale*.

During the first eight or nine years of the Société's existence, as we have already shown, Franck seems not to have been interested in writing chamber music, but was content without any self-criticism to trot out his juvenile works. His friends and supporters were anxious to direct his mind towards the composition of some major chamber-works, something that would lead them on a new path, something that would set him firmly in the front rank of the composers of the French musical renaissance. Such a change of outlook in his mind could not be effected without awakening storms among his family, whose tastes in music did not in any way tally with those of his circle in the Société Nationale.

The first outward manifestation of César Franck's new orientation in music proved to be quite extraordinary, even sensational, and it was certainly wholly unexpected by those who admired the religious atmosphere of his *Béatitudes*. On January 17, 1880, at the ninety-fourth concert of the Société Nationale, there was produced for the first time his *Quintet*, for two violins, viola, 'cello, and piano—a work of striking originality and of a stormy and passionate character hitherto unknown in chamber music.

CHAPTER XIV

The "Quintet" and "Rébecca": Two Symphonic Poems: A Scheme for an Opera

(1880–84)

IT was quite natural that, after the success of his 1840 trios at the Société Nationale and under the spur of his disciples and admirers, César Franck should turn once again to the writing of chamber music. Nor was there anything out of the ordinary in his election of an extended work for five instruments—a medium in itself somewhat orchestral. Quintets for piano and strings were common enough; the musical public had recently had opportunity to test the resources of the form in a quintet by Alexis de Castillon, a follower if not a pupil of Franck's, and every musician —even among those who had forgotten certain 'Grands Quintettes' by Félicien David and were above noticing the three dozen or so examples of the form by George Onslow—was an admirer of the *Piano Quintet* of Schumann. The prime cause of the general astonishment in January 1880 was the dramatic intensity, the frequently tragic quality, of the new work. The composer was a quiet-living organist, considered to be of retiring, religious, and even devout cast of mind; he had appeared so far to be willing to devote his gifts principally to writing church music and to improvising on the organ, for the benefit of the Church of Sainte-Clotilde, contemplative offertories or richly coloured outgoing voluntaries (*sorties*).

The surprise felt by the audience at the Nationale concert of January 17, 1880, showed itself in two quite opposite ways. One section of the public, the lovers of the classics, was shocked by the expressive force and emotional violence of the *Quintet*. Chief among the malcontents and the scoffers was the pianist himself, Camille Saint-Saëns. That famous composer was joined in the work by a string quartet consisting of Marsick, Rémy,

Van Waefelghem, and Loys. His own opinion of the work and of the public's enthusiastic reception of it he made abundantly clear by his ill-mannered behaviour. He walked off the platform at the finish of the work and left standing on the piano the manuscript which Franck had adorned with a dedication to Saint-Saëns himself (this precious document was later offered, bearing a second dedication, to Pierre de Bréville). All his ideals of abstract music, built on a traditional plan without any flights of imagination, were outraged by this freedom of form and development, this intense dramatic fever shown by his colleague, who was already ceasing to be his friend. We may not be so surprised perhaps when we realize that the most independent and rebellious of living musicians, Franz Liszt, himself later expressed the opinion that the *Quintet*, in its search for dramatic expression, had overpassed the legitimate bounds of chamber music.

The greater part of the public, on the other hand, was hedged in by no such formal restrictions and stylistic preconceptions. It was aware only of the glowing beauty of the new score, and allowed itself to be carried away by its extraordinary appeal; herein it found an unexpected and overwhelming display of a musical passion hitherto unsuspected.

No great time was allowed to pass before the specialists in musical form and texture applied their attentive minds to a minute examination of the score; we can read the results in the analyses made by Vincent d'Indy, Maurice Emmanuel, Robert Jardillier, and a host of others. They decided once for all on the formal plan adopted by the composer—after a slow introduction by the strings alone (almost an invocation to them) two allegro movements with a slow movement in between, but without the usual scherzo. They demonstrated his care to give unity to the *Quintet* as a whole by using a cyclic method of construction, with a frequent recalling of the chromatic main subject, which was continually expanded by means of widening intervals. They drew attention to the two main thematic ideas, distributed in a paradoxical style that the composer made use of again in the *Symphonic Variations*: the fiercely rhythmic first theme is assigned to the violins, which are by nature expressive, the broadly melodic second theme is given to the piano, which is by nature percussive.

To this second theme there was an introductory passage where, over the struck piano-part, the violin sings an alluring melody,

uncertain in its havering between a tonal and a modal basis, and
floating its song in a way that can be heard again in the opening
bars of the *Violin Sonata* of 1886. They remarked further that
the instrumental style was derived to some extent from the
technique of the organ—the first violin, as in the *Quartet* to come,
being given a part which made it into a kind of covering accompaniment for the rest of the strings. Vincent d'Indy went so far
in his *Traité de composition* as to suggest that the curious basic idea
underlying the finale (on the inexplicable key-basis of F minor,
B minor, F sharp minor, and F major) could only be properly
explained as the expression of a dramatic intention which Franck
himself never revealed. His colleague Charles Bordes firmly
asserted that the essentially dramatic character of the work was
steering French music towards a passionate conception of the art
which would never approach that of true chamber music, which
must always be a medium of pure delight.

Musical public and critics alike testified to the disturbing
vitality and command of the *Quintet*; they were swept off their
feet by the almost theatrical grimness of its address. Yet, so
obsessed were they with the accepted picture of Franck, the
mystical composer of *Les Béatitudes*, that it occurred to no one
to consider one central problem, which even musicologists of
the present day have not attempted, and perhaps would not dare
attempt, to solve. What in actual fact was the inner drama
behind this passionate outpouring of his soul? In its feverish
intensity Franck's *Quintet* stands alone and unparalleled among
his works. What was the cause of this sudden outbreak of
emotion, exteriorized in music of a kind never before heard,
which at the very opening carries the revealing expression-mark
tenero ma con passione? Sixty years after the Master's death we
venture to drop a gentle hint, indiscreet perhaps, but one which
throws light on that problem.

We gather together in later pages[1] some of the many personal
accounts of the Master as his friends and disciples knew him; all
bear witness to the fact that underneath his seraphic outward mien
Franck concealed a personality charged with vital human emotion,
sometimes violent in its passion. Hitherto no one has been bold
enough to observe that, according to the testimony of many
contemporaries of his, Franck never showed himself during his

[1] Chapter XVIII, "The Man."

youth and maturity in the least insensitive to the charms of the
young ladies who studied with him. We have recalled in our
account of his long years of betrothal that he was not only the
idol of his future wife but also "the ladies' oracle" among the
female members of his in-laws-to-be. In the early months of the
Société Nationale Franck was living in intimate association with
his younger fellow-workers in music, their mutual friendships
being at times troubled by the commanding charm and attrac-
tiveness of the young woman composer Augusta Holmès, who
joined the select little circle of Franck's pupils. Augusta Holmès[1]
(1847–1903) was born in Paris of Irish parents. She was a poetess,
an appealing singer, an all-round musician of remarkable gifts.
Of her personal beauty, then in the full blossom of her middle
twenties, the cold-blooded Saint-Saëns said, "We are all of us in
love with her!" After the start of the Société Nationale he
dedicated to her his *Rouet d'Omphale* and *Guitare*. Vincent d'Indy,
having heard her sing in the first version of the well-known piece
Danse Macabre, wrote, "I am completely infatuated with the
beautiful Augusta!" It is difficult to believe that Franck did not
also come under the spell of his attractive pupil. One day in front
of another pupil of Franck's a certain person claimed the Master
as a mystic. "A mystic?" replied the other. "Go and ask Augusta
Holmès."

Turn to the other side of the picture and you will see Mme
César Franck disliking the *Quintet*—detesting it and holding it in
horror. At times she would flare up in the presence of her husband's pupils, accusing them all as a group of having forced her
husband into the writing of such an abhorrent work. Her condemnation of it could reach the pitch of fury, according to Pierre
de Bréville's account of her. So exaggerated an attitude can
hardly be explained solely on musical grounds. The suggestion
may seem indiscreet or even startling, but there is nothing to
prevent us from looking to incidents of this or a similar kind to
find the key to the mystery of this passionate *Quintet*. Both in
inspiration and in actual execution it is a masterpiece; it is a
masterpiece, too, of emotional expression, subjective as well as
objective. Only a strong initial prejudice categorizing Franck as
a church musician could have closed the eyes and ears of those
listeners of 1880 to such a dazzling psychological self-revelation.

[1] The *accent grave* was an addition to her patronymic.

The public success of the new work was so great that the
Société Nationale broke its usual rule and arranged another performance of it in the same year, on May 2, 1880, with Mlle
Poitevin taking the place of Saint-Saëns at the piano. Further
performances of it were given on December 9, 1882, February
21, 1885 (with André Messager at the piano), and February 16,
1889 (with Mme Bordes-Pène). Each time the effect on the public
was equally forcible. Balthazar Claes (Camille Benoît) reported
in the *Guide musical* of February 27, 1889, about the last-mentioned
of these hearings, that the *Quintet*

> completely enthralled the audience, restraining them in silence at the
> end of each movement, not only from applause, but from any kind
> of oral acclamation, while at times it had drawn tears from the eyes
> of many among them.

One indirect consequence of the initial success of the *Quintet*
was the estrangement and before long the recession of Saint-Saëns
from the Société Nationale. He had been one of its founders and
most zealous early supporters, but from 1878, following upon an
incident related in our life of *Vincent d'Indy*,[1] the famous composer of *Samson et Dalila* began to grow suspicious of certain of
the younger members; at least, we may say, he began to lose his
authority over the more progressive believers in *Ars Gallica*. He
was gradually coming to a state of mind which could appreciate
little music but that of a time long past. Franck's position, on
the contrary, was that he could observe his own star in the
ascendant over the little world of the progressives exactly at the
same time that that of his old friend Saint-Saëns was waning.
Before long a campaign was started to exalt the former to the
exclusion of the latter, and became very pronounced among the
young Franckist party.

The lively and promising success of the *Quintet* was followed in
the later months of the year 1880 by two public disappointments.
Twice Franck was a candidate for the tutorship of one of the
composition classes, vacant owing to the retirement of Victor
Massé and the death of Reber. On both occasions, as we shall
recount more fully in Chapter XX, other men were chosen in
preference to him—Ernest Guiraud and Léo Delibes.

The work immediately following the *Quintet* was entirely

[1] Vol. i, pp. 240–241.

different in every way—*Rébecca*, a Biblical scene for solo voices, chorus, and orchestra on a poem by Paul Collin. Was it, one wonders, written for family reasons? Maurice Emmanuel relied on a confidential tale told to him by some one, probably by Franck's cousin and pupil Cécile Boutet de Monvel, when he wrote: "An incident of some significance took place within the family circle, and as a thanksgiving therefore Franck wrote this short oratorio." Mme Chopy, the composer's granddaughter, has herself told the writer that she personally had never heard a word of such an incident. We may legitimately imagine that in composing a peaceful oratorio in a style analogous to that of *Ruth*, written during his time of betrothal—in removing himself musically as far away as possible from the feverish mood of the preceding work—Franck had laid himself out to make some sort of apology to his wife, who was the sworn enemy of the *Quintet* as well as of its personal tone of speech and the source of its inspiration.

Rébecca occupied part of his holiday-time in 1880, which he spent at Marnes-la-Coquette, Seine-et-Oise. While there he added the date of September 29, 1880, below the sketched out version for voices and bass-line; the full score was to be completed early in 1881. One of the earliest of Franck's letters to be preserved discusses this work and gives us some valuable information.

> I have thought a great deal about *Rébecca*. I haven't had a moment to do anything with it to-day, but to-morrow I am determined to set to work again. You well know that I find it necessary to spend much time in thought over a work before putting the actual notes on paper. Up to now I have been casting round for the right colours, I have, so to speak, stocked my musical palette. But from now on I shall get down to active work, and I am in hopes that a fortnight or so will see *Rébecca* very nearly finished. I fancy I have struck a rich vein of work; since August 5 I have completed the first act of my opera [*Hulda*] and scored it as well.

The subject of the oratorio is the Old Testament story of Rebecca, chosen to be the future wife of Isaac by his servant Eleazar, who met her at the well. There are five sections: the first and last are choral, the second also, but with a solo for Rebecca; the third is a chorus of camel-drivers, while the fourth is occupied almost entirely by a duet between Rebecca and Eleazar. The most popular section of it is the central chorus, a

picturesque piece with characteristic rhythms; its oriental appeal
is due to the use of one of the old modes, with successions of
fifths and false relations. Throughout the score we find a certain
touching charm, serene and graceful, recalling the fresh candour
of *Ruth* with much firmer handling. It is indeed a moment of
relaxation after the tumult of the *Quintet*.

The first performance was given on March 15, 1881, in the
Salle Henri Herz, by the group named in the dedication: "To
the Amatuer Choral Society and its founder, Guillot de Sainbris";
the soloists were Hermann Léon and Mme Fuchs. At the same
concert were heard—all without orchestra—a choral piece by
Gounod and another by Saint-Saëns, accompanied by two pianos,
eight hands, with Cécile Chaminade, Vita Rousseau, César
Franck, and Maton. Two years later *Rébecca* appeared at the
Société Nationale, with Franck himself at the piano and the
choruses conducted by André Messager.

The reception of the public was warm, that of the critics
variable. The composer's supporters sang his praises in a number
of journals and reviews; thus the *Ménestrel* gave the opinion that
the work was

> well constructed in the style of an oratorio. . . . The dramatic scenes
> were less happily realized than the two choruses near the beginning,
> for female voices and for the camel-drivers respectively; the latter,
> a most colourful piece, was encored.

The reactionary *Art Musical* expressed a totally different view; it
considered that Guillot de Sainbris's choral society

> has a positive mania for dull music, for melodies in monochrome more
> or less spattered with Wagnerism. . . . M. César Franck's *Rébecca*
> one might name as a perfect example of their taste in music. Never
> have we heard a work more antimelodic, more outlandish, more
> utterly wearisome. One can only think that in writing this score
> the composer (who, after all, knows what he is about) compelled
> himself to produce the quintessence of the impossible. Nothing new,
> nothing to attract the ear, not even reminders of other works!
> There is a continuous stream of sound, and no more. . . . The duet
> between Eleazar and Rebecca made us feel quite sea-sick, so strongly
> does the music resemble the rolling and pitching of a ship at sea.

The parting between the young women and Rebecca seemed to
this critic to be "an appallingly sad lament," and only the camel-

drivers' chorus made any semblance of appeal to him: "Melodically it has the clarity and sparkle of a musical diamond."[1]

At the time of writing *Rébecca* Franck, as one of his letters has
shown, had begun to compose his first opera, *Hulda*, which was
to occupy his mind (though by no means exclusively) for four
or five years after 1881, but which actually represents no more
than eight months of steady work. We shall refer later to all
the troubles that were stirred up by this odd and unexpected
undertaking. The libretto was by a young poet and dramatist
named Grandmougin, who had already provided the verses for
Massenet's *La Vierge* and Benjamin Godard's *Le Tasse*. As a
drama it is wholly exterior, brutal in its realism, and lacking in
characterization. Of Björnson's original play on which Grandmougin based his script, only the barest outline is retained. The
action takes place in the eleventh century. It is a series of theatrical
tricks and incidents, including assassinations (at the final curtain
hardly one survivor is left alive!), a series broken up, to its great
advantage, by a ballet-scene presenting a royal park where the
dancers unfold an allegory on the struggle between winter and
spring.

At the Conservatoire, in proportion as his importance in the
concert world increased, especially within the Société Nationale,
so did the exasperation with Franck increase among his colleagues in charge of the composition classes. Their rising indignation was caused in part by exaggerated claims for their Master
made by his over-zealous followers, but very much more by the
peculiar, indeed unique, situation that had brought itself about.
Here was the professor of organ openly teaching the technique
of improvisation; here he was, also, continually widening his
pupils' knowledge of and love for the more austere classics, for
Bach's works in particular, which were either unknown to or
sadly neglected by the other professors! His seniority saved him
from unpleasantness to some extent. It was expected that his
age and position would before long be recognized by the award
of the *Légion d'honneur*; in the interim period he received at the
prize-giving of 1880 an academic wreath of honour. This petty
distinction irritated his pupils to the point of indignation by what

---

[1] Like that other Biblical cantata Claude Debussy's *l'Enfant prodigue*, *Rébecca* was turned
into a 'sacred drama' in two acts, and was produced on the stage at the Paris Opéra in
May 1918, with repeat performances in 1920 and 1921.

they considered its unworthiness. Nevertheless, the award was given to him, according to the usual practice, as "Professor of organ and a learned composer." A similar award was given to Massenet at the same time. Both the disciples of Franck and their Master experienced a new and even keener disappointment when (as we have noted above) the Directorate nominated first Ernest Guiraud and then Léo Delibes as professors of composition in those classes which Franck had long hoped to obtain for himself.

Franck was able to find some consolation in the thought that when his name appeared at the Société Nationale concerts he and his music were heard with interest and approval, not only by the music-loving public, but also by his fellow-composers; proof of this is to be seen in the minutes of the meeting of the General Assembly on May 23, 1881, six weeks after the second performance of *Les Éolides*. The business on the agenda was the election of seven new members of the Committee. Bussine the founder received forty-one votes, Vincent d'Indy thirty-nine, Gabriel Fauré thirty, Henri Duparc twenty-nine, while no less than fifty votes were cast for César Franck. In addition to that, every season saw the appearance in concert programmes of at least three or four works by him—whether chamber music, organ-pieces, choral or orchestral works—which the more friendly critics praised in various papers. He was, too, the acknowledged centre of an artistic group, of which Vincent d'Indy became more and more clearly each year the active and authoritative leader.

During the summer months Franck repaired to the country with his family, without giving up his regular work at Sainte-Clotilde. About his stay at Quincy, Seine-et-Marne, where he often spent his holidays, much interesting information has come down to us through several letters now in the library at the Conservatoire. The first of them, written in Paris on August 15, 1881, "between Mass and Vespers," describes in glowing terms the delightful house he was in and his walks in the pleasant surrounding countryside.

> We are half-way to Fontainebleau, and I am certainly going to make one or two excursions into the forest. . . . My life is strictly organized. Twice a week I go into Paris for my church-work, Sundays and Thursdays; so I have for myself the three days between Sunday and Thursday and two at the end of the week, during which

I get through an immense amount of work (when I am in the mood). At the present moment I am the bondslave of my opera [*Hulda*], which seems to me to be going along quite nicely.

A second letter, dated Sunday August 6, 1882, was also written from Paris, where he was detained for a day or two by prize distributions, examinations, end-of-the-year meetings, and other official Conservatoire business. He returned to Paris the following Sunday for the Sainte-Clotilde services and again on Thursday "to give a short series of lessons at home"; then he went to Quincy. "Now I am off into the country again, and to-morrow I shall settle down to work once more. As you know, work is the relaxation that I enjoy most of all." Then he tells us: "My class this year has had a success hitherto unheard of. Every single one of my pupils was given either a prize or some other award." The outstanding prize-winner that year was Gabriel Pierné.[1]

Round about the 1880's German Romanticism had taken a strong enough hold on French literature to have fired the musical imaginations of two of Franck's pupils. Henri Duparc and Vincent d'Indy adopted the ballads of Bürger and Uhland respectively as subjects for symphonic poems; the former in his *Lénore*, the latter in his *La Forêt enchantée* ("The Enchanted Forest"). Their master followed their lead. Franck picked on (or at least decided to illustrate musically) Bürger's poem *Le Chasseur maudit* ("The Accursed Hunter"). Such was his final title; at first he called the piece *La Chasse fantastique* ("The Fantastic Hunt"), but abandoned that designation on learning of the existence of another work of the same title written by Ernest Guiraud. During December 1882 he wrote to his future publisher Grüs, inviting him to come and hear his new score played as a piano-duet by Gabriel Pierné and himself. Pierné had just won the Rome Prize, and was holding himself in readiness for his departure to the Villa Médicis. The first public performance of *Le*

---

[1] Second prize, Grand-Jany; *proxime accessit*, Ganne and Paul Jeannin; runner-up, Kayser. The members of the jury, with Ambroise Thomas in the chair, were Mathias, Auguste Bazille, Théodore Dubois, Duprato, Diémer, Fissot, Gigout, and Guilmant. Franck wrote a letter about Gabriel Pierné on December 19, 1881, to Lefèvre, director of the École Niedermeyer, to recommend him as his most brilliant pupil with a view to the forthcoming competitions of the International Society of Organists and Choirmasters. On the evening of December 19, Franck left for Fougères, where he ran into Gigout, the object of the journey no doubt being the opening of a new organ.

Chasseur maudit was to be given in the provinces at Angers;
Paris heard it later at the Société Nationale, under the direction
of Colonne, on March 31, 1883, and again, at the Pasdeloup
Concerts, on January 13, 1884, this time conducted by the com-
poser. It was played in December of that year at the Liége
Conservatoire.

Bürger's ballad narrates the terrifying adventure that befell a
certain Rhenish count, who, one Sunday morning, defying the
holiness of the day, dashed forth upon a fantastic hunting expedi-
tion while all the bells and the chanting of the church choirs were
sounding on every side. A menacing voice sounded a warning:
"Sacrilege will lead eternally to the fires of hell." Frightened by
its tones, he races on even more quickly, pursued by a horde of
devils. Was such a subject, one may wonder, with its marked
satanic elements, really suited to a composer who in the opinion
of so many musicians was destined rather to sing the song of the
angels? The thought comes into one's head, remembered from
studying certain pages of *Les Béatitudes*—this depicting of human
wickedness always leads Franck into the quagmire of factitious
and conventional music. The finished score of the work, which
keeps closely alongside the German poet's text, has however very
considerable merits on account of its thematic ideas, its rhythmic
force, and even the richness of its orchestration, which only
reached its final form after careful consultation with Vincent
d'Indy. No cyclic experiments are attempted here as in previous
works; the musical form is fixed by the poem; there are but few
themes, most of them of a colourful character—the singing of the
church choirs, the bells ringing, the riding of the hunters—and
the picturesque story they tell in music can be followed without
any effort of the mind. Of all Franck's orchestral works this is
perhaps the most often played; it has even been made the basis
of a ballet.

Following the example of his pupil Vincent d'Indy, who,
railing against programme music, continued always to write
descriptive works, our apostle of pure music took up anew in
1884 the experiment of *Le Chasseur maudit*. He now chose as a
subject for musical illustration Victor Hugo's famous poem, *Les
Djinns*. This time the piano was allotted a leading part in the
score. The work was in fact written at the request of a well-
known solo pianist, Caroline Montigny-Rémaury (Mme de

Serres), who had made a great name for herself in Europe as well
as in France; she had expressed a wish for a short piece for piano
and orchestra suitable to fill up an ordinary concerto programme.
It was for Mme de Serres that Franck specially designed *Les
Djinns*: yet she never played it! Her relationship with Ambroise
Thomas (she was his sister-in-law) no doubt deflected her from
giving public hearings of a work written by a composer who was
mistakenly thought to be an enemy of the Director of the
Conservatoire.

Les Djinns was composed at high speed during the vacation
period of 1884 at Quincy, Seine-et-Marne. In September the
composer told his pupil Pierre de Bréville about it in a letter, of
which the first part is a composition lesson.

> I myself am working well here. Even so, I am not going along as
> fast as I could wish. *Les Djinns* is finished, and I am about to arrange
> it for two pianos: that will take till about Monday or Tuesday. I
> have orchestrated an entire act of *Hulda* (200 pages); I shall finish
> the scoring of another during the next month or so. I confess it
> greatly interests me!

Another very long letter, hitherto unpublished, was written in
November to Mme Joséphine Sanches, of Azille, and provides us
with more precise information about this holiday, about the
work the composer did, and his mental preoccupations during
that summer spent at Quincy among his children and grandchildren.

> I have been composing and working at enormous pressure during
> the holidays. I have written a symphonic poem for piano and
> orchestra, and I have almost finished my *Hulda*. There are already
> six hundred pages of full score, and I am going to start right away
> on the last act; but, alas, my time of freedom is nearly up![1]

According to Franck's letter to Mme Sanches, negotiations

---

[1] Charles Bordes, future founder of the *Schola Cantorum* and at this date twenty years
of age, went over to Combs-la-Ville in 1883 to submit a composition exercise to Franck.
In the *Courrier musical* of November 1, 1904, he jotted down this vivid memory of his
time there. "After lunch the two of us roamed about among the plough-lands that skirt
the forest of Sénart; following on our heels like a string of street-arabs were the master's
grandchildren, all firmly set on one object—the flying of a most unmanageable kite that
Grandpa Franck kept captive at the end of a string and did his utmost to tame." Bordes
told this little anecdote to his friend Pierre de Bréville, adding that "the children became
very excited about this new game, and kicked up such a racket with their bawlings and
screamings that one of the forest police interfered, charging Franck with frightening the
preserved game!"

were entered into with the Director of the Théâtre-Italien, "who," he wrote, "is considering staging my work, possibly in French, possibly in Italian. But all that for the time being is in the lap of the gods!" We find here another pointer towards his personal feelings about the *Légion d'honneur*:

> For some weeks I have cherished hopes (possibly even the certainty) of becoming the possessor of a little red ribbon, for I can assure you I stand first on the current list. I have even received anticipatory congratulations from my fellow-musicians; but for each vacancy another has been nominated. I do not think things will hang about long now.

The manuscript of *Les Djinns* shows precisely the dates of its composition. On the complete full score is noted "Combs-la-Ville, Quincy, 27/7/84"; and both copies of the transcription for two pianos are inscribed, along with the name of the lady-dedicatee, "Combs-la-Ville, Quincy, 6/9/84." Like *Le Chasseur maudit*, *Les Djinns* was originally heard at one of the symphony concerts at Angers, under the composer's direction. The first performance in Paris was given on March 15, 1885, by the Société Nationale in a programme conducted by Colonne, which also included the *Symphony in D*, by Gabriel Fauré, an *Orientale*, by Claudius Blanc, and the *Rapsodie d'Auvergne*, by Saint-Saëns. Mme Montigny was replaced by Louis Diémer, a faultless pianist, to whom Franck said by way of thanks as they left the hall: "You played splendidly; to try and express my gratitude I will write you a special little piece and dedicate it to you." The Master did not wait long before redeeming his promise.

The printed programme of the Société Nationale concert presented in the following manner, as a kind of epitome of the music, Victor Hugo's programme in his own words:

Mer grise
Où brise
La brise
Tout dort
Dans la plaine naît un bruit . . . La rumeur approche.
Dieu, la voix sépulcrale des Djinns.—Ils sont tout
près . . . Cris de l'enfer, voix qui parle et qui pleure.
Prophète, prophète, que ta main me sauve . . . Ils
sont passés . . . De leurs ailes le battement
  décroît.

J'écoute
Tout fuit,
Tout passe;
L'espace
Efface
Le bruit.[1]

A critic of sound judgment can find in this score, underneath
all its picturesque exterior, a moral intention on the part of the
composer—a philosophical basis familiar to us in his other works
which has positively obsessed him in *Les Djinns*. The opposition of good and evil spirits, of angels and devils, is strongly in
evidence here, unmistakably expressed in the music (as it is elsewhere in Franck) by the direct contrasting in the themes of
commanding rhythms against flowing phrases of the utmost
smoothness. The general design of the work, however, was
suggested by the lozenge-shaped typographical appearance on the
page of Hugo's famous *Orientale*. An equivalent plan in purely
musical terms suggested itself—both rhythmically and in emotional intensity there was to be a progressive enlargement and then
a retraction, in the visual manner of the poem. It was indeed a
tempting scheme, and the author carried it out in his music with
an exactitude that does not impair his symphonic style. On a
pencil rough, which is still to be seen, Franck made the following
note: "A coda . . . perhaps gradually increase the values."

At the same time, the score of *Les Djinns* contains very much
more than a single basic idea, be it philosophical or musical. The

---

[1] In rough translation:

"A grey sea, where the breezes have blown themselves out and are asleep.

"From across the plain a tiny sound rises to the ears. The noises come nearer. O God!
it is the sepulchral voices of the Djinns . . . Now they are quite near. I hear the shrieks of
hell, voices uplifted in talk and others in weeping. Prophet, prophet, I pray that your hand
will save me . . . They have passed by . . . The beating of their distant wings grows softer.

"I am listening; that fugitive noise, everything in the world passes by us. Space can
quiet all sounds."

whole orchestral registration is something quite new, one might even say "prophetic." The piano is not treated as a mere solo instrument; it glides about among the rest of the orchestra as a humble fellow-worker, mingling its sonorities with those of the other players and never taking upon itself too prominent a position—a pointed thrust at excessive virtuosity from one who as a virtuoso himself had in past years suffered cruelly from the efforts to maintain his place in the public esteem. The example Franck set in *Les Djinns*, which derived in the first place from certain works by Liszt, notably the *Danse macabre*, was to have a widespread influence. Within a year or two of the production of *Les Djinns* that faithful pupil of Franck's Vincent d'Indy wrote for the same instrumental combination his *Symphonie cévenole*, and another temporary pupil, Claude Debussy, also used it for one of his "envois de Rome"—the *Fantaisie*, for piano and orchestra, which he withdrew from public performance because in form and orchestral lay-out it followed too closely the teachings of his quondam professor of organ.

Les Djinns was sufficiently short and its appeal sufficiently direct to ensure a very favourable reception. The regular public of the Société Nationale concerts was, besides, always ready to admire unquestionably any work by their revered Master. The Press on the whole was good. What matter if *L'Art musical* omitted from its notice all reference to *Les Djinns* and mentioned only the Saint-Saëns Rapsodie and the Fauré Symphony? *Le Ménestrel* over the signature of an occasional critic of theirs, G. Morsac, gave it a eulogistic notice:

> An interesting work, if for no other qualities than the original simplicity of its ideas and the admirable uniformity of its style. Listening to the imaginative and logical development of the main themes and the unfamiliar sonorities produced by the marriage of piano and orchestra, we could not help thinking how sad it is that we do not more often see in our programmes the name of this outstanding composer, who is too little appreciated just at that moment when he has become (as he will undoubtedly remain) one of the great masters of our time.

During the period of *Rébecca* and *Les Djinns*, the Société Nationale often gave performances of transcriptions of Franck's works. On April 28, 1883, Mlles Poitevin and Haincelin performed *Les Éolides* on two pianos. On January 12, 1884, two excerpts from *Hulda*, "an unpublished opera," were heard, the March and the Ballet, with a chorus accompanied on two pianos by Mlles Haincelin and Cécile Boutet de Monvel; the same excerpts were to be heard again on April 17, 1884, at the Trocadéro, at the second concert of the newly formed Société Internationale de Compositeurs ("International Society for Composers"). Other performances were given: on February 23, the *Mass* with soloists and chorus, including for the first time the *Panis angelicus*, a work of some age which probably originated as an improvisation thought out during the sermon at the Christmas office in 1861; on May 3 a repeat performance of *Les Éolides* on two pianos; and on December 13 *Veni Creator*, performed by the singers Duc and Bérenger. During this year of 1884 Ernest Chausson organized two full evenings of Franck's music, during the course of which were performed the *Quintet*, *Les Éolides*, certain choruses from *Ruth* and *Rébecca*, as well as portions from the *Mass* and from *Hulda*. Both were invitation concerts arranged in the hope of speeding on the entrance of Franck into the membership of the *Légion d'honneur*.

In 1884, on March 2, Franck had the interesting experience of being present at the first performance, given by the Lamoureux Concerts, of the first act of *Tristan und Isolde*. During the performance, which aroused both surprise and enthusiasm, he attentively followed the score. Afterwards he told his pupils how much he admired so great a work, which he described as feverish in its intensity. So far he had not taken a trip to Bayreuth, nor did he ever do so. He held himself aloof, not (as Vincent d'Indy would have us believe) because he was frightened of taking sides in a musical dispute or of being classified as a Wagnerean. The reason was the far simpler one that his economic circumstances tied him during his holidays within an easy radius from Paris. Not one of his well-to-do pupils, who all knew Wagner's theatre inside and out, had ever conceived the notion of inviting him to go at their expense on a journey which would have thrilled him beyond words and might also have deflected him from the Meyerbeerism which manifested itself in his forthcoming works for the stage.

This same year of 1884 shows us Franck writing an 'occasional' piece with a special purpose in view. It was designed for

the inauguration of the organ at the Institute for Young Blind
Persons, in which he was inspector of musical studies and president at the yearly examinations. Many of its members had been
organ pupils of his at the Conservatoire, three of them (Adolphe
Marty, Jeanne Boulay, and Albert Mahaut) taking between 1887
and 1890 the first prizes for organ-playing. The work he wrote
for this event was his *Psalm CL*, which Breitkopf published after
his death. It is a short piece laid out for chorus, organ, and
orchestra. The choir expounds in great enthusiasm those words
of the Psalmist—"Praise the Lord"—which Debussy later chose
for the final chorus of his *Le Martyre de Saint Sébastien*. In form
the music quite simply follows the words of praise to God, with
many varied orchestral effects fitting to the text—strings, organ,
trumpets, the psaltery (reproduced on the harp), and cymbals are
all brought into service. The ending is a vast and exciting
"Alleluia," blared out by all the voices and every available
instrument. A worthy work, *Psalm CL* has all the accepted
characteristics of a 'festival' work, but nothing of novelty to
detain us.

CHAPTER XV

"Prelude, Chorale, and Fugue": "Hulda": The "Symphonic Variations": Trouble in the Société Nationale: The "Violin Sonata"
(1885–87)

THE next work Franck wrote was considered at the time to be of enormous importance: the *Prelude, Chorale, and Fugue*. Vincent d'Indy, in his unswerving desire to place his revered Master on a pinnacle, has considerably exaggerated its novelty of conception. In order to exalt the originality of the pianistic output of Franck's later years, he has sacrificed a number of French composers of the nineteenth century, and has resolutely forgotten that the flow of first-rate music for the piano had never been stemmed in France. Piano-works by naturalized foreigners and by composers of French blood were by no means lacking before 1885; nor did certain pieces by Charles-Valentin Alkan (of which Franck thought highly enough to transcribe them for organ), along with a large number of descriptive or emotional pieces by Stephen Heller, Gounod, Bizet, Saint-Saëns, and a host of others, leave any perceptible gap in the continuity of French piano-music. Franck himself, indeed, had an admiration for the fine piano-writing of his most distinguished pupil, Vincent d'Indy, who in 1881 had published his *Poème des montagnes* ("Mountain Poem") for piano solo—a work new both in thought and execution despite its obvious traces of others' influence. He had besides known since the spring of 1881 Gabriel Fauré's *Ballade*, for piano and orchestra, and was among those who had had the opportunity since 1883 of hearing that composer's *Romances sans paroles* ("Songs without Words"), his impromptus, nocturnes, and his *Barcarolle*—all distinguished works written with great subtlety and skill.

The writing of *Les Djinns* soon after the *Quintet* (in which the piano plays a particularly rich part), along with the recent example of Saint-Saëns and Fauré, seems to have reawakened in Franck his old interest in the piano, which he had neglected since the days of his boyhood and youth; his love for the works of Bach led him to adopt the formula of "prelude and fugue" familiar in *The Well-tempered Keyboard*. Having in mind, perhaps, the practice of the German master in one of his organ-works, he sought to enlarge the form, linking the two traditional movements by introducing a new intermediary element—a chorale; ushered in by a bold modulation from B minor to E flat major, this chorale was developed on broad lines and treated, as were the two other parts, in full cyclical form.

The result was a musical triptych in pure symphonic style. A number of analyses of it have been published. After Vincent d'Indy's in his *César Franck*, musicologists in France, England, and Germany have subjected it to the most minute dissection, which reappears often in books and lectures on the teaching of composition; one need do no more than refer to these studies any student anxious to discover the inner machinery that produces a masterpiece! In the formation of his later pianistic style Franck came under the spell of other influences besides that—both general and particular—of Bach; in the work as a whole one observes the Beethoven of the more important sonatas, the Schumann of the *Études symphoniques*, and, above all, the Liszt of the *Weinen Klagen* variations, which themselves came very near to realizing the true Franckist ideals.[1] One can find a close reminiscence even of Wagner in the melody of the chorale, which comes straight from the bells in *Parsifal*. The architecture of the work is solidly reared above German foundations; it is deeply tinged with foreign, and especially German, conceptions of musical colouring; yet this new triptych made a direct appeal to French musicians through firmly adhering to the cyclical plan, through its formal balance and, above all, through its potency of expression. The younger French composers, indeed, looked upon it as the starting point of the new movement towards the French renaissance

---

[1] Ever since his adolescence Franck had felt towards Liszt, not only a lively gratitude, but an admiration that never weakened. This admiration he clearly states in a letter of 1885, quoted by Maurice Emmanuel: "Liszt has the richest musical imagination of our time. His works whether for piano or for orchestra, are a mine of melodic and harmonic treasures."

in music for the piano. In its basic ideas, as well as their technical expression for the instrument, the *Prelude, Chorale, and Fugue* wielded a powerful influence over the rising generation of composers in offering them a kind of ideal to follow, a complete expression of the ideals that were opposed fundamentally to the superficial music then in popular favour.

The *Prelude, Chorale, and Fugue* was written during the summer of 1884 and was played for the first time at the Société Nationale on January 24, 1885, by Mlle Marie Poitevin, to whom it was dedicated. The audience at that concert welcomed the work with a devoted admiration, though it had no notion at the time of its future influence, both formal and emotional. Not a word of serious criticism was heard at the time, not even from Saint-Saëns, although a good while afterwards, in his pamphlet *Les Idées de M. Vincent d' Indy*, he roundly condemned the construction of the work, expressing the opinion that it was "abominably and awkwardly written," and declaring that "the chorale is not a chorale at all . . . the fugue not a fugue."

At the distribution of prizes at the Conservatoire on August 6, 1885, César Franck had the great satisfaction of receiving the cross of the *Légion d'honneur*. It was awarded to him in his capacity as professor of organ there, now in his fifteenth year as a teacher. The cross was the award habitually offered to the particular man holding Franck's post; for this very reason the most ardent of the Franckists considered it unseemly. They would have wished the honour to be attributed solely to his eminence as a composer. But public opinion made no similar mistake on this score. According to a report in the *Ménestrel*—a paper not as a rule favourable to Franck—the award was "above all things an act of homage paid justly if a little tardily to the distinguished composer of *Rédemption* and *Les Béatitudes*."

The official decoration of the ageing Master—he was then sixty-three—brought him in a large crop of congratulations: "a mountain of letters and cards, I assure you, at least four hundred!" This imposing total is given in a letter to the Sanches family at Azille, a long letter written on his return from Belgium in September 1885. He had been to Antwerp on the occasion of the Exhibition there to give a concert of French music; the programme included the March and Ballet from *Hulda*, and also *La Chevauchée du Cid* ("The Cid's Ride"), by Vincent d'Indy, to

whom he also wrote from Antwerp on August 14. The object
of his Brussels visit was to play through his opera to the director
of the Grand Theatre. While there he wrote an encouraging letter
to Mme Sanches.

> He (the Director) seems to me to be quite taken with my opera,
> and I have the greatest possible hope that it will be staged, not this
> winter, but a year hence. . . . I work on, meantime, indomitably,
> for I am really almost certain about the Brussels production. In the
> next eight to ten days *Hulda* will be all of it orchestrated. The full
> score will total between 850 and 900 pages!

It was a year full of hope. During its progress Franck had the
pleasure of seeing hung at the Salon his splendid portrait painted
by Jeanne Rongier—a canvas that has once and for all established
in our minds his image in the primary occupation of his musical
life—the organist of Sainte-Clotilde. Before brush and colour
were used the painter had made a number of sketches of Franck
the organist, without the subject's knowledge! At the same
Salon show was to be seen Fantin-Latour's picture, *Les Wag-
néristes* ("The Wagnerites"), showing a number of Franck's
friends crowding round a piano—in particular, Emmanuel
Chabrier and Vincent d'Indy.

An incident occurred during the summer which suggests that
the composer had in his mind some new musical project that was
never brought to blossom. Just before his vacation a letter from
Franck was addressed to the secretary of the Conservatoire asking
for permission to borrow from the library a number of volumes
of the works of Alessandro Scarlatti (mostly those containing his
religious works), and also of some of the old madrigals by various
composers. Not a note in any of Franck's subsequent compositions gives us a hint of the reason for this unexpected request.

By the beginning of the academic year 1885–86 *Hulda* was
finally completed; the orchestration was finished on September
15. Franck took steps to offer the score to the then Director of
the Opéra, but the latter found the subject too violent for his
taste, with its assassinations in every act (it is an incredible fact
that the kind-hearted César was delighted with the libretto!).
He refused the opera, but to soften the blow proposed that Franck
should write him a ballet; here the composer refused, for fear of
finding a cabal raised against him, as happened with Lalo's

Namouna, which would close the doors of the national theatre against him for ever. As a next step, Franck arranged a run-through of *Hulda* for the benefit of Dupont and Lapissida, directors of the Théâtre de la Monnaie, at Brussels, his singers being Mme Charlotte Damner, daughter of a former prefect of Strasbourg before 1870, and the amateur tenor Bagès, who regularly appeared at the Société Nationale. But neither were these directors interested: "Nobody," they commented, "can suddenly make his entry into the world of the theatre at the age of sixty-three." A journey to Brussels undertaken by the composer with the object of reopening the discussion had no greater success. The evening after this fruitless interview the editor-in-chief of the *Guide musical*, Maurice Kufferath, who later himself became director of the Brussels Opéra, ran into Franck and found him calm and smiling, completely resigned, showing no trace of bitterness, barely expressing a modest regret, and even finding the best of good reasons to justify to himself and others the rebuff he had just suffered.[1]

What does this score of *Hulda* consist of? The somewhat ridiculous libretto is written in the style of the 1840's, and conceived, at Franck's special request, in the spirit of Meyerbeer's operas. The music is a vast improvisation wherein passages of great beauty jostle up against pages of sheer mediocrity which nevertheless bear faint marks of the composer's genius. The persistent taste for Meyerbeer's works seems surprising to us to-day, but it was quite normal even during the later years of César Franck's life. Vincent d'Indy, as we noted on more than one page of the first volume of our biography of that musician, never lost his liking for Meyerbeer even after the revelation of Wagner in 1876. Claude Debussy, when a young student at the Villa Médicis, wrote from Rome to his friends the Vasniers on October 19, 1886, that his work *Zuleïma*, then in the course of writing, was too reminiscent of Verdi and Meyerbeer.

[1] Franck expressed his gratitude to Mme Damner and Maurice Bagès by dedicating to the one his song *La Procession* and to the other *Les Cloches du soir* ("Bells at Evening"). Soon after this run-through, as Pierre de Bréville has recounted, Mme Damner gave at her house an evening of Franck's music, at which she and Bagès sang extracts from *Hulda*. To sing one of the minor rôles she called in a certain lady-vocalist who, envious of the composer's success, insisted on singing the page's Cavatina from *Les Huguenots*. Franck accompanied her at the piano with the most solicitous attentions, and afterwards highly complimented her. Mme Damner, repeating without knowing the phrase of Castillon, cried out, "The old gentleman is truly one of the angels!"

The score of *Hulda* has been closely analysed by Charles van den Borren in his *Dramatic Works of César Franck*; in that treatise the Belgian musicologist attributes all the opera's weaknesses to the libretto, and considers that the music itself is on a level with that of *Les Béatitudes, Rédemption,* and *Psyché.* Vincent d'Indy despite (or perhaps because of) his filial admiration, dismisses the work as "an essay in dramatic music." Both opinions seem to be equally exaggerated. Van den Borren was very young when he wrote his book—the first from his pen—and allowed himself to be carried away by his devotion to his older compatriot, though he wrote to us as recently as 1947 that his admiration had not abated with the years. Vincent d'Indy went even farther in the opposite direction, the more readily because, first of all, the score gave him no opportunity to expatiate on new forms in music, and, secondly, because of his open hostility to Franck's school-master son, Georges, who was the instigator of this dramatic adventure. Both the son and his mother were musical, but their taste was for music of a completely out-of-date style. Their one desire was that the composer should devote himself entirely to writing music of the old school, music that would have a com-mercial value. Vincent d'Indy revolted against this idea. These two opposing forces that tossed César Franck about between his spiritual offspring and his natural offspring came into further conflict over another and more general question, this time political and religious; for Georges Franck was a republican and a disciple of Voltaire, while Vincent d'Indy was a royalist and a Catholic of burning fervour.

Two fragments from *Hulda*—the Royal March and the Diver-tissement—were played several times about the time of their composition: with piano at the Société Nationale, on January 12, 1884, as we have already recorded; and on January 9, 1886, with orchestra in Paris, Brussels, and Antwerp. Franck himself con-ducted them at the Trocadéro on April 17, 1884, causing the *Ménestrel* to bewail the bad acoustics of the hall and to declare:

> We are sincere admirers of the composer of *Rédemption* and *Les Béatitudes,* and it made us very unhappy to witness his vigorous and original ideas and his delicate and elaborate orchestration drowning helplessly among the interweaving echoes of that vast barn of a concert-hall.

Hulda was never produced as an opera during its composer's lifetime. Remodelled by Georges Franck and Samuel Rousseau (the latter chosen so as to avoid consulting Vincent d'Indy), it was put on the stage on two occasions, at Monte Carlo on March 4, 1894, and at the Theatre Royal, at The Hague, in March 1895. The Monaco production was given a most favourable and appreciative notice in the *Ménestrel* of March 11, 1894, the writer being that ardent admirer of Franck, Julien Tiersot. His critical opinion has the greater value in that it was informed by an actual stage-production of the opera, while others' opinions, published half a century later, were nearly all based on a mere run-through at the piano. The essential points in Tiersot's article are as follows: he considers the work lyrical rather than dramatic, leaning back towards an older type of opera, although the musical style is quite distinct from that past period. The music is direct and swift in its expression of passing emotions, the melody being spontaneous and coming straight from the heart. On the picturesque side he found a greater vivacity than he had expected; the level of tonal colouring is uniformly low and sombre, but the variety of the rhythmic and melodic patterns breaks up the monotony. He pointed to the wide diversity in the various numbers—a chorus of prisoners, savages chanting, women's choruses, a sword song, a solemn march, for example—all conceived in one consistent tonality, a mixture of the minor keys, the ecclesiastical modes, and chromatic harmonies; also to the Norwegian popular tunes and the ballet (the best thing in the work from the symphonic point of view). As for the emotional side, he mentions some beautiful lyrical outbursts and a strong use of declamation; the two love-duets, one of them occupying the whole of the fourth act, he considered to be the high point in the work.

An excellent piece of writing this! The orchestra is colourful, poetic, ever-changing, truly eloquent, as it continues pouring out its vigorous, passionate, and ardent melodies; the inspiration is sustained at a high level with an unbelievable flood of inventiveness.[1]

[1] Besides the detailed study of *Hulda* (and of *Ghiselle*, Franck's second dramatic work) made by Charles van den Borren, one finds in the *Rivista musicale italiana* (1895, fascicle No. 2) an analysis by Engelfred. There is also an important account of the Monte Carlo performance by Georges Servières in the *Guide musical* of March 11, 1894 (reprinted in that author's book *La Musique française contemporaine*).

To satisfy his family's desire to see him enter the world of the opera Franck had written *Hulda* with great speed, in a kind of prolonged outburst of extemporization, which was thus described by his son: "When my father was composing a scene for his opera some twenty or more musical ideas occurred to him for each situation; having jotted these down, he later could pick and choose the most suitable." The problem was to infuse some life into his libretto, which was crammed, as he had wanted it to be, with all the conceivable stage vicissitudes and startling events, in the worst tradition of popular opera. He found it necessary to prompt his musical imagination by playing *Die Meistersinger* from the piano score, and he let out the secret to some of his pupils—Charles Bordes in particular—during the summer of 1883:

> In the evenings I have been playing a little Wagner now and then, to warm me up: am I not now a theatre-composer? But, please notice—I have also *Les Béatitudes* to spur me on my way; I frequently re-read the score, and find that it puts me in the mood for writing for the stage.

The autumn of 1885 saw the completion of an orchestral work of major importance, the *Symphonic Variations*, which, like its predecessor, seems to have been written in a very short space of time, for the piano score is dated "Quincy, October 2, 1885," and the orchestral score "Paris, December 12." It is of course the "little piece" that Franck had promised to write to Louis Diémer in token of gratitude for his interpretation of *Les Djinns*. Like the last-named work, the *Symphonic Variations* set out to weld the piano and the orchestra into one substance in which neither element will predominate. *Les Djinns* was programme music, the new work absolute music. It entirely justifies its title, for it consists wholly of variations on a large scale, and Franck undoubtedly had Schumann's *Études symphoniques* in his mind, as well as the later works of Beethoven, when he was writing it. The work is divided into three linked parts; there are two contrasted themes—the first rhythmic and in its first announcement on the strings rough and violent, the second an exquisite and moving melody sung by the piano. The two themes are in continual conflict, but their struggles are controlled by the superb symphonic design, always clear and yet elaborate. Many careful analyses have been issued (by d'Indy, Cortot, Spalding, and others) of its various episodes, which all lead to the cheerful climax where one of the elements triumphs over the other. Technically the score is beyond criticism; musically it is perhaps César Franck's greatest achievement; expressively one cannot help imagining that once again the two motifs represent two personalities in spiritual conflict, one of them, representing gentleness of soul, being that of the composer himself.

The first performance of the *Symphonic Variations* took place under the Société Nationale on May 1, 1886, Diémer being the pianist, with Franck conducting; the audience was loud in its acclamations. The second performance, however, on January 30, 1887, under the direction of Pasdeloup, turned out to be regrettable; it then formed part of a festival about which more will be said later. Just previous to the Nationale concert a certain event gave Franck the warmest artistic satisfaction. His pupil Vincent d'Indy had won that highest of musical awards, the Prix de la Ville de Paris, with his *Chant de la cloche* ("The Song of the Bell"). In this connexion Claude Debussy, still resident at the Villa Médicis, wrote to his friends the Vasniers:

> There is a personal feeling, which you would perhaps not guess at, underlying old Franck's joy at his favourite pupil d'Indy's success with the prize. Franck has always vainly dreamed of having his own composition class, and therefore he is highly delighted to see his teaching methods triumph over those of the Conservatoire.

Such rivalry was normal and natural, and would have created no difficulties had not Franck's pupils obstinately maintained an attitude of contemptuous hostility towards the composition pupils at the Conservatoire. The favour in which Franck was held in the limited circle of the Société Nationale did not extend to other centres of musical activity. The newly acclaimed master had won in a few years a reputation too great and too unexpected not to arouse jealousies, which were aggravated by the behaviour of his clan, sometimes known as "the Franck gang." The profound Wagnerism and the passionate Franckism of these young musicians annoyed beyond measure the partisans of a musical style less complex and considered more truly French—that is to say, more superficial. It is no hard task to guess at whose head were directed such objurgations as those of a young critic on the

Revue des deux mondes, at that period the sworn enemy of Wagner
and of Franck, if not also of d'Indy, and later equally hostile to
his one-time fellow-student of piano at the Conservatoire,
Debussy: "Forget," wrote Camille Bellaigue on February 1,
1886,

> the good intentions of the composers of that generation, forget all
> their complications, their overloaded modernisms, and these obscure
> masters show up for what they are—mere gatherers of clouds.
> Beauty does not reside in them; she cannot hide herself behind their
> enigmas.

In the autumn of 1886 Franck found himself mixed up, much
against his will, in a musical plot hatched for their master's benefit
by his friends and supporters.[1] The Société Nationale was by now
fifteen years old; like every other organization, it had reached a
stage when it needed rejuvenating, especially as the most influential of its founders, Camille Saint-Saëns, no longer came with
any regularity to its meetings now that Franck had become
powerful within its circle. The astonishing success of the *Quintet*,
in the first performance of which he had occupied so important a
part, was the crowning point of his ill will. Saint-Saëns was now
in his fifties; though younger than Franck by thirteen years, he
was already becoming a reactionary figure, characterized by his
anti-Wagnerean, anti-Franck feelings. The younger musicians
who up to then had greatly admired him and sought out his
advice had come to the point of regarding him as the opponent
of all their ideas and tendencies. The Société needed a new leader
of indisputable popularity and with a full belief in the new ideas,
bred from the solid stock of Beethoven and Wagner. César
Franck, a professor at the Conservatoire, a famous organist, and
publicly accepted through his recent successes as a composer, was
the obvious choice for the presidency, and was elected thereto.
He was able to leave all matters of direction and administration
in the hands of his two secretaries, Vincent d'Indy and Ernest
Chausson. But his influence was not thereby lessened.

A very different account of these startling changes has been
given by Vincent d'Indy. Thirty years after their occurrence
d'Indy gave a lecture, in April 1915, which was published by *La
Renaissance* on June 12, 1915. In the course of it he stated that

---

[1] The full story is told in our *Vincent d'Indy* (vol. ii, pp. 11–16).

alongside the founders of the Société Nationale there had grown up

> a musician of genius who, without the least knowledge of it himself, gradually became the moving spirit of the new association and then took the leading part in the movement: that genius was César Franck.

Saint-Saëns vehemently contradicted this statement in a counter-statement in the issue of the same review dated September 4, 1915, in grossly exaggerated terms. "César Franck," wrote Saint-Saëns,

> whose works were then mostly unheard, seized the propitious moment to emerge from the shadows of obscurity and hurry off to the proper office to become a naturalized Frenchman in order that he might be eligible to join the Société. He was welcomed therein with open arms, and I myself, as President of the Société, often gave him my help and co-operation in getting his works performed. No long time passed before I began to be aware of the underground work going on with a view to sapping my influence and substituting for it that of Franck and his pupils. By a continued series of petty annoyances they succeeded in causing the resignation of their most troublesome opponents, like Bizet and Massenet. At committee meetings César and his pupils formed an exclusive circle of their own, plotting in low voices in dark corners. In short, the situation became such that I myself in my turn handed in my resignation. From that moment onward the Césarean and Wagnerean party had imperial power, and the Société became, what it is now, a closed shop, whose value and aims I know nothing of, but which is entirely out of touch with the intentions of the founders.

Such verbal commentaries, whether sympathetic or antipathetic, are but the outward manifestations, with more or less directness of statement, of an inner reality—the existence of what is known as "Franckism." That doctrine, founded on the noble examples of Bach, Beethoven, and the German Romantics like Schumann and Wagner, became more and more opposed to the traditional lightness of style of French music in the theatre and the concert-hall, and sought to bring about the creation of a new art of music, more inward and personal, more austere, more consciously national for all that its roots were in German soil. César Franck, Germanic by race, Frenchman at heart and for a dozen years or more by nationality, was thrust forward as the champion and leader of the French musical renaissance, the *Ars*

Gallica, according to the motto of the Société Nationale. While
the Salles Pleyel and Erard were to become the high places where
public sacrifices to the gods were offered of the cyclic sonata and
symphony, the private meetings of the committee of the Société
were (so to speak) consecrated in part to the work of spreading
the new symphonic gospel, preached less by Franck himself than
by his disciples. Master and pupils marched together towards
the same objective, but the pupils led, the master followed. The
truth about this paradoxical situation was crystallized in a casual
remark by Charles Bordes: "Father Franck is the offspring of his
pupils!"

This pert epigram is in no way contrary to the facts, and the
truth it contains may be pinned down in various ways. We may
for example observe the parallelism (already referred to above)
between the productions of the Master's later years and that of
certain young musicians whom he had taught. Duparc and
d'Indy led the way along the new path, to all extents and purposes guiding Franck in the composition of large symphonic
poems on literary subjects, usually borrowed from German
Romanticism, and setting before him, too, some fine examples
to follow; thus, five years ahead of Franck, d'Indy with his
Symphonie cévenole had demonstrated for him the potentialities
of a new kind of symphony, truly modern in spirit, and (as well)
of the use in major orchestral works of the piano as a principal,
but not the leading, partner. At their meetings in private and
public these Franckists could talk only of the future; they were
dumbfounded that Franck in his natural humility could rest
contented with playing the trios of his youth, forty years out of
date, or motets and church music lacking in any personal character. They goaded him on to compose large-scale works, not for
the theatre, as his family wanted, but for the concert-hall—
sonatas, quartets, symphonic works; they encouraged him to
develop his natural instinct for cyclic form, of which he himself
was barely conscious, but which was to develop into the principle
ruling a strict system of musical composition. Everything was
done to make him assume the full leadership of the new school
of thought by setting for future composers to follow creative
models of high symphonic value.

The Master, it is obvious, showed himself perfectly willing to
be led by his zealous disciples along the path which followed the

direction of his inner tendencies, but from which he had been
deflected, early or late, by the material conditions of his life.
The unceasing displeasure expressed by his family with his new
orientation in music forced him to modify his creative plans by
the composition of operas, with a view to winning popular
success and so financial reward. During the few years of life
that remained to him he strove to maintain the balance between
the contrasting desires and ambitions of his two personal circles,
with the result that he found himself alternately improvising
music for the theatre and elaborately constructing symphonic
works of lasting merit, solid in technique and worthy of his own
teachings.

While this minor revolution in musical taste was in progress,
Franck completed, in 1886, a new work of outstanding beauty
and great importance, the *Sonata*, for violin and piano. Was it
actually a new work? Or was it merely the realization of that
earlier product of the summer of 1858, the sonata which he
proposed to write for Cosima Liszt, at that time the wife of
Hans von Bülow? During the autumn of 1886 the *Sonata* suddenly appeared out of the blue at the house of Eugene Ysaÿe
under somewhat curious circumstances. That great violinist was
getting married on September 26 at the small town of Arlon, in
Belgian Luxembourg. César Franck was prevented from being
present, and so Charles Bordes represented him at the wedding,
which he attended in company with his sister Mme Bordes-
Pène. In the course of the wedding breakfast he handed to the
famous virtuoso, on behalf of his Master, the manuscript of the
Sonata, which had been read through in Paris with Mme Montigny-
Rémaury. At the first available moment Ysaÿe and Mme
Bordes-Pène played it through again before an invited audience
which included Théodore Radoux, Director of the Liége Conservatoire, Sylvain Dupuis, his future successor in that post, the
oboist Guillaume Guidé, future director with Maurice Kufferath
of *La Monnaie* at Brussels, Théodore Lindenlaub, a journalist on
Le Temps, and Jules Laforgue, the poet, just back from Berlin.[1]

The *Violin Sonata* did not have long to wait for a public
performance; it was played two months later in the course of a

[1] The incident is described by Antoine Ysaÿe in his biography of his father. Laforgue
had been French tutor to the German Empress Augusta at Berlin; he was an associate of
Théo Ysaÿe, who first introduced him to the world of music.

Franck festival at Brussels. The Belgians took a great pride in their one-time compatriot, now become a French citizen; the Arts Club at Brussels therefore organized a concert on December 16, 1886, the programme consisting entirely of compositions by César Franck. The principal interpreter was Mme Bordes-Pène, who played the *Prelude, Chorale, and Fugue*, and was joined by Ysaÿe in the *Violin Sonata* and by the Ysaÿe Quartet in the *Quintet*: the only other item was the forty-year-old song *L'Ange et l'enfant*, sung by Mlle Gavioli. Franck and Bordes arrived in Brussels the night before to attend the rehearsals and the concert. The success was enormous. Gevaert, the Director of the Brussels Conservatoire, was much affected by the passionate feeling of the *Quintet*, and said to the composer, "You have transformed chamber music: thanks to you a new vision of the future has been revealed to our eyes."

It may seem odd that the new sonata should have had to wait five months in silence before its first performance in Paris. One reason for this neglect may be found perhaps in the shower of musical problems rained down upon the heads of Vincent d'Indy and other lesser workers over the rehearsals for the Parisian production of *Lohengrin* and its tremendous reception at its first performance, conducted by Lamoureux, on May 3, 1887. Another reason was the labour involved in organizing, for the coming January in the Cirque d'Hiver, a Franck festival, its expenses defrayed by subscriptions raised among his supporters. This festival concert was planned in two parts. The first would be conducted by Pasdeloup, and would include *Le Chasseur maudit*, the *Symphonic Variations* with Diémer as soloist, and certain portions of *Ruth* sung by Mlle Gavioli and M. Auguez with a supporting choir. In the second part the composer himself was to direct the March and one of the Ballet tunes from *Hulda*, Nos. 3 and 8 of *Les Béatitudes*, sung by Mmes Leslino, Gavioli, and Balleroy, and MM. Auguez, Dugas, and Gaston Beyle. The advance notices in the Press made much of César Franck's achievements as a composer; one of them, the longest and most significant, appeared on January 15 in the *Revue Wagnérienne* over the name of Alfred Ernest; therein one may read the striking phrase that the French composer, while openly a great admirer of Wagner's music, "honours him at the proper moments in his inspiration, but never imitates him."

The performances under these two conductors were execrable, particularly those directed by Pasdeloup. He was an ageing man, almost exhausted by his labours in music; six months later he was dead. He was discouraged, moreover, by the failure of his concerts to fight any battle against the newer organizations reared up by Colonne and Lamoureux, whose competition proved fatal to his efforts. He was entirely incapable at his time of life of giving a balanced performance of the *Symphonic Variations*; the finale became a public disaster! The second part of the concert was no better. All the composer's friends were horrified. In response to those who made adverse comments on the quality of the performance he merely replied (according to Vincent d'Indy), "No, no, my children! You are too exacting! I myself was very delighted with all of it!" A family anecdote may, however, not be out of place here: Georges Franck, returning home to the Boulevard Saint-Michel after the concert, tells how he found his father sitting in an arm-chair in a state of collapse; he spoke but few words: "The music is beautiful, believe me, my son! Those performing people do not understand it." Some of Franck's sympathetic critics did their best to hide from the public the manifest failure of the festival concert. Thus, Victor Dolmetsch, in the *Ménestrel* of February 7, began his report by saying that "M. Franck, who was conducting the second half of the festival, was warmly applauded after each of his works, and the public gave him a prolonged ovation at the close of the concert." Then he added:

M. Franck's position as a composer has long been established. One can find in his works much that is poetic and no more; but we are well aware that this composer has those imaginative powers over musical construction that only come from years of study and practice in the art, while his artistic conscience never allows him to substitute a cheap and obvious effect for one that, however remote it may seem, is more closely connected with the meaning of the music as a whole.

Then there was printed a complimentary account of the works played in the programme.

Eventually the *Violin Sonata* was played in Paris by Mme Bordes-Pène and Eugène Ysaÿe at the third concert of the Société Moderne—an organization founded only two months before by these two artists in collaboration with the 'cellist

Fischer. The new society did wisely in reserving for itself the
first performance in France of a sonata of which the two main
performers had given the original first performances in Brussels,
and their choice was justified, for the work won an instant
success. It is surprising that no one thought of giving the new
sonata an immediate public hearing at the Société Nationale,
though in 1887 the Société's concerts included a transcription for
two pianos of certain extracts from *Rédemption* and also a second
performance of *Les Djinns*. Thus, the first performance at this
society of the *Sonata* was heard on December 24, 1887, Rémy
replacing Ysaÿe in the violinist's part. Again, a great success
greeted the work: the public applause was so persistent in its
enthusiasm that the finale had to be played twice. The critics
were also favourably impressed with the performances of the
Sonata at the Sociétés Nationale and Moderne. Guy Ropartz in
L'Indépendence musicale of May 15, 1887, paid tribute to the
breadth of its artistic scope and the high quality of its ideas, as
well as to the richness and novelty of its harmonic basis. An
anonymous writer in the *Ménestrel* (conceivably Julien Tiersot)
wrote about the score:

> It is modern in its formal design, and yet it retains the attractive
> qualities of the best of the classical sonatas. The first movement,
> somewhat legato in its general style, is constructed entirely on the
> basis of a persistent 9/8 rhythm, which makes one think of what
> Bach might have written had he lived in our nineteenth century.
> The *recitativo, quasi fantasia*—very free in form—is superbly lyrical.
> And the finale, which is treated almost throughout in canonic tex-
> ture at the octave, reveals beneath its outward shell of academicism
> an ease, a grace, and a charm seldom equalled by anyone.

Written more than sixty years ago, the *Violin and Piano
Sonata* has become Franck's most popular work, and, in France
at least, the most generally accepted work in the whole repertoire
of chamber music. In his *Traité de composition* Vincent d'Indy
puts it under the microscope of analysis—an exaggerated labour
of love, no doubt, but justified in its maker's eyes by the fact
that it was to be "the first and the purest model of the cyclic
treatment of themes in the form of the instrumental sonata."
One of Franck's supporters, Albert Groz, delved deeper into the
dissection of the work in his contribution to *Le Courrier musical*
of June 15, 1908. Robert Jardillier, in his book, did not lag behind

the two composers above-named. His central proposition is that the entire work is developed out of an embryonic cell of three notes—a node, or, as the Gregorian terminology names it, a *torculus*—with varying intervals. This point of view is disputable; at its best it is one of sight and not of hearing—of reading eyes, not listening ears! Franck himself would have been stupefied by it; his whole method of composing was to invent, spontaneously almost, and without calculation or any system, a large number of kindred themes—"cousins," as he called them.

A far greater interest exists in the musical form of the work, with its triple design of sonata form so carefully managed—in its changing harmonies, too, in its rhythms, in its melodies that alternate between tender and assertive moods.

The *Violin Sonata* has four movements. The first is an allegretto in normal sonata form; the second, allegro, is built also on two main themes, which are developed with much personal feeling; the third, irregular and entirely free in its musical progress, is aptly marked *recitativo, quasi fantasia*; the finale is for the most part concerned with a plain and flexible canon, and is directed to be played allegretto poco mosso. Harmonically, the sonata is extremely varied, with an inexhaustible suppleness of resource. We can observe in the very first lines of the score a pre-Debussy subtlety of balance in sound between violinist and pianist —a kind of rhythmic and melodic decoy that leads us on against our wills—which Franck had long sought to produce, but never found until he committed the whole of this sonata to paper. Rhythmically, the *Sonata* is fully charged with pulses that are always exciting, sometimes even brutal, as the *Quintet* is. The broad and moving melodic thought is typified by the first subject of the first movement, which the violin takes twenty-six bars to expound. The same kind of emotional feeling inspires both the *Sonata* and the *Quintet*—a hidden drama of the soul, undefined in its unfolding, strong enough, indeed, to exorcise from our thoughts any preconceived judgments, any images that may have arisen in the minds of his unthinking admirers of Franck the organist, the sweet-natured mystic, nearly attaining the state of true holiness.

In performance, the sonata presents a number of problems. We will cast a passing glance at two only. The first of them (which has come in for the most general discussion) turns on the metro-

nomic speed of the opening bars. Franck's own direction is
allegretto ben moderato: Ysaÿe played it considerably faster than the
composer had first imagined it, but so moving was the emotional
reaction he received from the performance by Ysaÿe and Mme
Bordes-Pène that he discarded his original notions and completely gave way to them. And then, secondly, should those
opening pages be interpreted *vibrato* or *amoroso*? Would it be
the best plan, perhaps, to leave this opening at rest in a serene
and dreaming mood of half-heard mysteries, in order that the
next part of the work, with its passionate outpourings, should be
given wing to fly to its predestined heights? No one solution to
the problems can be set coldly on paper. Great masterpieces can
be subjected to the most diverse readings in performance, to
musical interpretations from entirely opposite points of view, and
still remain immune from any need to bring charges of treason
against the performers.

CHAPTER XVI

Piano Pieces and Songs: "Psyché": The "Symphony"
(1887–89)

ONE of Franck's rare journeys out of Paris for any considerable distance occurred at the end of 1887. His destination was Bordeaux, where two performances of his compositions were announced—a symphony concert given by the Saint Cecilia Society at the Grand Theatre on November 20, and his *Mass* at the Church of Notre-Dame on November 22. The orchestral programme, conducted throughout by the composer, consisted of extracts from *Ruth*, *Rédemption*, *Rébecca*, and *Hulda*, and three major works, *Le Chasseur maudit*, *Les Éolides*, and the *Symphonic Variations* (with Theo Ysaÿe at the piano). The public, no doubt adversely affected by the monotony unavoidable in a one-composer concert, proved cold in its welcome; but when certain of Franck's loyal friends gathered round him and complained of the Bordelais' reception the composer answered, "Don't talk about such things! They were most kind, and anyhow they let me go on right to the end of the concert." The local Press was more kindly in its attitude. The reporter of the *Gironde*, Paul Lavigne, concluded his long account of the concert with these words:

> This artist seems to me to be quite plainly the leading symphonic composer of our age. M. César Franck, I have not the slightest doubt, will be considered in the twentieth century as one of the really great composers of the nineteenth.

The *Mass*, for three voices, was equally highly praised; for the Offertory Franck interpolated a brilliant and majestic improvisation. Admiration was also expressed for the composer's command of the situation when, having noticed the choir's hesitant entries at the beginning of the *Sanctus*, he stopped them and made them start again. Up to this time probably the only provincial French town that had given Franck a welcome as a composer was Angers, where he had been invited to conduct a concert of his own works.[1]

During 1886 and 1887 César Franck had been writing a long work for piano solo, a kind of counterpart to the *Prelude, Chorale, and Fugue,* which he published under the corresponding title of *Prelude, Aria, and Finale.* The manuscript, which he presented to Mme Bordes-Pène, bears the finishing date of September 6, 1887. Despite its title, the work is in truth a sonata in one movement, and original in its design: an andante, exceptionally long in its melodic invention, takes the place of the normal allegro; an extended air with variations forms the slow movement; and the last recapitulates the thematic material of the two preceding movements. The Prelude is a kind of chorale, in which, however, the melodic elements are not confined to the traditional four-bar phrase, but are expanded to twelve bars by the treatment of one of them in rosalia. The Aria is also a chorale, with a typically Franckist subject. The classical allegro-form of the Finale is enlarged in a novel way by means of the cyclic return of already heard themes and by an elaborate scheme of tonalities. It is an outstanding work, written more in the style of the organ than of the piano, and bearing once again traces of the influence of Beethoven, Schumann, and Liszt: comparison of its merits with those of the *Prelude, Chorale, and Fugue* would lead to interminable discussions.

The new work, dedicated to Mme Bordes-Pène, was first presented in public by that pianist at the Société Nationale on May 12, 1888, in a programme that included among other things a portion of Vincent d'Indy's *Wallenstein* in a duet transcription played by Mme Bordes and the composer. Franck's quasi-sonata seemed to have caused some disappointment in those who admired his *Prelude, Chorale, and Fugue.* A serious critic on the *Ménestrel* staff, Amédée Boutarel, dismissed it with the bare words "a piece by M. César Franck, long and tedious." Another journalist, Julien Torchet, wrote with some scorn in the *Monde artiste,* "a composition, new if in no way a novelty, by this master whom I

[1] The library at the Paris Conservatoire contains a letter written by Franck on November 29, 1887, to one of his friends in Bordeaux, telling him about the two concerts devoted to him in that city. The letter shows the great pleasure the composer derived from the favourable reception of his works.

prefer to worship at a distance than listen to," and went on to express the wish that its creator might be added to the list of boring composers published by Camille Bellaigue.

Actually, on May 19, 1888, just before Boutarel's and Torchet's opinions were printed, Bellaigue had devoted a second article in *Figaro* to the subject of 'Boredom in Music.' The first article dealt with Bach—'king of all bores'—Beethoven, Wagner, and Hummel; the second article was reserved for living composers. In this later gallery of bores, Bellaigue prophesied,

> there will assuredly be a space reserved for the composer of *Le Chasseur maudit*, of the *Symphonic Variations*, for piano and orchestra, of *Ruth* and *Les Béatitudes*—that composer whom his zealous disciples call the "French Bach," the "Master," but who in reality is no more than a capable teacher.

However, no actual name was quoted, even when the moment came to discuss the Société Nationale (also unnamed in the article):

> I can see them all ranged before me in hierarchical order—the composer-bores, the apostles, and the priests of boredom. I know who is their pontiff, but, as Heine once said, I will write nothing against that man, nor against his acolytes, nor against his faithful worshippers.

Alongside this opinion held by a musical critic we may set the opinions of one or two conductors. Édouard Colonne did not like Franck, and he had frequently shown his dislike ever since the first performance of *Rédemption*, in 1873. Charles Lamoureux held him in no higher esteem. In a letter written in 1888 to Paul Poujaud, Ernest Chausson gives an account of some meetings with Lamoureux at Biarritz. "Lamoureux is much interested in us," he writes, 'us' being the younger Franckist composers; he adds:

> We spent an entire evening solidly discussing Franck. Lamoureux does not begin to understand him at all. He recognizes in him some technical ability and some fine moral qualities, but that's all. He cannot see anything even in *Les Béatitudes*. Franck's influence appears to him disastrous—we must (in his view) throw him overboard or we shall sink. . . . Naturally, at the end of a couple of hours, neither of us had changed his opinion, and all we could do was to cry quits and go off in search of a wash and a drink! Poor Franck is greatly hoping to have his Symphony performed at the Lamoureux Concerts; I very much fear his hopes will not be realized.

The ablest and most devoted supporters of Franck did him considerable and continuous harm by their sincere but exaggerated eulogies, by the excessive harshness they poured over those who were not among the devotees of the Société Nationale, and by their merciless condemnation of all who would not share their whole-hearted faith. By such means they aroused against their god all the fanatical fury of the iconoclasts.

Another work was about to stir up a new controversy, this time again, as before, to intrude itself within the family circle of the Francks. On March 10, 1888, the composer conducted at the Société Nationale a symphonic poem for chorus and orchestra; its musical importance was too great for it to be neglected, but the subject matter came in for endless discussion. The score of *Psyché* was based on a short literary sketch by Sicard and Louis de Fourcaud (the latter had already provided Franck, in 1884, with the poem of his beautiful song *Nocturne*). Both the authors' names were printed in the March 10 programme of the first performance at the Nationale, but they do not appear on the title-page of the printed score. In view of these clearly established facts, certain lines in a letter written by Vincent d'Indy on February 4, 1901, to Hugues Imbert are distinctly surprising:

> I have never exactly known the origin of the poem of Franck's *Psyché*. To the best of my belief, however, it was written by Georges Franck (the Master's son) and put into verse by one of Franck's pupils at the Normal College whose name I don't know.

Another letter, addressed by d'Indy on October 20, 1918, to Henri Rambaud, again attributes to the same source the paternity of the short poem underlying the symphonic work, at the first public appearance of which d'Indy had been present. Part of the letter runs thus:

> The Master's eldest son was a university man and a schoolmaster at the Lycée Lakanal. He did everything in his power (if I may dare say so) to turn his father aside from the path of religion, which up to then he had followed, at least in all his compositions with verbal texts. Georges raved ecstatically about the beauties of the classical mythology and recounted the story of Psyche, providing his father with a sketch-plan for an opera on the subject. Franck was delighted with the legend itself, but had no desire to treat it dramatically; he therefore begged his son to reshape his text in a form suitable for a choral symphony. That was eventually done. All

the same, César Franck (as you have observed as well as I) was incapable of seeing the subject from anything but a Christian point of view, and so treating the libretto as a mystical rather than an erotic poem. The result was indeed worthy of the composer of *Les Béatitudes*, and not at all what had been hoped by those who strove so hard towards the end of his life to deflect the Master from his religious inclinations. . . .

Most of *Psyché* was composed during the vacation period of 1886; the sketches, written on three staves, have survived, bearing the following figures of dates and duration:

"Sommeil de Psyché," (August 9–13), duration 6 minutes; "Psyché enlevée par les zéphyrs," August 14 (2 minutes); "Jardins d'Éros," August 18 (4 minutes); "Amour," Quincy, September 27 (6 minutes 30 seconds); "Souffrances et plainte de Psyché," Paris, October 13 (total length, 24 minutes).

The cause of the waves of discussion that broke over the choral symphonic poem was not the music itself, but, as one might guess from Vincent d'Indy's second letter, the philosophical and religious significance of the subject. In the ancient myth of Psyche happiness deserts her from the moment she conceives a longing to look on the face of her lover. Franck, always sensitive and ingenuous, was no doubt entranced by a story in which there is not an evil thought, and where innocence, for a time unhappy, is rewarded in the end; he looked upon the fable without doubt as the expression of perfect love. Vincent d'Indy was the dedicatee, and always regarded the work as his own personal property. In religion d'Indy was an uncompromising absolutist, and at this period was moreover roused by the opposition from Georges Franck. The love scene he firmly believed to be

an ethereal dialogue between the soul, as conceived by the mystical author of *The Imitation of Christ*, and a seraph descended from heaven to make known on earth the eternal verities.

A totally different interpretation was put on the work by the Franckist Julien Tiersot; for him the final scene was a platonic commentary on "a procession of the gods and of lost souls, tremulously soaring upward towards the conquest of the Idea." From both these views, one Christian, one pagan, Franck's mind was (we may be sure) equally far distant.

The discussions spread until they developed into a quarrel between the Franckists and the composer's family circle. The Francks were not religious; it was their one ambition that the head of the family should devote himself, not to costly works for chamber and orchestral concerts, but to music less refined, with a less specialized public, wider and more popular in appeal, and altogether more commercial—that is, to operas. The veteran composer did all he could to satisfy both parties. The conflict raged unceasingly; a number of incidents indicate that; many of them are easily verified, and therefore give proof positive of the seriousness of the struggle between the two families, natural and spiritual.

Mme César Franck disliked the new work, which she regarded as too sensual, quite as much as she disliked the *Quintet*, whose excessive emotionalism she found quite shocking. She never ceased to rail against the former, just as she refused to listen to the latter. Her antagonism was based wholly on moral grounds. Alfred Cortot recalls a characteristic incident. Franck was talking with a friend one day about *Psyché* and the ecstatic rapture of certain passages therein; whereupon Franck, putting his hand on the score of *Les Béatitudes*, said: "What I like most about *this* work is that it does not contain a single bar of sensual music." This question of sensuality in the score of *Psyché* long occupied the attention of the critics, and was to turn up anew years later in one or two essays. As an example, we quote Gaston Paulin from the *Guide musical* of November 16, 1890:

> In *Psyché* . . . Franck has depicted the beauty and the sorrows of the lover of Venus's son, and after that her repentance. He has deliberately omitted from his picture any reference to Psyche's hour of happiness, and thus has held himself aloof from any kind of carnal thoughts. But, even so, he fully expresses himself in a way that is at once masterly and cold, and gives us the picture of the people in the ancient legend—a spiritual picture of an ideal chastity.[1]

To anyone considering the problem of *Psyché* without a bias

---

[1] The Master's granddaughter Mme Chopy wrote to us thus in May 1944: "My grandmother took a dislike to *Psyché*, particularly to certain of its harmonic progressions, and many a time she tackled César Franck on the subject." In addition, she has told us the story of how Mme Franck once allowed herself to be taken to a concert to listen to *Psyché*, but when she arrived found she had forgotten to bring her admission tickets, and returned home with the firm intention of not being noticed by anyone. No doubt she did it on purpose so as to avoid hearing the performance.

in either direction it is at once apparent that what Franck found appealing in the ancient legend was above all the subject herself, and also the varied pictures offered to him in his collaborators' short poem—pictures which he realized in music to the best of his ability and with all his heart and soul. The work is laid out on the following plan. Part I: "Sommeil de Psyché" ("Psyche asleep"), where three melodies (so alike in appearance as to be sisters rather than cousins) express the sleep and sweet dreams of the heroine of the story; the music is exquisitely tender: "Psyché enlevée par les zéphyrs" ("Psyche awakened by the breezes"), a short and swift allegro based on two themes, the second caressing in character, the first borrowed from *Les Éolides*, where it represented "les brises flottantes des cieux" ("the floating breezes of the sky"); the choice of this theme, already used in a different connexion, was made on the advice of Henri Duparc. Part II: "Les Jardins d'Eros" ("The Garden of Cupid"); here, mingling with the zephyrs, there appears a new theme vigorously hammered out and representing Eros (or Cupid), after which the voices enter in a chorus celebrating first "Love, the source of Life," then the charm and beauty of marriage; finally, the sopranos in long-held chords utter a warning of danger that reminds one of *Lohengrin*; "Psyché et Eros" ("Cupid and Psyche"), a love-duet in symphonic style, with a number of kindred themes of a character at once ardent and tender; it was no doubt their interlacing and their passionate appeal that shocked the composer's wife. Part III: "Le Châtiment (souffrances et plaintes de Psyché)" ("Punishment: Psyche's sufferings and griefs"), a tragic episode, the main subject being a long, sad melody, sung first by the sopranos, then by the full chorus, and then discussed by the orchestra in a brief interlude; "Apothéose" ("The Apotheosis"), characterized by a new theme representing the forgiveness of Eros (or Cupid), and with all the preceding themes mingling together across voices and instruments.

Throughout the work there is an incessant outpouring of melodies, unified in their design, each so closely resembling its neighbours that they all seem to be no more than fragments of one single vast and endless melody. Another astonishing fact about this love-symphony is the absence from it of any uneasiness or anxiety, indeed, of any element that could recall the restlessness of the *Quintet*; the thought behind the music is glowing, but always serene. Yet another surprise—the orchestration lacks any kind of heaviness; indeed, in the hands of a Toscanini it would develop a paradoxical lightness of texture.

It is the abundance of its melodic invention—so marked a feature of the work—that has always made *Psyché* readily acceptable to the public and to the critics, even the most reactionary of them. After the first performance, on March 10, 1888, *Le Ménestrel* found in the work "an interest that continually grows from bar to bar," and praised it "not only for its formal beauty and its admirable lay-out, but also for its high-mindedness sustained throughout the music." The same paper, it is true, published two years later, on March 2, 1890, a very curious article by Barbedette:

> Melody reigns supreme with the most exaggerated tyranny. Across an uninterrupted series of harmonic abracadabras, there wind in and out tunes formulated on no ordered plan, which, having no good reason for beginning, can find none for ending. The orchestra moans and murmurs; the choir behind the scenes imitates the vague sounds of Æolian harps hanging in the pine-trees. M. Franck is the most mystical of our composers; he excels in depicting divine hypostases, celestial beatitudes, impalpable shapes, the bottomless abysms and the limitless expanses of the universe. There is in him something of the *Pater extaticus* and the *Pater seraphicus* of the second *Faust*.[1]

The publisher of *Psyché* (father of the composer Alfred Bruneau) asked César Franck for some songs: Enoch, who had published the *Symphonic Variations*, commissioned him to write two duets for equal voices: a choral society at Liége made known to him their wish to have from him a male-voice chorus to follow up the well-known chorus of camel-drivers in *Rébecca*. These various requests delighted the composer, but were not so pleasing to Georges Franck, who had constituted himself his father's adviser in literary matters, for both Bruneau and Franck himself decided to apply to Paul Poujaud to choose the texts for them. To the latter the composer wrote on January 27, 1888, repeating

[1] A letter from Vincent d'Indy to Guy Ropartz, written from Avignon on September 27, 1898, gives some information about the positioning of the chorus: "As for the singers in *Psyché*, I know that dear old Franck wanted them not to be seen, according to the advice given him by his son; on the other hand, if they are in the wings it is impossible to make out a single word they are singing, and in that case why have a chorus at all? At the Société Nationale we let them remain on the platform, and he did not seem to mind."

his urgent need for words for young women's choirs and describing a new and also urgent need: "a chorus for men's voices, of the character of a prayer or a hymn, something very broad and calm." Poujaud sent him the *Hymne* of Racine, a translation from the Roman breviary, which Franck set to music immediately and sent to Sylvain Dupuis, conductor of the Liége choir. To Poujaud, once more, on March 13, 1888, the publisher Bruneau wrote off a request on Franck's behalf for a poem which could be suitably set as a companion to *L'Ange et l'enfant*: "We want something very noble in thought and at the same time very child-like, very simple in its inner meaning." Poujaud sent him *La Procession* of Auguste Brizeux. On September 3 of the same year occurred another letter to Poujaud about Enoch's commission for six choruses for equal voices: "Forgive me for thus approaching you so often. My excuse is that you have such an unfailingly happy touch!" The answer was *La Vierge à la crèche* ("The Virgin at the Manger"), by Alphonse Daudet, and *La Chanson du vannier* ("The Basket-maker's Song"), by André Theuriet.

Four or five years had passed since the previous vocal work was written—the *Nocturne*, to verses by Fourcaud, which the poet had published in 1885 in an album issued by his paper *Le Gaulois*. *Nocturne* is a pleasant, dream-like song with a broad melody and a typically Franckist accompaniment: the first three verses, in the minor mode, are practically the same, save for some slight variations of the first in the second and third; the fourth verse, in the major, has about it a warm radiance. The songs of 1888–89 all have charm and even beauty. *La Procession*, performed at the Société Nationale's concert of April 27, 1889, has a certain religious grandeur expressed in a symphonic manner of easy mastery. Of the pleasant duets for women's voices, two were sung at the Nationale on January 19, 1889. The more majestic and purely choral *Hymne de Racine* Franck heard sung at Tournai in the course of his last journey to Belgium.

An important first performance early in the year 1889 was to attract the attention of the musical world and also to arouse new controversies. For two or three years past César Franck had been working on a symphony, a project possibly inspired by the recent success of the "Symphony with Organ" (No. 3, Op. 78), by Saint-Saëns, which was published by Durand in 1886 a short time

before its first performance at the Conservatoire on January 9,
1887. Another incitement may have been the success of the
Symphonie cévenole, by Vincent d'Indy, at the Concerts Lamoureux
on March 20 and 27, 1887. Franck thus seems to have been led
on by his former friend and rival and by his pupil, both of whom
he admired. He recognized the former's symphony as a fine
piece of music beautifully scored, and, according to the testimony
of his disciple Louis de Serres, he expressed surprise only about
one point: "The critics," he is reported to have said,

> "have one and all picked out as something new the use of leading
> themes all through the course of a work; but more than forty years
> ago I did that very thing in my *Trio in F sharp*!"

Franck simply settled down to the composition of the symphony without being able to foresee that one day in the future
the composer of the *Cévenole* would make every effort so to
arrange its chronology as to attribute to his master the renaissance
in French music of a form that had never been abandoned—
which, indeed, had outstanding representatives in Bizet, Gounod,
and Lalo, to name but a few. Both in his *César Franck* and in his
Treatise on Composition d'Indy has falsified history. The Saint-
Saëns symphony with organ, asserts d'Indy, cannot have been
known to Franck before its initial public performance, and at
that date, he tells us, Franck's work on his symphony was complete. There are two errors here, since the score of Saint-Saëns
appeared in 1886, and since d'Indy himself has given the dates of
its composition by Franck as the years 1886–88. The sketches for
Franck's symphony were jotted down during two months of the
summer of 1887—that is, six months and more after the publication and performance of the Saint-Saëns—and the last page of
Franck's finished manuscript bears with its dedication an exact
date: "To my dear friend Henri Duparc. César Franck. Paris,
August 22, 1888."

Franck would have liked the first performance of his symphony
to be given by Charles Lamoureux, but after the mishaps with
Les Éolides in February 1882 that conductor declared Franck's
orchestral music to be impossible. One day at Chausson's house
the composer went up to Lamoureux, and said to him, probably
with no hint of ill will, "Monsieur Lamoureux, you are very
kind to my pupils; you so often play their music, and I should

like to thank you for that." Pierre de Bréville took occasion to tell the conductor that Franck did not know to whom to offer his *Symphony*. "Not to me!" replied Lamoureux. "Let him take it along to the Conservatoire! That is the sanctuary of the symphony." César Franck followed his advice; he passed his score to Jules Garcin, the head of the Société des Concerts du Conservatoire, who was able to smooth out all the difficulties, including the resistance of his committee. Two performances were arranged to take place on Sundays, February 17 and 24, 1889—a decision which, even before the first hearing, loosened a number of controversial tongues.

At the final rehearsal Franck was present with his son; his former and present pupils at the Conservatoire had received permits to attend, and they were joined by some of the more fervent admirers of *Les Béatitudes* and the *Quintet*. His friends completely encircled the composer so that he should not hear any unsympathetic comments, but the Master had ears for nothing but the music. He was enraptured. At certain moments in the symphony he could be seen turning to the enthusiastic Ernest Chausson and with a broad gesture pointing out to his friend the return of the themes from the first and second movements in the finale.[1]

Was it this rehearsal or was it the concert that Gabriel Marie (one of the conductors of the Société Nationale) had in mind in the story he relates in his book *Pour la musique*? Gabriel Marie was seated behind the players; he tells us that Franck came up close to him with a score in his hands; while they were playing, certain passages seem to have pleased the composer, whereupon he pointed to them in the score, saying under his breath, "How good that bit is!"

On the day of the concert itself the audience proved to be ice-cold; the work seemed to them to have an audacity unwarranted in a practically unknown composer whom at least one lady-subscriber thought to be a teacher of the harmonium! One has

---

[1] Information about the event was published by Pierre de Bréville in the *Revue S.I.M.* of November 1913 and in the *Mercure de France* of January 1, 1938. We may take it to be authentic, since it comes from notes written at the time by this pupil of Franck's. Another pupil, Louis de Serres, is not so readily to be believed in his account of the rehearsal. According to him, Ambroise Thomas, sitting in the front row of the stalls, remained unmoved during the playing of his professor's symphony, but warmly applauded the 'Unfinished' Symphony (which was not on the programme) and congratulated Bourgault Ducoudray on one of his works (which was not on the programme either!).

often heard people quote the remark that Charles Gounod is alleged to have made about the work: "It is the assertion of impotence pushed to the lengths of dogma." Both the opinion and the meaningless jargon in which it is couched seem improbable in the last degree. According to another anecdote, told by Georges Rodenbach in *Figaro* on December 24, 1896, Gounod is reported as saying "It is the negation of music." That remark too seems hardly credible. Whatever differences in outlook and taste separated the two old friends, Gounod always recognized the mastery of his fellow-musician. If at times he criticized certain of Franck's tendencies—his excessive refinement and his lack of simplicity—he never ceased to acclaim him as a great artist. One need attach no importance to certain solemn pontifical utterances of the composer of *Faust*, bandied about, distorted, and twisted out of recognition by the malignancy of the public. It is nevertheless true that the majority of Franck's fellow-composers did not form favourable opinions of a work which by its general style and even certain details (for example, the use of the cor anglais in a symphony) outraged the formalist rules and habits of the stricter professionals and amateurs.

Franck was totally oblivious of the attitude of his listeners. On leaving the hall he said to his friend Paul Poujaud, "What a lovely sound it makes! And what a splendid reception it had!" He was counting on an even greater success for the repeat performance, the subscribers for the second series of concerts having the name of being less reactionary than those for the first series. In actual fact there were two distinct currents among the public: the stronger was that of the regular subscribers, who were either unconcerned about the personality of the composer or hostile to his trend of thought, and so condemned the new style outright; the weaker, but also the more noisy, was that of Franck's pupils and the supporters of the Société Nationale, to whom the work appeared as a revelation.

The Master had frequently shown people his score and as frequently aired his intentions. One pupil, Louis de Serres, asked if the symphony had been inspired by any poetic idea; to him Franck replied:

"No, it is just music, nothing but pure music. At the same time, while I was composing the allegretto, especially the first phrases of it, I did think—oh, so vaguely—of a procession in the olden times."

Then he added, aware of the novelty of the work, "I have been very daring, I know; but you wait till next time, I shall go much farther in daring then!" A precise and detailed statement Franck made about his symphony is given here in the form recollected by Pierre de Bréville. "The work is a classical symphony," he said.

"At the end of the first movement there is a recapitulation, exactly as in other symphonies, for the purpose of more firmly establishing the main subjects, but here it is in an alien key. Then follow an andante and a scherzo. It was my great ambition to construct them in such a way that each beat of the andante movement should be exactly equal in length to one bar of the scherzo, with the intention that after the complete development of each section one could be superimposed on the other. I succeeded in solving that problem. The finale, just as in Beethoven's Ninth Symphony, recalls all the themes, but in my work they do not make their appearance as mere quotations. I have adopted another plan, and made each of them play an entirely new part in the music. It seems to me successful in practice, and I fancy you will be pleased!"

A minute analysis of the symphony is extant; it was written by Franck himself, and appeared in the programme at the Concerts Lamoureux of November 19, 1893. The composer, much to our surprise, makes no reference to the connexion between the themes, nor to important points in the cyclic form; nor does he say one word in the note about his ingenious plan for combining the andante and the scherzo. The secrets of his methods of composition which he was proud and delighted to reveal to his pupils did not appear to him to be of the least interest to the general public, who would be carried away only by the eloquence of the music.

Critical opinion was very diverse, ranging from unreserved enthusiasm to systematic disparagement, which included a good measure of violent opposition. A former pupil of Franck's, Camille Benoît, printed in the *Guide musical* an article full of devoted admiration; first he established that the new work

had introduced into the middle of a coterie of semi-somnolent people an entirely new conception of music—wide awake, young, burning with vitality; the warm applause accorded to it contrasted not a little with the usual behaviour in that place—behaviour notable for its well-mannered flabbiness and its torpor considered to be 'good form.'

After expressing his musical views on the work, he wrote words that throw some light on its obscure psychological background.

> For myself, I am happy when I see reflected in this music the nobility and beauty of soul of a Master worthy of all reverence; I am happy to be able to perceive there so many splendid qualities; to find—alongside the manly sorrows of a lofty spirit, alongside outbursts of a vigorous faith and an unexhausted energy—so much of tenderness, of the delicate feelings of a heart still young. I am happy that I can find in it, yet once again, the courageous lightness of heart which in life's combat boldly confronts the meannesses, the tyrannies, the cruelties of the world. Here are the superb, all-absorbing single-mindedness of the martyr, the joyous detestation of virtue for vice, the scorn of the high for the low, the inevitable triumph of righteousness.

Arthur Pougin, reactionary as usual, and faithfully adhering to the æsthetic ideals of his youth, considered the work worthy, well conceived, well written: "Everything," he wrote,

> that study and knowledge of music can bring to a composer is comprised within this score. The one thing lacking is the fire of genius, of inspiration; what we miss is freshness and (if not abundance) a generous provision of ideas.

He found the orchestration lifeless and colourless, the harmonic warp and woof drab and overshadowed by mistiness, and the melodic texture thick.

An article of some significance was published by another conservative critic, Camille Bellaigue, in the *Revue des Deux Mondes* of March 15, 1889, and was reprinted in the book *L'Année musicale*. Some part of it, despite its unwarranted severity, deserves quotation here. Bellaigue opens by assuring Franck of his respect and esteem and regard; then he reviews the two performances at the Conservatoire.

> On the first Sunday the *Symphony in D minor* by M. Franck gave us some feeling of hope. There appeared to be something in it—certain serious and accomplished qualities. There were a few clouds as well, but they broke apart a little and later evaporated. On the second hearing all the clouds had disappeared, but there was nothing hidden behind them. Their veil was a deception, their mystery an illusion; and so the second performance, so far from confirming our first hopeful impressions, completely effaced them.

Bellaigue cannot resist comparing Franck's symphony with the recent symphony for organ by Saint-Saëns, which he held in unreserved admiration. "The one is night, the other day. In the Saint-Saëns one can breathe freely; in the Franck one is stifled and dies." His opinions are then broadly developed.

Oh, what arid and drab music, without any touch of grace or charm, without a smile! Even the themes are often lacking in interest. The first subject, a kind of musical question-mark, is hardly above the level of the themes given to Conservatoire students to develop. Another theme has more attraction and more daring, but the composer has not made the most of it. The opening of the second movement is an oasis in the desert. One feels for a moment or so refreshed by a pretty song on the cor anglais, supported by chords by the harp and strings. One evening in his organ-loft, no doubt, M. Franck has hit upon this tune, which partakes in some degree of a religion that is neither insipid nor mystically sensual. Why has he not built the whole movement on this felicitous theme, in the way the composer of the "Italian" Symphony did with another religious theme? Because, simply, M. Franck is not a Mendelssohn; and we shall be disappointed if one day soon one of his adepts does not cease to congratulate himself on that deplorable fact. The finale of the D Minor Symphony seems to us its most distressing movement. In a high fury it summons back all the motifs of the preceding movements. This system is much in favour these days, but it is essential that it should not be misused. What M. Franck accepts as unity and cohesion turns out to be nothing else but aridness and poverty of invention.

To-day, in France at least, unanimous opinion places Franck's Symphony in, or near to, the front rank of the great compositions in this form, but one may recognize in it faults of both detail and conception. The recapitulation of the introduction of the first movement, for example, has few to defend it; all find it superfluous in the extreme. The orchestration also has come in for fairly general criticism, although it is palpably better than that of Les Béatitudes and Rédemption; it seems to be grossly overloaded, with the basses eternally plodding along like the pedal notes on the organ, with the parts too often doubled; the woodwind is expected to do nothing more than a crescendo and diminuendo, while the brass insistently punctuates the loud passages when it is not, as at the end of the introduction, weaving thick patterns in canon. All that is easily explained, even excusable,

when considered in relation to the organ; the orchestration
derives all the time from registration of stops on the organ.
Franck never ceased to be an organist, and also, as one hears in
the course of certain dull passages and pointless repetitions, an
improviser.

Franck profited by the lessons he learnt from the performance
of his first and only symphony. If he enjoyed having—as he
fondly believed—broken down the hostility of the conductors
and the public, if he was happy planning out schemes for new
works, at least he felt he had been taught much by the experience.
He confided in his pupils that from thence on he would never
write like that again; especially, he would never provide the
brass with parts like those he had written for them in the finale.

CHAPTER XVII

"Ghiselle": The "Quartet": Improvisation: Chorales: Death
(1889–90)

I N the meantime César Franck still clung to his hope of raising the standards of those colleagues of his at the Conservatoire who were composers of operas. In this ambition he was at one with his family in their urgent desire that he should produce a popular and profitable theatre-piece.

Through his son's introduction he made the acquaintance of Gilbert-Augustin Thierry, a writer of historical novels and son of the historian of the Merovingian period. Franck took much interest in the ancient history of France; his first idea was to find therein some story suitable for treatment in a symphonic poem, but under pressure from his son Georges he accepted a libretto offered to him, a drama about the dynasty of Merovius. This libretto, it will be readily imagined, was in the style of Meyerbeer's operas; in literary quality, if not in dramatic, it was (luckily) a good deal superior to that of *Hulda*. Hence came about the opera *Ghiselle*, with a text by the son of Augustin Thierry.

The principal character, Ghiselle, is an Austrian princess, long held prisoner by the savage Frédegonde, regent of Neustria, and subjected to all manner of ill-treatment. The libretto pleased Franck by the conflict in the sixth century between paganism and Christianity, so attractive to the composer's spiritual ideals; nevertheless, it is packed full of violent episodes and incidents, of which Georges Servières made a list (no doubt incomplete):

> Choruses of victory and a triumphal march, drinking songs, the captive princess insulted by a haughty and pitiless queen who looks on her as a rival lover, a duel between two men in love with the same lady, a sorcerer searching for his daughter and finding her in the last act, a religious scene of novices taking the veil, a lover who

has just snatched a nun away from the altar, the bishop's solemn curses, the pursuit of the fugitives, the great fire, a scene of madness, a double suicide. . . .

All these wild and melodramatic events were presented in an unrelieved succession, without the ballet and extraneous incidents that had done much to lighten the atmosphere of *Hulda*.

During the autumn of 1888 César Franck occupied his mind by setting this terrifying drama to music, not at first in score, but in rough sketches from which eventually to orchestrate the work. A fragment of the music, preserved in the Conservatoire Library, would seem to show that the actual process of composition moved along with some rapidity. The third act bears the dates August 7–28, 1889; the fourth September 11–21. The opera was a kind of improvisation, and the hastiness of the writing is confirmed by a study of the score, not the less because it is full of reminiscences of *Rédemption*, *Psyché*, and *Le Chasseur maudit*. Franck himself orchestrated only the first act. The remainder, on the Master's death, was entrusted for instrumentation to several of his pupils: the second act to Pierre de Bréville (the sorcerer's scenes), Ernest Chausson (the love scene), and Vincent d'Indy (the ensemble scene); the third act to Samuel Rousseau; the fourth act to Arthur Coquard. This collaboration turned out to be the cause of further friction between Georges Franck and Vincent d'Indy. One can follow the development of the quarrel by reading in the Franck dossier at the Bibliothèque Nationale a letter from Georges Franck dated January 6, 1896. On the other side, Pierre de Bréville wrote the present author a long personal letter on March 1, 1944, giving the real facts of the dispute, which had a political and religious, rather than a musical, basis.

According to a statement by Georges Franck in the twenty-line preface at the head of the score (1896), the published edition "was designed to reproduce with exactitude the outward appearance of the original manuscript." That manuscript of 294 pages is in fact no more than a rough sketch, not fully written out; one thus knows exactly how little faith one can place in the accuracy of the definitive printed edition. As a work *Ghiselle* has been generally neglected, even by Vincent d'Indy, who, despite his boundless admiration for his master, could see in it no more than an operatic endeavour of no historical importance. Nevertheless, one serious critic, the Belgian musicologist Van den Borren, studied it deeply, as he did *Hulda*. He wrote enthusiastically about the opera in his first book, *L'Oeuvre dramatique de César Franck*, and to us personally he not long ago declared that after forty years his admiration for *Ghiselle* has lost no force, either as an opera or in its personal appeal to him, and he has reiterated that opinion in his admirable booklet on César Franck published a few months ago. Very few musicians are to be found who had the privilege on March 30, 1896, at the theatre at Monte Carlo of seeing and hearing the "lyric drama" in four acts written in collaboration by César Franck and Gilbert-Augustin Thierry. This misunderstood score can never be properly judged until it is produced once more on the stage; only from the theatre could one derive some idea of the thoughts and intentions in the Master's mind.[1]

But shall we ever be allowed to see it, to hear it, in a revival on the stage? The festivals arranged in 1922 to celebrate the centenary of the Master's birth passed by without any lyric theatre in France or Belgium giving a performance of either *Hulda* or *Ghiselle*. From *Hulda* we occasionally, but rarely, hear played the charming ballet to which Franck, when composing it, found himself dancing!

Of *Ghiselle* one never hears a note, although more than one page of considerable merit could easily be extracted from it: among others, the picturesque scene—admittedly somewhat conventional—where Gudrune is gathering herbs to make her love-philtres, or the incidents in the baptistery: the latter presents before us a noble religious scene of a kind entirely suited to Franck's genius, for the sacred edifice has become a prison where the lovers are confined; we perceive at once the violence of that opposition between the Christian Church and paganism which had first aroused César Franck's interest in the libretto.

One cannot but wonder whether a complete performance of the opera will ever be found practicable. There will be grave difficulties in the way, largely on account of the excessive romanticism—so localized and out of date—which dictated to Franck his choice of subject and its realization in musico-dramatic form. But could one not begin with extracts from *Hulda* and *Ghiselle*, perhaps without any visual stage-setting, but at least in a concert

[1] Under the musical direction of the conductor Léon Jehin, the following artists appeared: Mme Eames, soprano (*Ghiselle*), Mme Deschamps-Jehin, mezzo-soprano (*Gudrune*), Mme Adiny, dramatic soprano (*Frédegonde*), the tenor Vergnet (*Gouthram*), the baritone Melchissédec (*Theudébert*), and the bass Mauzin (*the Bishop*).

version of an hour or two's duration? Out of these two scores of a past era, not suitable for revival in their entirety, one could compile a delightful anthology of music. Such a compilation would joy the hearts of the Franckists, still very numerous to-day, and would give all musicians the opportunity of appreciating the dramatic force in the great master, that force which the difficult circumstances of his life never allowed him to develop into its full power.

While working on *Ghiselle* Franck set himself the task of simultaneously undertaking the composition of a string quartet, and thus was able to hold an even balance between the ambitions of his family and those of his followers. To his collaborator in the theatre, G. Thierry, he actually wrote about the project: "I have a vague impulse stirring within me not to write our fourth act until after the quartet is done. But I'm scared of being haunted by *Ghiselle* while I am composing the quartet." The two projects were altogether too diverse to be jumbled up together—that grandiose Meyerbeerian drama and the pure style needed for the chamber-music work which the violinist Ysaÿe, in company with other Franckists, had begged him to produce. In the end Franck finished the opera before undertaking his work on the score of what turned out to be a masterpiece, the highest outcome of his new style.

The last page of the manuscript of *Ghiselle* shows the date September 21, 1889. Three days later Franck wrote to Paul Poujaud: "I am anxious to apply my mind to my quartet. Shall I be able to, I wonder?" For months he had been casting his mind about for ideas and surrounding himself with the best models for reference. In 1888, somewhat to their astonishment, d'Indy and his friends had noticed on the Master's piano some scores of the quartets of Beethoven, Schubert, and Brahms; in addition, at the weekly home-sessions of music Franck arranged for the performance of all the Beethoven string quartets by the chamber-music group of his friend Léon Régnier, an important member of the society known as La Trompette, to whom as an expression of his thanks the composer eventually dedicated his new work. Sufficiently primed in his own view, he began work, not without difficulties and a number of false starts. The opening movement he found particularly troublesome; the first important task was to invent and establish a motto-theme, a central creative idea, and at the same time to plan ahead and settle in his mind the cyclic interplay of the various elements. The search for the right ideas for the larghetto took him some time. "I have been trying vainly," said Franck to Bréville, "to think of the right expressive phrase; it has got to be very long, all on a single stem of growth, without repetition and without turning back on itself." Vincent d'Indy has reported that one could see the composer "any morning, nervously removing with a piece of india-rubber the ideas he had finally decided on the night before." Among others who saw him in this same state of mind in August 1889 was the young Belgian composer Guillaume Lekeu, who writes enthusiastically of Franck in his letters. The library of the Paris Conservatoire possesses the sketch-copy of the work, with many variants, that was given as a present to Ernest Chausson. In the margin of the finale a note is to be found: "A new phrase needed here; see the E flat quartet of Beethoven, Op. 127."

As with the majority of Franck's works, the *Quartet* has been subjected to a number of analyses, ranging from æsthetic discussion down to its dissection into the minutest details. The length of the main subject has been generally appreciated; it extends over some fifteen bars, with the first violin singing over harmonies sustained by the three lower instruments, and is characterized by a rising leap of a tenth. Its various transformations have been remarked on—the fugal exposition in the minor mode, its swift and fugitive appearance in the scherzo, its return in the finale, with a new rhythmic pulse and a quite other character despite the retention of the rising interval of the tenth. In a conversation with Bréville Franck himself made some comments about one of these remarks, analogous to that already quoted in connexion with the finale of the *Symphony*. "As in the Ninth Symphony," he said,

"I begin by calling up again the thematic ideas of the preceding movements, but after their recall I do not leave them alone and in silence; I make use of them in the development of the movement."

No one has yet attempted to probe into the originality of the *Quartet's* architectural design; yet musically it has provided a model for a number of later composers. Especially worthy of admiration is the complex pattern of the first movement, which is based upon the continual interweaving of two tempi, one allegro, the other andante. No less admirable are the melodic richness and the vitally glowing counterpoint. On the opposite scale of the balance one finds oneself at times wondering whether the string-writing is really in the true quartet-style. Often one is aware of the influence of the organ; the four instruments are combined without any relief, their polyphony is unceasing, and their harmony is inclined to develop into multiple parts, into rich and heavy chords, involving the frequent use of double-stopping. Here and there one finds the four instruments relapsing into the orchestral tremolos which, in 1846, we have already criticized as overworked in *Ruth*. Regretting this excess, certain musicians have expressed their surprise that all the movements save the scherzo, which is neat and Mendelssohnian in style, are haunted by the spirit of the later quartets of Beethoven.

The first performance of the *String Quartet* took place at a Société Nationale concert on April 19, 1890, the interpreters being the Quartet Hermann-Gibier-Balbreck-Liégeois. The reception was triumphant; twice Franck was called on to the platform to respond to the public applause, both times showing as much surprise as joy in his demeanour. The few critics who came and wrote notices of the event were, as usual, of the Franckist persuasion, and expressed their enthusiasm as often before in a feverishly high tone of voice. In the *Ménestrel* Julien Tiersot firmly asserted the continuity existing between Franck and the musical tradition of the last Quartets of Beethoven, the new work appearing to him as their natural successor; he stressed the beauty of the introduction, the dexterous cross-currents of the scherzo, the return of the themes in the allegro molto.

The journal *Art et critique* had six months before begun to publish a series of articles entitled *Lettres de l'ouvreuse*.[1] "Willy," its titular signatory, transcribed into his column the feelings of several of his informants, notably those of Alfred Ernst, the future adapter of the librettos of Wagner, and of Pierre de Bréville. Thanks to the helping hand of the latter ex-pupil of Franck's,

---

[1] There is no exact equivalent of the word 'ouvreuse' in current English, for 'box-opener' means nothing in the modern concert-hall. 'Theatre attendant' is a poor substitute and 'programme girl' insufficient, while an even worse one is the cinema's debased and pretentious word 'usherette.' The "Willy" who wrote the *Ouvreuse* articles was in fact Henry Gauthier-Villars, the husband of the well-known French novelist Colette Willy.

L'Ouvreuse was able to print certain exact and detailed observations on the work:

> This *Quartet in D major* is (we say it in all earnestness) a masterwork, and one that comes from a great master. M. Franck is carrying on into our time the Beethoven tradition; but it is from the third period of that giant mind's development that he takes his point of departure. Re-read the Beethoven Quartets from No. 13 to the last of the series, and you will at once realize that M. Franck's new work is their heir by natural right.

The Franckists obstinately insisted on the importance of the close design of the work, and also on its profound conception of the cyclic ideas of form—to such an extent indeed that their admiration blinded them to the faults in the work. *L'Ouvreuse* added: "I only wish you knew how heartfelt our applause was!" The applause was no less cordial ten days later when the Ysaÿe Quartet gave a Franck festival, under the composer's presidency, at Tournai, in Belgium, the principal items in the programme being the *Quintet* and the *Quartet*. Franck had the pleasure, on the same occasion, of conducting at Tournai his *Hymne*, for four-part men's chorus, sung by the local concert society of that town.

The public's recognition of his *Quartet* was not an isolated incident. In face of much opposition, especially in the limited circle of the Conservatoire, César Franck had for the past year enjoyed a series of successes which surprised him no less than they delighted him. His pupil Camille Benoît, writing in the *Guide musical* about the triumph of the *Quartet* in February 1889, said:

> I can only wish that certain of the recalcitrants from the Conservatoire had been present at the concert. Dare one really believe that justice is beginning to be done to Franck during his lifetime as a composer of music?

The elderly composer's frequent appearances at the piano in the concerts of the Société Nationale had established anew his former reputation as a pianist. The most reactionary of the chamber-music societies, known as La Trompette, which had only given one work of his (*L'Ange et l'enfant*), invited him to collaborate with them on March 16, 1889—though it is true that that day five other pianists were also invited. On June 6, 1889, the Colonne Orchestra performed his eighth 'Béatitude' at their concerts in the Universal Exhibition. On February 23 and March 2, at its concerts at the Châtelet, this orchestra gave *Psyché*, which had not been heard in public since the first performance on March 10, 1888. *L'Ouvreuse* wrote in the letter of March 2:

> The public was swept quite off its feet, and Franck, the proud father of *Psyché*, sat glowing with happiness in his box, and listening in wonder to the prolonged and unanimous applause freely sprinkled with 'bravos' that saluted his 'Apotheosis'—which, I should perhaps mention, is the only part of the work of which I myself am not a fanatical admirer, and that only because it shows somewhat marked traces of Gounod's influence.

The previous letter of *L'Ouvreuse*, that of February 23, is worth quoting:

> It is a ravishing work; and yet, oh mighty Cæsar, the meanest of your sonata-works gives us a greater glow of satisfaction! You were sent down to live on this earth by the special will of the Almighty (oh, believe us, we beg!), not to preach in music the Word and the Deed, not to produce *Ghiselle* in collaboration with Gilbert-Augustin Thierry, but to pour out endlessly preludes, fugues, symphonies, quintets.

An impudent remark no doubt, but in some ways interesting! These *L'Ouvreuse* letters were the outcome of a collaboration between various Wagnereans and Franckists, and were the mouthpiece for a small group of them who claimed to direct the production of the veteran composer. As the great exponent of pure music, the Master (according to their intentions) should stick to the writing of works in the 'absolute' manner, and not stray off into the realm of the theatre or the symphonic poem. So, once again, we see certain of his admirers endeavouring to control his musical output, to nail him down to one style, to decide for him his future actions. Luckily, the great man, happy as he was to enjoy the admiration of his pupils and always interested in their views, had no intention of letting himself be treated like a child, neither through the well-meaning importunacies of his friends nor by the imperious instructions of his wife. All he tried to do was as far as possible not get on the wrong side of either party.

The Franckist group took in very bad part the contempt for Franck shown by Lamoureux in his obstinate refusal to conduct any of his music after the failure of *Les Éolides* in 1882. Their

justifiable complaints found vent more than once in the *Lettres
de l'ouvreuse*, which repeatedly warned Lamoureux that he was
keeping the Franckists away from his concerts in increasing
numbers: "If M. Lamoureux will believe what I say," one reads
in the letter of December 1, 1889,

> he will at once put down for performance Franck's *Symphony*—a
> work of such superlative construction (save perhaps for the short
> superfluous repetition in the introduction), so luminous, so beauti-
> ful in its seriousness! That, he would find, would bring back all
> those people into his concert hall.

Another complaint appeared four weeks later:

> Lamoureux played the other day some music by pupils of Franck:
> all to the good! But will he not deign to put a stop to a nameless
> scandal going about the world of music, and to remember for a
> moment that Franck himself is still alive?

On March 12, 1890, *L'Ouvreuse* once again reproached the conductor with having borrowed from Camille Bellaigue "the
impertinent views he airs everywhere about my poor César
Franck."

A letter addressed by Franck to Albert Cahen on April 15,
1890, has been preserved and was reproduced in facsimile in
Musica of March 1907; from it we learn that the Master travelled
to Rouen to be present at the first performance of his pupil's
opera *Le Vénitien*. "Monday evening," he wrote therein, "was
of the the best moments in my musical life." This enthusiastic
opinion of Franck's is but one example among hundreds of the
affection, sometimes a little blind, in which he held his pupils
and supporters.

Eight months later Franck found a new outlet in the provinces.
He journeyed to Lyon to take part, on December 15, 1889, in a
performance of his *Mass* at the Church of Saint-Bonaventure. A
choir of 150 voices was gathered together under the baton of
Léon Reuchsel: "the vital harp parts" (a reporter informs us)
"were entrusted to the skill and care of two professors and their
best pupils." The three singers all came from Lyon. César Franck
arrived in the city the night before the performance and was
present at rehearsal, which to his ears sounded so good that
he had no comments to make except congratulations to his
performers. The performance itself, too, seems to have been

excellent, and the work was well liked. Opinion favoured the
Credo, "in itself," we read, "an oratorio complete, noble in style
and unity of design"; also the *Panis angelicus* and the *Agnus Dei*,
which were hailed as "masterpieces of restrained emotion."
Franck himself played the organ for his *Mass*, and afterwards
added a piece or two and a couple of improvisations for the
moments of the Offertory and the out-going. The proceeds
were devoted to the poor of the parish, and their large total is a
good guide to his personal success on this occasion.

This visit of Franck's to Lyon raised certain hopes in the breast
of the Director of the Conservatoire there, Aimé Gros. He
conceived the idea that through the visit of the organist of Sainte-
Clotilde, who was also the Conservatoire professor of organ, the
town council might be induced to found in that music-school
an organ-class of the kind he had been longing for during the
last twenty years.

During the latter years of Franck's life a large number of
musicians, pupils, and admirers of his were in the habit of repair-
ing on Sundays to the Church of Sainte-Clotilde to hear him
improvise on the fine organ there. Among these consistent
listeners were Vincent d'Indy, Henri Duparc, Ernest Chausson,
Camille Benoît, Charles Bordes, Pierre de Bréville, Maurice
Emmanuel, and Paul Poujaud; at times one might also have seen
the brothers Eugène and Théo Ysaÿe, and also their friend Jules
Laforgue. Gabriel Pierné (who was to succeed him) has left us
in *Le Ménestrel* of December 1, 1922, a precise account of the
Master's habits and methods of improvisation. Franck, never
late but always in a hurry, arrived at the church (he tells us) a
little after 9 o'clock in the morning, and went straight through
into the sacristy to consult the week's order of services so as to
be able to regulate his own time-table of lessons. His pupils
began to arrive towards 9.30, after service, in time for the improvisations of the Offertory, the Communion, and the Reces-
sional. The Master would select a theme from one of the little
note-books kept by the side of the organ, which were filled with
melodies and themes out of Bach, Beethoven, Schubert, some
carols, some folk-songs from France, Scandinavia, and Ireland,
and the like; sometimes the chosen theme was a musical idea of
the organist's own, or one perhaps suggested by a visitor in the
organ-loft.

Then, the theme decided upon, Franck would reflect before beginning to extemporize; with his right elbow in the cup of his left hand, he would tap his forehead with the third finger of his right hand; from that moment nothing else existed any longer for him except music, and when he translated his thoughts into terms of the organ the result was something unimaginable—the themes linking themselves together in logical continuity with an ease and certainty of touch never heard before or since, the whole taking on an appearance of solidity only to be expected of a major composition. I have never heard anything so wonderful in all music. Shall one ever hear the like again? I doubt it.

All who listened to these improvisations of genius formed the same enthusiastic opinion of them; from the point of view of technique, the testimonies of Vincent d'Indy, Bréville, and Emmanuel, and those of his organ pupils Vierne, Mahaut, and Tournemire, are in complete agreement. From d'Indy we hear: "Franck was the supreme genius of the art of improvisation, and no organist of modern times can be compared with him, by a very long way, in this branch of music." At Mass the extemporizing of an Offertory or a Communion caused him some effort, "some hasty but concentrated moments of thought," while at Vespers the musical realization of one of the versicles of the *Magnificat* was spontaneous, a source of delight to the composer.

The *Magnificat* was for him a smile, a smile radiating a happy face, a smile full of confidence and free from all doubt. . . . It was in truth like the smile of the venerable Franck himself.

Pierre de Bréville has described how during a few minutes of meditation the great organist would mentally visualize his piece-to-come, settle on the main course of its musical journey, decide on the actual route to follow—that is to say, the tonalities along which he would guide his theme—and the stages at which he would make temporary pauses. According to Tournemire, the forms selected by the Master were usually the sonata-form allegro, the *lied*, or the developed *fantaisie*. In the actual execution at the keyboard there were sometimes movements that seemed a little long in their search for the real secret: the preludial matter was perhaps a little errant up to the moment when inspiration arrived and irresistibly gripped the mind of every hearer. Vierne's account is not dissimilar, in that it repeats the suggestion that

Franck was sometimes slow in starting his improvisations. Vierne
has written:

> Never have I listened to a player who could rival Franck in
> improvisation from the point of view of sheer musical invention.
> In the church he seemed to need a little time before he got under
> way; he would put out his musical feelers, he would ask questions of
> himself and us. Then, once in his stride, he poured out over us a
> prodigality of musical invention that was quite miraculous. His
> polyphony was remarkable for its richness, and yet all the time he
> presented us with melody, harmony, and formal balance which vied
> with each other for the position of first importance; there were,
> too, always those great moments and those astonishing outbursts
> of musical ebullience which can be provided only by palpable
> genius.

Acknowledged as leader of the younger French school, accepted
as a composer of genius, Franck had at long last reached a height
of reputation when he was the idol of a particular section of the
musical world. There was opposition too, of course, but that is
the normal price paid by success. The often over-assertive adora-
tion of some of his disciples set up violent reactions that were
understandable, if not excusable. The little world of the Conservatoire was then (as it always will be) an eddy of seething
human passions, raised to boiling point by the inevitable academic
conditions of rivalries between pupils in the various classes and
between professors of various subjects. The musical papers kept
the battle continuously raging at its height. Certain of them
were, at least to some extent, in the hands of the Franckists; for
example, the chief Paris correspondent of the Franco-Belgian
Guide musical was that Franck pupil Camille Benoît, who, under
the pen-name of Balthazar Claes, lost no chance of glorifying his
master with an enthusiasm that was no doubt touching, but was
also highly irritating to the anti-Franck party. One wonders,
were the attacks on Franck really as violent and uncouth as the
phrases below would lead us to imagine? They are quoted from
a book by Alfred Bruneau, entitled *La Musique française* (Paris,
1900). The author was an ardent Franckist; both composer and
'cellist, he won the Prix de Rome from Massenet's class and was
later to collaborate with Zola. Discussing Franck, Bruneau writes:

> He was greeted with blind indifference and underhand hostility
> by those to whom he offered with open hands the sublime splendour

of his music. . . . He seemed not to belong to the world that thus spurned him. . . . Insulted, vilified, dragged in the thick mud of falsehood and back-biting, he met every attack of fury and envy with an unchanging serenity that was magnificent.

No doubt the above description of the opposition reared against Franck is exaggerated, but it had the effect of spurring him to a more active and more varied production in music. *Ghiselle* (that family concession!) and the *Quartet* behind him, he planned to write two or three major works in various forms: some large-scale organ-pieces and a new sonata, for example. An accident hindered him from realizing his projects.

At the beginning of May César Franck was riding in a cab on his way to see the pianist Paul Braud and to attend a rehearsal of the *Quintet* at his house. On the crown of the Pont Royal the side of his cab was hit by the carriage-pole of a passing omnibus: struck on his right side, Franck fainted for a short moment, recovered himself, and was able to go on to the rehearsal. He even played twice through the second-piano part of his *Symphonic Variations*, and returned home delighted with "the lovely music" in which he had been taking part. He attached but little importance to the accident, but it nevertheless prevented him from attending the last concert of the Nationale, and he thus had to forego the pleasure of hearing his sixth 'Béatitude' conducted by Vincent d'Indy, who, reported *L'Ouvreuse*, "was only prevented by one remaining spark of respect for the opinions of others from conducting it on his knees!" Neither was Franck able to go to the end-of-year banquet, an annual event (as he wrote to the committee) he had never before missed; his disappointment was sharpened by the fact that after the dinner there was to be a new performance of his *Quartet*. He made courageous efforts to keep his Conservatoire lessons going on uninterrupted; walking was painful, but he was active and had no fear for the future. However, he could not continue his courses after July 7, and was unable to serve on the adjudicating panel for the examinations in piano and fugue. In a letter addressed to Ambroise Thomas he wrote with some deference:

MY DEAR MASTER AND DIRECTOR,

I am a great deal better by now, but still not well enough to be able to accept the honour you have done me by inviting me to serve on the panel at the piano examination of July 25. This is the first time, my dear Director, when I have not responded to your appeal. Believe me, it causes me a very keen regret.

On the day of the organ-tests Pierre de Bréville came to fetch him and took him to the session in his brougham: during the examination the Master appeared to be normal and did all he could to encourage the entrants. The examiners were presided over by Ambroise Thomas and comprised Ernest Guiraud, Auguste Bazille, Théodore Dubois, Henri Dallier, Alexis Fissot, Eugène Gigout, Alexandre Guilmant, and Raoul Pugno; they awarded the first prize to Mlle Prestat and *proxime accessit* to Charles Tournemire, who was to become one of his teacher's successors at Sainte-Clotilde after Gabriel Pierné.

For the vacation period César Franck went off as soon as possible to Nemours (Seine-et-Marne) to stay with a cousin of his wife's, Mme Désiré Brissaud.[1] Hers was a quiet house with a garden, and there were a piano and a harmonium at the composer's disposal, so that (should he care to) he could get some work done. His main intention was to compose some important organ-pieces, and he had also a commission from the publisher Enoch to write an album-full of pieces for harmonium or organ —a commission that highly delighted him, and which he wanted to appear under the title of *The Organist*.

A letter to one of his friends at the end of August gives us some news of his labours during the holiday:

> I am ever so much better nowadays and am hard at work. On the other hand I have just taken a fortnight of semi-holidays, during which I worked now and then, but without keeping my nose to the grindstone. I have written a large piece for organ which I have named simply *Chorale*; a chorale it is indeed, but with plenty of fantasy: then I've also done fifty pieces for the harmonium, about half the promised volume. I am hoping next to compose two other organ chorales, the second half of the harmonium book, and a sonata for piano and 'cello.

This sonata was in fact never written.

The letter makes no reference to *Ghiselle*, and the opera remained unfinished, at any rate as far as the orchestration was

[1] Mme Désiré Brissaud, daughter of the singer Féréol, was described by Franck as "the most charming of my cousins"; since 1846 he had dedicated several of his works to her. Authoress of the memoirs already quoted in Chapter VII above, she was the grandmother of M. Jean Chopy, the husband of César's granddaughter Thérèse.

concerned. However, in 1890 Franck played it over to Danbé, who had conducted *Ruth* at the Grand Hôtel Concerts, which he had founded in 1871, and who since 1877 had been the conductor of the Opéra-Comique. His word carried great weight.

The pieces for harmonium, in all the major and minor keys, were planned to work out to a total of ninety-one—that is, thirteen groups of seven each in a chromatic series from C to C', each seventh piece containing in itself the essential elements of the other six. No more than fifty-nine were completed, the last-written being noted down only in pencil. Among them we find some versicles (relics of past improvisations) intended for interposing in the *Magnificat*, according to the Parisian tradition; many of the pieces are based on the same themes, themselves not seldom of folk-origin and taken out of the little note-books that Franck kept beside his organ. Some are dated, and from them we can deduce the composer's tonal plan: on August 21, 24, and 28 and September 5 he wrote the pieces in D flat major and C sharp minor, D major and D minor, E flat major and minor, F sharp minor and G flat major; on September 26 the pieces in G major and minor "for Christmastide."

A detailed study of this set of pieces by Amédée Gastoué can be read in the *Revue de musicologie* of May 1937; they are not lacking in interest. But on no account must they be confused by the reader with that other harmonium collection, of far less musical value—the *Pièces posthumes pour harmonium ou orgue à pédales pour l'office ordinaire* ("Posthumous pieces for harmonium or pedal-organ designed for the daily services"). Of the latter the first edition appeared with a prefatory note by Georges Franck, in the following terms:

> Many years ago a pupil of César Franck's who lived in the provinces asked his advice about how to keep going with his organist's work in the parish where he lived. My father gave him that advice as requested, and from time to time supplemented it in a practical way by producing examples for him to use and follow. These are the pieces César Franck wrote under those circumstances.

The pieces themselves come from the years 1858 to 1863. All different in design, they range in merit from the quite lovely to the mediocre and even worse—thirty pieces in all, entitled *Sortie, Elévation, Préludes pour l'Ave Maria Stella, Offertoire,*

Pièce symphonique, and *Grand chœur*, others being named by a mere indication of the pace. One is tempted to imagine that they were intended by Franck for his friend Sanches, the wine-merchant at Azille, who was in charge of the music at his village church. From among the number of more commonplace pages a few stand out as the product, not of a master-hand, but of a provincial pupil of the composer's. This is no doubt the reason why in the new and latest edition, edited by Tournemire, some of the less worthy pieces have been omitted as not attributable to Franck himself.

A number of musical manuscripts were preserved at Auguste Sanches's house at Azille, both of his own writing and of Franck's, as we mentioned in connexion with *Les Éolides*. A study of these papers enables one to establish the origin of certain posthumous pieces for harmonium as the product of Franck's pupil. The instrument Franck used during his Azille visits was chosen by the Master himself; it was a Vygen, and is still to be seen at Azille, in the house of M. Albert Morel, Sanches's grandson.

A quite other enterprise, smaller in scale than the fifty-nine harmonium pieces, but of no less significance, was the completing of the *Three Chorales*, dated respectively August 7, September 17, and September 30, 1890; only the first was written at Nemours, the two others in Paris. They are the realization of an idea spoken of by Franck to his personal friends in the previous year: "Before I die I am going to write some organ chorales, just as Bach did, but on quite a different plan." Their beauty and importance are such that they may be properly considered as a kind of musical last will and testament, or (to use a cliché) a swan-song.

These *Chorales* raised certain technical problems in the act of composition which were solved with supreme skill. About the first Franck warned d'Indy that the difficulty of disentangling the theme might confuse some listeners, "for, you see," he said, "the chorale itself is not really the chorale, which creates itself in the course of the piece." A comparison arises in the mind with his pupil's work *Istar*, in which the theme is at first only vaguely defined, and then sheds one by one the veils enveloping it, to appear at the end entirely nude; the Franck chorale-theme, however, never appears in its barest form, but develops itself in the subtle process of passing from the minor key into a final brilliant revelation in the major. The second *Chorale* consists of a series of variations on a theme which passes and repasses incessantly across the musical scene to find calm after restlessness towards the end. The third is a kind of sonata with two allegros surrounding an adagio; it is built on a chorale-theme which, as in the companion pieces, is an original melody untouched by any influence from Protestant church music.

All three *Chorales* are complex in the extreme, both in design and in tonality; the older and more rigorous forms have been set aside; so too has the musical style of the 1860's and that almost theatrical picturesqueness which can be found in other previous works by the composer. In this highly personal music Franck has succeeded in combining harmoniously the spirit of Bach with the spirit of Beethoven—the style of the one, the expressiveness of the other, and the genius for variation of both of them.

The musical specialists admired with good reason the beauty of their design—so original and yet adhering so closely to tradition; the form is, admittedly, here and there somewhat confused, yet so striking in its novelty. One cannot help recognizing the fertility of invention in forming these three models, which for more than sixty years have exercised a profound influence on organ music. It is permissible, moreover, for one listening to them not so much to regard them as magnificent examples of original architecture as to feast on the richness of their inspiration, to discover in them emotional elements that animate and sometimes perturb their firm yet supple construction. Maurice Emmanuel rightly emphasized their personal interest when he observed in these pieces "sudden gusts of sound, dramatic in the extreme, like the memory of burning passions long past." Ten years separate the *Quintet* from the new trilogy by the aged Master, and yet the two works stand very near to each other; the final effect of the three later pieces is one of the supreme calm and serenity of true religion.[1]

On his return to Paris at the beginning of October Franck found himself well enough in health to start work again both at the Conservatoire and at the Institute for Young Blind Persons. Two

---

[1] Immediately after Franck's death the dedication of the *Three Chorales* caused yet another clash between the composer's family and his disciples. The Master had dedicated his three works respectively to Alexandre Guilmant, Théodore Dubois, and Gigout. For personal reasons of his own, Georges Franck replaced the first two names with those of Durand and Augusta Holmès. The Franckists, perfectly aware of their Master's intentions, wrote and told the truth to the three original dedicatees.

days before commencing, he had the pleasure of welcoming several pupils at his house, when he played to them his *Three Chorales* on the piano, Guillaume Lekeu undertaking the bass-part. On October 17 Franck caught cold; nevertheless the next day he went out to his usual day's work. It was the last time he was able to do so. He was obliged to stay in his room, but insisted on getting up from bed to give some lessons; pleurisy set in, complicated by pericarditis. There is no doubt that he was quite aware of the gravity of his condition, but not one outward sign of his awareness did he then show. There was a temporary improvement at the end of the month, which was announced in the Press; at the beginning of November the illness took a turn for the worse, though there was a rally of several hours' duration on November 7. The sick man, with his accustomed hopefulness, did all he could to reassure the relations and faithful friends round him. Canon Gardey, the parish priest of Sainte-Clotilde, was sent for; according to the priest, Franck spoke about the versicles for the *Magnificat* which he had not succeeded in completing for his publisher, and said, "May God grant that I shall finish them in heaven!" He then entered upon a period of great agony, during which a fugue began to develop itself in his brain while he followed all its ramifications; he begged and prayed the doctors (his cousins Féréol and Brissaud) to deliver him out of this musical obsession. Before long the power of speech left him, save to utter repeatedly the words "My children, my poor children!" On Saturday, November 8, at 5 o'clock in the morning, he passed away.

Musical politics and intrigues were the cause of a false account of César Franck's funeral; the story was circulated that on November 10 very few people attended the Mass at Sainte-Clotilde and that the Conservatoire was not even represented there. The actual truth is that a very large number crowded into the church and the Conservatoire was represented, if not by a group of professors, at least by one of them, Léo Delibes; that musician (a former rival of his dead colleague for the composition class) had been officially requested to deputize at the funeral for the Director, Ambroise Thomas, who, in his eighty-fourth year, had some excuse for not walking in the funeral procession during the cold, damp weather of November. The pall-ribbons were held by Delibes, Saint-Saëns, the organist Gigout, and Dr

Féréol. From among the numerous musical personalities present the *Guide musicale* of November 16 singles out Gabriel Fauré, André Messager, Victorin de Joncières, Alexandre Guilmant, Charles-Marie Widor, Alfred Bruneau, Camille Benoît, Cahen (from Antwerp), Édouard Lalo, and Augusta Holmès. In the cemetery at Montrouge (whence two years later the remains were moved to Montparnasse) Emmanuel Chabrier gave a short and moving funeral speech, in the place of Vincent d'Indy, who was detained in Valence by a concert of French music. It was a simple and balanced tribute of homage to the memory of a much revered musician whom his disciples considered to be one of the greatest masters that had ever contributed to the glory of their country and the country of his adoption.

Immediately after the funeral a new crop of troubles sprang up between Franck's family, his pupils, and a society in process of formation under the presidency of Édouard Colonne, each group wishing to take exclusive possession of the deceased composer's music. Meanwhile, however, enthusiastic articles poured out from the Press—some of them veritable panegyrics, some needlessly extravagant in their praise—to render tribute to the Master and his genius. The most important of them appeared a month after Franck's death; it was a booklet by Arthur Coquard, one of his older pupils, presenting a clearly stated survey of the composer's life, his struggles, and his achievements. Such reservations as were made here and there in the Press were all at least respectful. A typical example may be quoted from the *Ménestrel* of December 21, 1890, where the writer was Arthur Pougin, hitherto one of Franck's severest and most reactionary critics:

> There are those who cannot share the admiration, almost fetishistic in quality, which the very name of César Franck seems to create in his former pupils; I count myself among that number, yet even they and I cannot but be touched by the filial affection the composer was able to inspire among those who had the benefit of his lessons, his general teaching, his advice. But this is not the right moment to voice a discordant note among those heated *apologia* that now are springing up on all sides, nor to express those reservations which any sane mind is bound to have regarding a man whom some have represented as a genius misunderstood.

The high enthusiasm and admiration proved to be of lasting duration, at any rate in France, though at the same time it

exasperated a large section of the musical world. However, sixty
years have enabled us to find a proper focus towards the figure
of Franck. The general opinion seems to be that as a composer
Franck was not (as d'Indy's influence would have us believe) the
equal in greatness of Bach, of Beethoven, or of Wagner; rather,
we hail him, in the company of Johannes Brahms, as one of the
leading figures among the great composers of the second rank.

CHAPTER XVIII

The Man

THE Franck legend is the product of hagiolatry and even iconolatry. The pious and voluminous writings of Franck's pupils have combined with the one visual representation of the man known to the public—Jeanne Rongier's beautiful and life-like painting—to build up in the popular mind a touching portrait of the composer, both mentally and bodily. Unfortunately that formal and largely imaginary portrait is neither accurate nor complete.

Franck's physical appearance could never be forgotten by those who saw him, even if they saw him only once. In daily life the Master had none of that magnificent allure, that sovereign command, which hold our attention in the famous portrait of him at the console—an allure, however, which was certainly his when, improvising at Sainte-Clotilde, he was lit up by the aureole of the splendid music that gushed forth from his keyboards. At ordinary times his appearance was far less striking, even banal on the whole, but with some marked characteristics.

Short in stature, he had an intelligent head covered with long waving hair; his face was serene, not handsome, but radiant in its expression, with a broad forehead and a thick nose; his small eyes, deeply set under the eyebrows, were lively, expressive, and penetrating in their glance; he had a very wide mouth and his chin was hidden by the whiskers that he had worn since his youth—all his life his whiskers remained with him, black, grey, or white, and gave him the appearance, not of an impetuous artist, but of a quiet-living provincial lawyer. "That face," Vincent d'Indy has written, "which we have known and loved for twenty and more years, never changed in a detail, save only for the whitening of his hair, up to the day of his death." Always in a hurry, he would trot rather than walk on his daily rounds, passing through the streets as distractedly as he passed through

life. Without noticing changes in fashion, he always wore a
black frock-coat above grey trousers that were too short for him,
and in the same way he remained faithful to the high hat, the
old-fashioned 'topper,' which sometimes without noticing it he
brushed against the nap!

In moral character, Franck was far less simple—complex,
indeed, to a contradictory degree. There was little in him of that
systematic and carefully organized personality with which the
majority of his admirers of yesterday and to-day have invested
him after a hasty reading of certain writings on his music—
notably those central words by d'Indy. There he is portrayed as
the saint in music, pious and devout, rapt in dreams of mysticism,
soaring (whatever his circumstances) far above the coarse exi-
gencies of human life. On certain sides of his nature Franck
showed himself indeed to be the Fra Angelico, the *Pater seraphicus*,
of the public's imagination. Was he not also (surely and above
all) a man of passionate human feelings, vibrant with life, incessantly reacting against the petty happenings of daily life, even in
the presence of those who sought his company?

Better by far, we think, to avoid these preconceived and sum-
mary conceptions of a Master who for sixty years was more or
less publicly mixed up with the musical life of his time. Better
by far to think of him realistically as he was among the drab,
daily round of teaching, among the political, social, and intellectual happenings in his lifetime—as a man, indeed, who never
shut himself up in an ivory tower. Franck must be regarded, as
we have tried so far to regard him in this book, from the angle of
his whole life, and not seen only through roseate glasses, from a
distance, as that calm and saintly figure of the time of his tardy
glory, which illuminated him only between his sixtieth year and
his death.

Even his panegyrist Vincent d'Indy, who more than any other
person has focused his eyes on the halo of the musical saint, has
shown himself aware that Franck was not of a placid temperament, so disinterested or indifferent that he could look down
from a height on our petty human struggles. D'Indy has declared
—what the works clearly testify—that his Master had a passionate
nature of violent reactions, of swift impatience, of sharp temper,
and was capable too of righteous wrath. All that is established in
fact; two or three of Franck's pupils are still living (the most

famous of them is Guy Ropartz) and can tell us how often he manifested his intense and exuberant side, how frequently in personal conversation he allowed himself to be carried away by violent emotions. His son Georges has asserted:

> My father was the incarnation of life itself—always active and ebullient. His nervous energy was immense, and was controlled only by clear thinking and instant will-power.

D'Indy's well-meant legend has overlaid the real Master with a permanent and precious patina, which has hidden many of his most salient characteristics and erased all his eccentricities. We must no longer allow this artificial vision of an evangelical serenity, of the resigned meekness of his religious works like *Rédemption* and *Les Béatitudes* to dull our eyes and ears to the restless and passionate ardour of soul, the dramatic insight, that inspire so many pages in the *Violin Sonata*, in *Psyché*, *Hulda*, and *Ghiselle*, in the *Symphonic Variations*, above all in feverish assaults on our souls—violent and explosive, but also well regulated— made by the astonishing *Quintet*, which even that Hungarian and romantic Franz Liszt found to have overstepped the bounds of chamber music.

Like all artists, Franck derived from the fashions and style of his early days: he began as, and always remained, a romantic. His father's strictness had disciplined his childhood with no relaxa- tion of the trainer's whip during his adolescence and even up to his twenty-fifth year. His personal internal feelings, however heatedly they seethed within his soul, were tamed by the rough- and-tumble of a hard life as a musician and by the grinding neces- sities of maintaining a family. After this first period the most powerful of his emotions were continually held in leash by a new and insensitive authoritarianism—that of his wife, his elder son, and certain of his pupils. Yet, long before that day (not far from his sixtieth birthday) when he suddenly threw all his habitual reserve to the winds, he had shown clear signs in his music (and even in his conduct) of his romantic leanings, of the emotional turbulence of his temperament. In every line there is a fluttering of his innermost soul, a quivering hint of longing or unrest.

Franck's childhood was spent in an atmosphere of romanticism. As with Méhul, his education (most of it on the German side of the Rhine) had familiarized him with the music of Beethoven,

Weber, Schubert, Schumann, and Liszt; it is likely, too, that about
1830 he came into contact with the productions of the revolutionary painters of the period; though no one ever applied him
to the pictorial arts, Franck clearly exhibited expressive and
dramatic tendencies which can be summarized in Berlioz's word
'volcanic.' Little exact information about Franck's character as a
child is available to us, and what little we know is overpainted
(in the theatrical sense) by the worldly ambitions of his father,
who was determined to confine him to the supposedly money-
making career of a touring composer-pianist. In a previous
chapter, however, we have recorded the criticism of one of his
professors that his piano-playing showed an excess of emotional
warmth. Yet, cast a passing glance at any work written by
Franck during his adolescence, and you cannot but be instantly
struck with the emphatic power and force of his inspiration,
which, in the opinion of an experienced critic of 1843, brought
to his mind (as we have noted) visions of lugubrious, tumultuous,
"cannibalistic" scenes, forcing him to compare a trio by the
peace-loving César Franck with the lurid gloom created by the
English novelist Ann Radcliffe.

The moment when one can clearly see the true Franck in the
round comes late in his life. Then he no longer figures in our
imaginations as the daily practitioner of music, the ordinary person going about his business, shy, timid, restrained in his musical
invention. About the years 1870 to 1880 Franck found himself in
some degree freed from the obligations of the family drain on his
expenditure and of remuneration by pupils' fees. After a long
period of retirement from the public places of music he was able
once again to devote himself to serious composition. His inspiration at that moment of rejuvenescence was fired by romantic and
fantastic legends of the past—by the 'Accursed Hunter' who
chased through the forests of Germany, sounding the hunting-
horn of Oberon, by the Æolids envisaged by Leconte de Lisle
and the Djinns of Victor Hugo's imaginings, by the grim stories
of the Middle Ages which were the basis of *Hulda* and *Ghiselle*
and which engaged his affections precisely because they retained
the nostalgic and lasting aroma of Scribe and Meyerbeer. In
every score, even among those of the latest works, we can perceive a picturesque reminiscence of Mendelssohn's *Midsummer
Night's Dream* and, less obviously but with equal emotional force,

some influence from *La Damnation de Faust*. In certain passages we can trace the music back to the impassioned intensity of *Tristan und Isolde*, from whose poisoned philtre our composer had (despite himself) been forced to take a draught.[1]

In nearly every one of Franck's essays in absolute music—his masterpieces—we can see the same thing (and, indeed, we need hardly draw attention to it). Everywhere we find the expression in music of a strong and ardent personality, of a soul tortured by thoughts burning with a brilliant flame within him, but veiled before public gaze by an outward appearance of resignation and calm acceptance of life's conditions. In every score we can observe a violent conflict of emotion, a fight to the death between two opposed enemies—the brutality of fate against man's capacity for suffering, which, battered by crushing blows, maintains to the end of life (and to the end of Franck's music) an indomitable hopefulness, a firm and smiling optimism. Man's endurance is greeted with a hymn of faith and hope for the future. Think for a moment of the *Symphonic Variations*. The work is surely anything but a study in musical texture for piano and orchestra—it is rather a great tragedy expressed in music! Whatever work we examine, we find no difficulty in throwing a limelight on those passages where joy and sorrow are placed in contrasting poses by the composer; he writes of such elemental things with the eloquence of simplicity. That subject—evil versus good—is his real programme. All Franck's works that are classed as 'absolute music' can without paradox or awkwardness take a suitable place among the symphonic poems of the nineteenth century, precisely because of their dramatic and emotional background in the composer's mind.

Most clearly of all, the Franckist romanticism asserts itself in his actual style of writing—dominates and spreads itself across the whole musical texture, not so much in early works, but certainly in those of his maturity and old age. It is characterized by obstinate and incessant modulation ("Modulate, modulate!" Franck would cry to his organ pupils at the Conservatoire), by a continual chromaticism derived from sources as various as Bach and Frédéric Chopin—no one yet seems to have remarked that

---

[1] A score of *Tristan* which belonged to César Franck was at one time extant. On its cover the Master had written the one word—"Poison." The whereabouts of that score is to-day unknown.

it was one of the latter's posthumous mazurkas that provided
Richard Wagner with the unique style of *Tristan und Isolde*.
Franck's chromaticism gives his musical thought freedom to
roam where it will with the utmost smoothness, to follow the
most subtle divagations of his fluid mind, to explore all the
corners and hidden places of his ever-changing emotions. Listening to Franck's major works without prejudice or preconceived
ideas, one is aware that one is standing far away from, far outside, that serenity so often vaunted by the eulogists of the musical
Fra Angelico—a serenity sometimes actual, but frequently artificial, adopted as a counterpoise to the instinctive excitability of
his nature or as a mask to cover the despair of a tormented soul!
Nowhere is this clearer to the senses than in the *Quintet*.

From childhood César Franck had been fettered by the harsh
discipline of his father; on his marriage, at the age of twenty-
five, he came under the new controlling influence of his wife.
She was musical, and had been his pupil, and was helping him
with the artistic instruction of the children; in these and other
ways she was closely mixed up with César Franck's practising
life in music. At first all went smoothly, for the two shared a
liking for the style and tendencies of a past period, so long as he
remained faithful to the æsthetic ideals of his early years. Dis-
sensions arose round about 1880, to become accentuated and even
angry at times, for the wife adhered obstinately to his early
modes of expression, and was unable to keep pace with her husband's evolution. Nevertheless, she sought to keep a controlling
hand on Franck's production. Once they had moved into their
flat on the Boulevard Saint-Michel, she occupied a room adjacent
to that containing the piano, and thus could continually exercise
a close supervision over his musical utterances. If his music
tickled her fancy she could not resist coming into the room to
listen to it at a closer hearing; but if the Master poured out sounds
that seemed to her too complex or bold she would throw open
the dividing door and call to him: "César, I do not at all approve
of that piece you are playing!" This surprising story was related
by Constance Elizabeth Maud in the English monthly *The Nineteenth Century* of November 1922; we sent her text to Mme
Chopy Franck, who replied to us: "Her account is strictly
accurate!" This granddaughter of Franck's, who had just reached
nine years of age on the Master's death, has told us her own

memories of her grandmother's superintending her grandfather's original work, and can recall too how little liking Mme Franck had for the scores of *Psyché* and the *Symphony*.

Pierre de Bréville throws further light on this family situation in two incidents which he has recounted to us. One day Félicité Franck gave tongue to a violent and heated indictment of her husband's pupils: "You have no need to tell me that Franck has written some beautiful works, for I am a musician myself; his organ-pieces are everything that is admirable; but that *Quintet*! Ugh!"—her gesture clearly showed her disgust. Then she added (what was true): "It is you pupils who have aroused all the hostility shown against him." The other occasion concerns the *Prelude, Chorale, and Fugue*, which Franck had at the moment just completed. He was playing the finale fugue to Bréville in his own house when the door was thrown open and Mme Franck burst in on them in a state of great excitement, crying out, "Is all that hubbub going to stop soon?" Poor Franck merely said in a somewhat sad tone of voice, "You see! What I write now is regarded as an unpleasant noise!"

After Mme Franck's, the next influence Franck was subjected to was that of his elder son, Georges, a teacher of the history of art, whose general culture and amateur musicianship the father much admired. Like his mother, the son wanted the composer to turn out simpler and more saleable works, and especially music for the theatre, as we have noted in our account above of *Hulda* and *Ghiselle*. Directly counter to the machinations of mother and son were ranged all the forces of 'the Franck gang.' The Master was caught between two fires, and continually suffered under both attacks. Traces or memories of this antagonism are to be found in those many works of his based on a sharp musical contrast, which represents, or at least recalls, the personal struggles of his inner soul.

Franck's belief in his son's abilities—he was a university lecturer—can be explained by the poverty of the Master's own general culture; even his musical culture was far narrower than one might imagine. Up to his last years his musical background was that of the average organist—that is to say, commonplace and very restricted. One is surprised to find, for example, as we have found, that this master of counterpoint was almost totally ignorant of the great polyphonic composers of the sixteenth and seventeenth centuries, even of those whom two of his pupils, Charles Bordes and Henry Expert, did so much to make more widely known. But, further than that, Franck seems never to have taken any deep interest in them. It was only late in his career that he acquired a knowledge and love of the greater works of J. S. Bach; Boëly's playing of them came to him as a revelation. Familiar though he was with the Opéra-Comique repertoire of his youth, he never showed any of the cultured musician's interest in the treasures of the older French music.

Outside music his culture was distinctly limited, almost non-existent (one might say) during his childhood and adolescence. Neither literature nor science had a place in the curricula of his early studies in Liége and Paris. That family tormentor, his father, had sentenced him to an unlimited term of hard labour as pianist and composer; locked in the work-room, he was given no leisure, was not even allowed the normal comradeships and friendships with boys of his own age. After separating from his father, about 1847, César-Auguste had a lucky encounter with the Abbé Charles Gounod, his temporary friendship with whom gave him for some months an opportunity of opening the windows of his mind. In 1848 (as we have shown in Chapter VIII) his wife's family introduced him to a new intellectual environment; he frequented the theatre, in particular the Comédie Française. But, tired out with teaching all day, he derived little pleasure from the plays he saw, especially as the amorous intrigues in Racine and the subtle psychology in Musset passed over the head of one who was by nature simple, kindly, and ingenuous.

Hardly before the period of the 1870 war did Franck find leisure time to broaden the narrow boundaries of his literary knowledge; during the last eight years of his life he found more time for reading, for visiting art exhibitions, and for exchanging ideas with the intellectuals whom his son Georges, specialist in the history of art, gathered round him during his visits to Paris. In the letters written during the last part of his life we read many times the words "I am reading . . . [so and so]." His literary studies cannot have been either abundant or carried to any great lengths—were limited, indeed, at times to the *Revue des deux mondes*; nor could they accustom his mind to appreciating the refinements of thought or the expressive style of modern or 'advanced' writers. Now and then one or other of the symbolists and impressionists would write him a letter of admiration couched in a refined or even affected prose: Franck's reaction was always: "I can't understand a word of all this; I am quite out of my depth!"

He was proud of the academic honours won by his elder son; the younger son, Germain, was of lesser intellectual capacity and was content to remain a respected official on the railways.[1] Into George's hands therefore he was quite willing to entrust himself regarding the choice of books worth reading. This literary father-confessor passed as a Voltairean, and to him was due the recommendation of (among other things) *Vie de Jésus*; Ernest Renan's historian's approach to the Gospel narrative fascinated and enthralled Franck, to the point possibly of inspiring him with the idea of writing *Les Béatitudes*; later, under the influence of Vincent d'Indy, he became troubled in his mind, until he reached the point where he renounced the book entirely and on his death-bed spoke of his earlier absorption with Renan's ideas as one of his faults.

One day some one saw in his hands a copy of *The Critique of Pure Reason*; Kant's treatise seems to have given him keen pleasure, and even became one of his favourite bed-side books. How much did Franck understand of that great German's confused thinking, expressed as it was in an abstract style and in all the usual philosophical jargon? One wonders how Kant could be comprehensible, and apparently attractive, to a mere musician-dreamer, unprepared by any special reading. That he can have understood much seems very improbable; but no one can tell, so different and so contradictory are the reactions of each human mind. An illiterate may be as a thinker quite at his ease among the meanderings of an abstruse philosophy. In any case Franck had about him nothing of the æsthetician; he was incapable of sustained thought about the æsthetic problems of music. On one occasion his Belgian pupil Guillaume Lekeu asked for his opinions about programme music. Franck, a little embarrassed by the question, replied thus:

"It is a matter of little importance whether music is descriptive—that is to say, sets out to awaken ideas about a given external subject

[1] In 1874 Germain Franck, then a railway inspector at Valence, was recommended by Vincent d'Indy as a friend of his: "I am very fond of Germain; he is a charming young man with very nice manners, who has only one fault—that of being too retiring" (letter to Roger de Pampelonne of January 2, 1874).

—or whether it limits its intentions to the expression of a state of mind that is purely internal and exclusively psychological. What is of the first importance is that a composition should be musical, and emotional as well."

Lekeu repeated this somewhat vague opinion to his former Belgian Director Kiéfer, adding the comment: "It seems to me that Franck the Master has not thought about the problem either very often or very deeply."

César Franck at least showed that he was as easily moved by poetry as he was by painting and the other arts. Victor Hugo had delighted him in childhood and had inspired him to write (as well as *Les Djinns*) that uncompleted symphonic poem *Ce qu'on entend sur la montagne*; he also appreciated Leconte de Lisle, whom he met sometimes at his son's house and whom he had translated into music in *Les Éolides*. Unfortunately he seems to have perched at the same level as those two poets the lady-rhymester who had provided him with the verses for his *Béatitudes*. He was unable to show the smallest critical sense in the choice of his literary collaborators.

'Critical sense': that is precisely what Franck lacked in the domain of music, as he did in that of literature. It is a fault often to be observed among Anglo-Saxon and German composers, a fault too that is readily explainable in a composer whose formative years were passed during a period when Scribe and Meyerbeer were rulers of the French stage and imposed thereon their deplorable style, when the majority of dilettantes were ready to gorge their fill on 'fantaisies brillantes' based on poor-quality operas, and when the stupid and often ridiculous librettos written in their hundreds for the Opéra, the Opéra-Comique, the lyrical theatre generally, or the Théâtre-Italien provided the normal standards of literary and dramatic art.

Just as Franck was not a sound assessor of literary merit, so was he incapable of a balanced judgment of musical interpretation, particularly with his own works. He was always satisfied with the performances given to him—and many were the deplorable performances he had to accept! He seemed to follow nothing but the unfolding of his musical dreams without hearing anything of their vocal and instrumental realization.

Of his lack of critical sense, at least in literature, Franck began to be aware during his later years. Acting on the advice of his most cultured pupils, who had expressed regret at his pitiable choice of texts after the unfortunate dramatic experiments of *Hulda* and *Ghiselle*, about 1887 he jettisoned his adviser Georges, who had been more or less directly responsible for his acceptance of those two pompous librettos. He then had recourse to an amateur, an intimate friend of Vincent d'Indy's and a most active member of the Société Nationale—Paul Poujaud. An admirable literary adviser of many composers, Poujaud suggested to him poems by Jean Racine, Marceline Desbordes-Valmore, André Theuriet, Auguste Brizeux, and Alphonse Daudet. The composer was amply rewarded for his modesty and trustfulness since the texts provided by this music-loving barrister inspired him in 1888–89 to write the *Hymne*, for male-voice chorus; the beautiful *Procession*, for voices and orchestra; and three delightful duets for equal voices—*Danses de Lormont, Chanson du vannier,* and *La Vierge à la crèche* ("The Dance of Lormont," "The Basket-maker's Song," and "The Virgin at the Manger"). To Poujaud he confessed quite simply in a letter of September 24, 1889, "I have searched for texts on my own, and I have seen for myself what a difficult job it is."

The extreme modesty of the Master shown in the above literary example extended itself into the realm of music. Vincent d'Indy has recorded:

> When he was hesitating over the choice of this or that tonal relation or over the progress of any development he always liked to consult his pupils, to share with them his doubts and to ask their opinions.

His young Belgian colleague, the conductor Sylvain Dupuis, met with a typical instance of this simple-mindedness. Not long before his death Franck travelled to Belgium for a concert, and presented Dupuis with the printer's proofs of his charming duets for equal voices. But he broke off in the middle of their talk to submit to Dupuis two different versions of a certain passage. "Which do you prefer?" he asked; and, on receiving the opinion he sought, said, "That's settled—I will adopt your view."

Nevertheless, Franck was not without a sense of his own value: "I am not modest!" he went so far as to say. There are several stories extant that show him to have been quite alive to his merits as a composer and as a teacher. One day Franck was showing one of his scores to his pupil Paul de Wailly, who naïvely said to him, "At such and such a place in Wagner you will find something very like that." Franck's tart reply was: "I have no need to be aware of what Wagner does." To the same pupil he confided in a mild voice that a certain pupil had given up taking composition lessons with him. "He has left me to go and work with Massenet; he is entirely wrong."

This mingled pride and modesty allowed Franck to judge his colleagues' works without the least jealousy. He had a great fondness for Chopin, his rival as a pianist, admiring above all his harmony. He never ceased to pay homage to the sovereign mastery of his friend Liszt, frequently in similar terms to those we have quoted earlier. He was an admirer of Berlioz as a powerful composer, though he was disturbed by the latter's character and surprised at Berlioz's ignorance of musical grammar and his amateurism; he took none the less pleasure in paying tribute to the orchestral genius informing all his works, to the originality of the *Symphonie fantastique* (the finale, at least) and of *La Damnation de Faust*, whose failure, followed by a long neglect, occurred some months after the one-night success of *Ruth*; he also liked the enchanting melody in the duet from *Béatrice et Bénédict*. He felt a great sympathy for Massenet, his successful rival in 1873, and for Saint-Saëns, who was a little younger than he and had enjoyed continual success with his symphonic and dramatic works and also as an organist; in particular he had obtained, read, and studied the full score of the last-named's *Symphony in C minor*, for organ, at the time when he was writing his own *Symphony*. Franck's own friendliness towards Saint-Saëns, which was not always returned, had been shown in his dedicating to the composer of *Samson et Dalila* one of his principal works, the *Quintet*. He much appreciated the gifts of his friend Charles-Valentin Alkan—"the poet of the piano" Franck named him—and publicly showed his favourable opinion by transcribing for organ and publishing in 1889 some *Préludes et prières* ("Preludes and Prayers") by this remarkable, but now almost forgotten, composer. The imagination and pianistic style of Gabriel Fauré delighted him to an equal extent. He was sympathetic towards the young revolutionary Achille Debussy, winner of the Prix de Rome in 1884 and for a time a transitory pupil in his organ-class; he thought highly of his subtle talent. "Pointed and delicate music, I find it," he confided to Pierre de Bréville. He had much respect for his seniors—Gounod, for example, friend of twenty-four years' standing (though latterly the two had separated), and Ambroise Thomas, the "Director," and regretted that his pupils should so unrestrainedly dispute the latter's authority and his merits as a composer. His interest and good-will embraced, not only his best pupils—Duparc, d'Indy, Chausson, Lekeu—whose work he praised, but also those of more mediocre achievement, for he was well able to sympathize with their good intentions and their efforts to carry them out in music.

This natural good-will was extended to all men in every walk of life. In contrast to his closest pupils, he refused ever to take sides. He closed his eyes against petty struggles about fashions, class, and race, against all that ranged men into opposing factions. He was untouched by any feeling of the anti-Semitism which was rife among his artistic circle; he maintained cordial relations with the musicians of the synagogue and with his few Jewish pupils, like Albert Cahen—indeed, it was Franck who put Vincent d'Indy into touch with the official musical head of the Paris synagogue, Samuel Naumbourg, which resulted in their collaboration.[1]

One can well imagine that this ingenuous and disinterested nature made Franck incompetent and even defenceless in his dealings with librettists and publishers. As regards *Le Valet de ferme*, *Rédemption*, and *Les Béatitudes*, it seemed to him the most obvious behaviour to buy his texts at an agreed price without first making sure of their suitability, while the moneys due to him from his various publishers were liable to dwindle down to practically nothing. *L'Ange et l'enfant*, written in 1846, was engraved in 1889, and then only on the promise of his pupils' purchasing a stated number of copies. He thought himself lucky to be offered a hundred francs for the score of *Le Chasseur maudit*. When his pupil Lekeu expressed surprise in 1889 that the full score of *Rédemption* had never been engraved and printed, he rejoined:

> "It would be a heavy expense for the publisher! If ever the work is played again in Paris that may bring it into public notice, and then Hartmann might agree to publish it. Or perhaps, by chance, I might become famous! But I am not counting upon any such lucky stroke of fortune."

[1] See our *Vincent d'Indy*, vol. i, p. 131.

Neither the *Quintet* nor the *Symphony*, not even the *Sonata*, brought him in a penny of financial reward. The *Sonata*, it was agreed, should be published without any subsidy from the composer, subject to the composer's promise (never kept!) to make a transcription of it for two pianos. He was positively flattered when Enoch, the publisher of *Les Éolides*, *Les Djinns*, and the *Symphonic Variations*, gave him a firm commission to write six choruses for equal voices and a hundred harmonium pieces at a pettifogging price for the entire rights.

Financial questions meant little to him in his later years, when he found he had no need for money; despite all his daily expenses and his charitable gifts, he considered himself very well-to-do. He could hardly be called that, yet with quantities of lessons at fifteen or twenty francs a time, he was able to make some 20,000 francs a year—about £800 sterling at that time. On his death, it has been stated, he left something like 10,000 francs.

The republican enthusiasms which (as we have shown) Franck naïvely manifested in 1848 were snuffed out under the disappointments of the Second Republic and the Second Empire. It was not long before he turned up his nose at politics; a single characteristic incident proves the point. In November 1867, during the period of (so-called) 'Boulangism,' Franck went to Bordeaux to conduct some of his works there. At the dinner after the concert the guests could talk of nothing else but the hero of the hour; he asked one of his friends, "What exactly *is* this General Boulanger?"

César Franck's religious views have been much discussed, and by those who knew him best; yet his disciples have put him into different categories in the religious world according to their own personal tendencies. A believing, but not a practising, member of the Christian Church—so his children and grandchildren have always described him—he appears in Vincent d'Indy's distorting mirror as a devoted Catholic, without any of those backslidings which, at least during one period of his son Georges's influence, had led him down the slope towards Renanism, only to climb quickly up again to orthodoxy. We have given in connexion with *Psyché* some sketched-in picture of the debate—Christianity or Platonism?—which divided his two pupils d'Indy and Tiersot.

The evangelical morality evolved by Tolstoy had a great interest for Franck; he liked reading certain books by the Russian writer, taken up first, no doubt, on the advice of Vincent d'Indy, who was himself overwhelmed by them in and about 1886. But Tolstoy stands a very long way distant from modern Catholicism. `Our composer's somewhat uncertain religious leanings did not prevent him from sometimes showing—in Romain Rolland's phrase—a lovingly pagan soul. It is this aspect of Franck's nature, in all likelihood, which Charles Bordes was depicting in his review of Vincent d'Indy's *César Franck* (*La Tribune de Saint-Gervais*, November 1906): we may accept as veracious, or approaching very near to the truth, the following carefully chosen phrases:

> Franck was indeed a *Christian artist*, but more Evangelical than really Catholic, whatever M. d'Indy may say, for the latter firmly presents us with the image of an artist of profound faith. Faith Franck certainly had, but he was above all things Evangelical, and the Jesus who sang to him was rather the Jesus of the first centuries of the Christian Church than the Christ of Catholic doctrine. His nature overflowed with charity and altruism, but had nothing in it of the casuist or the medieval mystic: in that respect his genius differed entirely from that of his disciple and biographer.

In adopting this view of Charles Bordes, a man well placed to form a true opinion of his Master, we can escape from the gilded legend which Vincent d'Indy, with some lasting success, set himself out to foist upon us.

CHAPTER XIX

The Teacher[1]

THOSE who studied under César Franck at the Paris Conservatoire have frequently set down their memories of him
in books and periodicals. It is thus no difficult task to reconstruct
the atmosphere of his classes in organ and improvisation from
February 1, 1872, the date of the new professor's appointment to
succeed his former teacher François Benoist, down to the opening
of the academic year 1890–91, when Franck through illness had
finally to relinquish the position he had occupied for nineteen
years. Without much effort of the imagination we can conjure
up the whole scene of those courses—the background, the little
daily events, the teacher's affectionate attitude, so full of sympathy
and charm, towards his pupils, his general and highly personal
methods of teaching.

The interior of his class-room remained unchanged in visual
appearance throughout the entire nineteenth century. It was a
small hall in the old Conservatoire, in the Rue Bergère, standing
next to that other more historic hall where the concerts were
given. The organ was placed opposite the royal box dedicated
to the Empress Joséphine. What exactly was this organ? It was
an old instrument, or rather half-instrument, the other half
standing in the adjacent concert-hall: broken-winded and cracked-
voiced like the late cuckoo, it had been moved in two sections
from the Palace of the Tuileries. The previous professor, Benoist,
had been satisfied with it for more than fifty years; there César-

---

[1] We have here drawn on a number of the recollections of César Franck written by his
pupils and colleagues at the Conservatoire: Pierre de Bréville, *Fioretti de César Franck*
(*Mercure de France*, 1935–38) and *Encyclopédie de la musique*; Alfred Bruneau, *Massenet*,
pp. 12–13; Gaston Carraud, *Magnard*, p. 27; Arthur Coquard, *César Franck* (1890);
Maurice Emmanuel, *César Franck*, pp. 104–106; Vincent d'Indy, *César Franck*; Albert
Mahaud, *L'Oeuvre d'orgue de César Franck*; Gabriel Pierné, *Souvenirs*, in *Le Ménestrel*,
December 1922; Louis de Serres, *Quelques souvenirs sur le père Franck mon maître*, in *L'Art
musical*, 1936; Charles Tournemire, *César Franck*, p. 71; Louis Vierne, *Souvenirs*; Paul de
Wailly, *La Vie et l'âme de César Franck* (Abbeville, 1922); Ch.-M. Widor, *La Classe
d'orgue du Conservatoire*, in *Le Ménestrel*, June 3, 1921.

Auguste had worked in 1841–42, and won his remarkable second prize; there he was to be in charge for his nineteen years of office; there it remained as a legacy for his successor, Widor. Louis Vierne draws attention in his memoirs to its unbelievable combination of stops and its mechanical deficiencies. Sometimes the organ class-room would be taken over for examinations; on these occasions teacher and pupils would remove themselves to a piano class-room where they were left with nothing to do but to study the accompaniment of plain-chant according to the regrettable practice of the period—that is to say, note against note.

Franck was a model member of the staff; he arrived for his class at the hour stated in the time-table, 8 A.M., maybe a little before. His pupil Gabriel Pierné has told us that he came in

> by the back door with a springing step, dressed in his usual clothes that had the regularity of a uniform—the frock-coat, the tall hat, the grey trousers held up so high by his braces that they had the semblance of being cut too short; also his umbrella, which he never forgot and which he either carried hooked over his left forearm or allowed to trail negligently on the floor (but still always on his left side).

Often he found no pupils awaiting him, a few at most, sometimes because the careless organization of the school had arranged the organ-professor's class at the same hour as that of Massenet, the composition-professor, although a number of students were enrolled in both classes. As a result occasional jangles—picturesque, but in no way serious—occurred between the two musicians.

While he was waiting for the late-comers Franck would take his seat at his wretched instrument with its pipes all out of shape, and, once there, of course he would improvise. If no one at all arrived he would before long leave the class-room in search of the young delinquents, some of whom would be in the middle of listening to Massenet's fascinating discourse. Then he would open the door of his colleague's class-room (the two were always on friendly terms) and ask "in a voice at once calm and serious but surprisingly loud" (we are told), " 'Isn't there anyone for me?'; or else he would murmur through the partly opened door, 'Please won't one of you gentlemen come to my room for a minute or two, just to keep me company?' " Massenet would give the necessary permission in a somewhat peevish tone of voice, for he was not without vague fears about the general influence of the organist on his pupils which might well lead them in a very different direction from his own.

Once settled down, the class presented (as indeed did the instruction poured out to them) a rather irregular, even eccentric appearance. In part it was composed of genuine pupils for organ-playing; but there were also certain composition-students who came, like the young Debussy in 1880, to seek light on the writing of 'absolute' or 'pure' music, but seldom stayed long in a course so out of touch with their theatrical tastes and ambitions. One might sometimes see, too, visitors of some note, like Georges Bizet, organ prize-winner in 1855, who at the time of his writing *Carmen* was one of Franck's most assiduous listeners.[1]

Franck always maintained that his organ-class was devoted to what it was intended to be—a class for technical study of the organ. To a new pupil, Louis de Serres, he said: "When you join my class, young man, your job is to play the organ," and repeated slowly "to play the organ!" Something about this emphatic repetition suggests that it was an indirect and more or less conscious reply to the reputation he had gained in the Conservatoire, and of which his successor, Widor, gave confirmation, that he had turned his organ-playing class into a class for composition. The facts are, according to his pupils' accounts, that he had six hours a week for his class, in three two-hour sessions, and that at least five of them were devoted to improvisation. As a player Franck was but a moderate technician himself, though in the heat of improvising at Sainte-Clotilde he sometimes attained a surprising degree of virtuosity; and thus he was not greatly concerned with the executive achievement of his pupils. Louis de Serres—a great admirer of Franck's—makes the point himself: "Franck was never meticulous or exacting about technical details, though he would give almost too much help with registration or expressive pedalling." Louis Vierne went so far as to say that Franck did not give his pupils much chance for accurate manipulation of the instrument:

> He would pull out the stops, work the combination pedals, manage the swell-box: everything was made easy for one and reduced to mere finger-work on the manuals and attention to musical style. That no doubt is the reason why, save for Dallier,

[1] See our book *Vincent d'Indy*, vol. i, pp. 201–202.

Marty, Mahaut, and Letocart, none of the prize-winners in Franck's class ever spoke of him as a first-rate player.

Both Vierne and another brilliant pupil, Tournemire (Conservatoire students in 1889 and 1890, in their professor's last months before his death and so before Widor's taking his place) have regretfully stated that they did not learn from him much of the technique for which they are held to be masters—in fact, that under their new teacher's strict methods they had to undergo anew a severe executive training not required in his predecessor's days.

It was to improvisation above all other branches of organ-playing that Franck gave his closest attention. He would never check a pupil during the process of working out a theme—Gregorian or otherwise, of his own invention or set by the teacher, whether a fugue or a sonata movement in contrapuntal treatment. A quantity of interjections would be hurled at him in that heavy, vibrant, arresting voice, which sometimes took on "a formidable crescendo," in order to prevent the young player from losing his way in the jungle-growth of counterpoint, or to ejaculate remarks of criticism or commendation: thus one would hear:

"Modulate! . . . Now some flat keys. . . . Now some sharp keys! E, if you please, in the bass! . . . Back to the tonic! . . . Now something quite different! . . . I dislike that intensely. . . . Ah, that was a good bit! . . ."

and so on.

"Sometimes," according to Vincent d'Indy, "these apostrophes would be thundered out at us when our clumsy fingers stumbled at the keyboard on some incorrect harmonic combination." One day Franck was seen in a towering rage with one of his worst fumblers, when he hurled on the floor the text-book of plain-chant; but later he very gently apologized for his loss of control! When he wanted a phrase to balance the principal theme he would call out for 'a cousin.' Seated alongside his pupil, he would help him in every possible manner, and sometimes would allow his active collaboration to go to too great a length. Gabriel Pierné's account is: "He would take hold of one note, then of another, until he gradually was sitting in your place, improvising for you and teaching you by his example—and what a magnificent

example he gave!" No system of instruction could be more
vivid. It was all a splendid and attractive game, educative in the
extreme; but it did not please all comers. The case of the youthful
Debussy is well known. His free and restless spirit, unamenable
to discipline, could not for long remain still in a class where,
though the musical quality attracted him, the incessant modulation
enjoined by the Master soon put him off.

   Dexterity and ingenuity in counterpoint were the special
delight of the professor. He himself, in the distant days of his
own studentship at the Conservatoire, had caused untold surprise
among those judging the organ competition by this astonishing
readiness of his contrapuntal skill. He showed it frequently
during his professorship in dealing with the set pieces and improvisations played by his pupils within the strict demands of the
syllabus—that is, fugues, academic and free, on a single subject.
While his pupils were in the process of elaborating their ideas at
the keyboard Franck, with his marvellous fertility of mind, would
join in the fray, and would combine some quite new theme with
the principal in the course of its development, or in a fugue of
Bach, perhaps, he would add a new entry of the subject, even
some countersubjects to those originally set down by the composer. These continual flights of musical technique, always
interspersed with a string of remarks from teacher to pupil,
Franck would pursue with all the burning force of his passionate
temperament—a temperament so different from that remotely
mystical character which, up to this moment, has always been
attributed to the Master, with an exaggerated simplification of
his real nature. As a teacher, Franck was inclined to lose sight
of one of the important objects of his instruction in organ-playing
and improvisation. Thanks to his unquenchable enthusiasm, his
class increased in its numbers; but educationally it was of less
technical value to the mere instrumentalist than it was of general
value in the formation of a fine musical and general culture.

   It could not be expected that such exceptional pedagogic
methods would be welcomed by every one belonging to the
grand school in the Rue Bergère. The secretary of the Conservatoire, Émile Réty, appealed to the Director, Ambroise
Thomas, who was above all such petty worries, and made no
secret of his uneasiness. His tone was reprobatory: "In this school
we have at the present time a professor of organ who makes so

bold as to turn his organ-class into a class for composition!"
Nor were the composition-professors themselves pleased when
they found that certain of their pupils who had been frequenting
the organ-class were well grounded in principles of composition,
and especially of musical construction, which were opposed to
all they were being taught in the classes taken by Guiraud,
Massenet, or Delibes. Guiraud, a man always in the clouds, paid
little heed to this circumstance; he was sufficiently pleased that
his pupil Achille-Claude had shown a lively reaction against the
Franckist ideals of modulation. Massenet, as we have said, was
a touch irritated. Delibes was unwilling to admit that so inconvenient a conflict actually existed; he put the matter shortly in a
letter he wrote to the parents of his pupil Maurice Emmanuel:

> I have a high respect for M. Franck, but I am conscious that he
> shows some dangerous tendencies in music, and moreover he wants
> to persuade every one else to share his tastes in such ways; thus his
> policy contradicts that of his colleagues who are charged with the
> preparation of pupils for the Rome Prize. Your son must choose
> for himself between our two conflicting methods of teaching
> composition.

No such antagonism, however, subsisted between Franck and
one of the harmony professors, Théodore Dubois, who gladly
paid tribute to the original and rich harmonic invention of his
friend and colleague at Sainte-Clotilde.

Before long there crystallized at the Conservatoire a firm
opposition against Franck—spontaneous in origin and not
organized by any one group. Vincent d'Indy, along with several
others of his comrades-in-arms, has no doubt exaggerated its
importance; it existed nevertheless, and they were responsible for
it. Yet it is easy to explain.

Franck appeared to them as the champion of 'pure' music, in
rivalry against 'theatre' music, which was the central subject of
study in the ordinary composition classes; he was the man of
fugues and sonatas, while his colleagues were representing the
traditional cantata, the only gateway into the competition for
the Prix de Rome. In teaching harmony Franck had strict rules
of his own, but apart from that he preached a harmonic freedom
far removed from the formalism of the other teachers. He
was once heard to state: "At the Conservatoire a thing like that
would not be allowed for a moment . . . but, for myself, I like it

enormously!" About his fleeting pupil Debussy he said, "Consecutive fifths! Yes, I find them very attractive; but the great thing is to know how to make proper use of them!"

His contrapuntal learning and skill were recognized by all, and conferred on him a manifest superiority over many of his colleagues, over Delibes, for example, who—incredible as it may sound—had in truth had no formal teaching and practice in counterpoint when he was appointed in 1891 to teach those subjects. All the respect and admiration and affection Franck inspired—amounting sometimes to filial piety—led his pupils on to show up in the brightest light the deep chasm which lay between the two different systems of instruction, which should in fact have never been riven in twain; and their next step was to light up the differences between the pupils as well as those dividing the teachers.

The original members of the organ-class took some hand, no doubt, in keeping up its numbers of newcomers at a higher level than in those classes reserved for the more ordinary (or 'proletarian') frequenters of the school. Alexis de Castillon (though never himself a pupil under Franck at the Conservatoire), Vincent d'Indy, Paul de Wailly, Pierre de Bréville, Louis de Serres, all came from the upper classes and were members of the Société Nationale; they very soon imprinted their aristocratic seal on this organ-class; through their birth and the culture they attained they imposed upon their comrades—even on their successors—a stamp of elegance, of attractive distinction, which added greatly to a scheme of instruction already distinguished in itself. Out of Franck's class-room there emanated a kind of superior and condescending aura which diffused itself about the other teachers and pupils, especially those concerned with the writing of cantatas, who were considered to belong to a lower class of society altogether.

Even the pleasant-mannered Massenet came under the anathema on the grounds of the long-past rivalry between *Rédemption* and *Marie-Madeleine* (in 1873) and also because of his success in writing and producing operas whose value had been at first underrated. Ironies and even insults were often thrown from one class to another, and the loud invective of Franck's own class, having first splashed the General Secretary, later spattered mud on the clothes of the Director himself! Ambroise Thomas must have often found good reason to regret his choice for the organ professor-ship. He did not understand Franck at all, and evinced no sym-pathy towards him. Furthermore, the musical rancour between the two parties was embittered by the violent disagreement between them on all matters political, religious, and racial—a situation analogous to that we have often referred to in our biography of Vincent d'Indy.[1]

Far above all this discord—secret or noised abroad—soared the spirit of César Franck in all its natural good-will, simplicity, and candour. The Master was, nevertheless, the victim. He must have been aware of it all (or, perhaps, not even then?) when, hopeful of being appointed a professor of composition, not organ, he twice thought himself a likely nominee, and twice his hopes were dashed. Many causes contributed to this double disappoint-ment (such is the complexity of Conservatoire politics!); one of them was undoubtedly the opposition of those on the staff already teaching a specialized subject in which Franck's pupils considered their Master the only competent authority.

In 1880 Victor Massé, the second-rate composer of *Les Noces de Jeannette*, retired from his post as composition-teacher. Franck had then been the senior teacher of organ for eight years, and applied for the vacancy. The Minister of Public Instruction sup-ported his application, possibly with a view to excusing himself for his absence, in the previous year, from the private performance of *Les Béatitudes*. Though Franck disliked private intrigue, he spoke about the matter to the organist Ch.-M. Widor, who has himself reported the conversation, with Franck speaking in such terms as the following:

"Look! One of the three composition classes is vacant; you know the Minister; put a word in his ear about me, and if I am nominated for it, then you can take on my organ-class."

At the same moment Ernest Reyer was approached; Reyer, the composer of *Sigurd*, has told an amusing story which shows him to have been as firm an admirer of the Master as of the young Vincent d'Indy. Franck tackled Reyer, and said to him, "Master,

---

[1] On our last visit to Pierre de Bréville, in September 1945, we said to him, "All you people at the Conservatoire caused irreparable harm to your master, Franck." His reply was: "I quite agree; we spent our time blackguarding Ambroise Thomas!" Mme César Franck made it abundantly clear to her husband's pupils that it was they who had been responsible for all the enmity shown towards him by others.

I come to you——" Reyer instantly interrupted him: "No, it is you who are the Master!" Franck's longings came to nothing; he was not elected, and in preference to him Ernest Guiraud became the professor of composition, and in this way, later, the teacher and the friend of the rising young Debussy.

At the end of the same year another composition class fell vacant upon the death of Napoléon-Henri Reber. Franck once more put in for the post, yet, though he was considered the most important of the candidates, saw Léo Delibes appointed in preference. This second decision against Franck was the result of a whimsical notion taken by Ambroise Thomas—one might call it a bet; Thomas was sensitive to the pulse of the public and quite willing to submit therefore, as a man of the theatre, to any professional irregularity. He turned away his most suitable candidate from a post for which he was eminently fitted; in so doing he suffered no qualms of conscience in choosing a man of little educational ability and, indeed, of some lack of academic knowledge, a man, however, of undeniably brilliant talent who had composed the startlingly successful *Jean de Nivelle*, an opera played one hundred times during the preceding year at the Opéra-Comique.

Franck, the composer of *Les Béatitudes*, seems to have abandoned all hopes in this direction. Holding on to his usual courses in organ and improvisation at the Conservatoire, he resigned himself to the task of gathering together a few outstanding pupils to study composition with him privately. These special students appeared to him as witnesses to his methods of teaching, as personal champions, as the opposites of those who, in the national school, enrolled themselves under the collective banner of Delibes, Guiraud, and Massenet. We have quoted in a previous chapter (p. 191) the characteristic remark of Debussy's on Franck's pride at d'Indy's success with the *Chant de la cloche* and the Prix de la ville de Paris—his pupil had done one better than win the Prix de Rome!

The regular teaching of composition (apart from improvisation at the organ) thus was confined in César Franck's life to personal and private lessons. His pupils, however, far outnumbered the small circle of his exceptionally talented and most devoted supporters; the latter, completely satisfied with what they had learnt from him, continually refilled his roster with new, young, and promising recruits. The most assiduous propagandists were (one can guess) Henri Duparc and a little later Vincent d'Indy; we enlarge on the point in our book about the latter.

Many of his disciples he regarded with a paternal affection—"Father (or even "Daddy") Franck" replaced about 1880 the former polite address of "Monsieur Franck"; in addition, he regarded many with warm admiration: Henri Duparc he called "the most gifted of my pupils"—Duparc, who was unhappily to give up the practice of music almost immediately after he had written his celebrated songs. Gabriel Pierné's facility seemed to Franck quite exceptional. Camille Benoît, he thought, retired too soon from active music, though he simultaneously recommended him and was suspicious of him as a critical writer on music. Ernest Chausson, Guy Ropartz, above them all Vincent d'Indy, he held in the highest esteem. The last named, indeed, from about 1873 became Franck's self-appointed standard-bearer. It was with a legitimate pride, as well as a lively appreciation, that Franck heard and applauded d'Indy's *Chant de la cloche* and *Symphonie cévenole*—they presented an equal triumph for the master and the pupil!

A broad liberalism was the keynote of his teaching of written composition, as it was with that of improvisation at the keyboard. He showed it unreservedly on one occasion by expressing his view of a certain passage in a student's counterpoint paper which had been heavily blue-pencilled by one of the Conservatoire: "Ridiculous!" he cried; "every student must be allowed the chance of writing music, even in his exercises." Franck was strict enough, on the other hand, during the months or years of first apprenticeship for so long as the student had not acquired a basic technique. He laid down a gruelling course of studies, with continual practice in academic fugue strictly adhering to the rules and principles of the Conservatoire; his view was that a sound technique would equip the student to cope with all difficulties. But he adapted his methods to suit the natural gifts of each of his students; some, like Paul de Wailly, had to remain a whole year under this partly mechanical discipline; not so Vincent d'Indy, as we have shown in our book on him.[1] In 1872 d'Indy had made up his mind to "write fugues till I drop down dead," but he was exempted from this laborious process and wrote no more than

[1] Vol. i, p. 126.

two or three fugues. The same with Charles Bordes, who was made to write none at all; in his case the Master had perceived the fantastic and wayward quality of mind of an exceptional artist whose genius lay in improvisation, not in calculation or reflection.

On the subject of form and the construction of extended works Franck wielded an inexorable authority. He demanded from his pupils a rigorous formal plan, a ruthless logic in the succession and relationships of tonalities, and an absolute purity of style. At the same time he took into consideration the personality of each student and readily adapted himself to it, leaving the pupil to choose the kind of music he wanted to write—theatre music, symphonic poems, or 'absolute' music. His famous phrases "I like that," "I don't like that at all," were the spontaneous expression of his feelings, and not in the least brutal or despotic. His terse comments might be kindly and understanding, impressive and fair-minded; they all contained a criticism or an encouragement that was of high value to the student. Saint-Saëns in his *Idées de Vincent d'Indy* would have us believe that Franck's teaching

> consisted almost always of compliments and encouragements which, coming from so exalted an authority, delighted his students and turned them into enthusiastic disciples and proselytes of the Master.

The churlish spirit shown by Saint-Saëns from 1886 on against his successor in the artistic direction of the Société Nationale does not encourage us to place any faith in his asseverations.

Certain letters written to Pierre de Bréville contain some precise indications of the way Franck's mind worked; they were published in the *Mercure de France* of September 1, 1935. One of them, dated September 1884, runs thus:

> For stage-music always be melodic, and you well know the kind of melody I mean. For trios and quartets I want you to be more daring, but do not forget these points: (1) Don't be too complicated. (2) Your tonality must *never* be in any way doubtful. (3) Your basic formal plan once settled, stick to the classical mould. (4) Never be overlong.

One of his last pupils, Guillaume Lekeu, gave further detailed information about Franck's ways as a teacher in a letter written on

December 15, 1889, to his former teacher in Belgium, Kiéfer. "As for text-books of counterpoint," wrote Lekeu,

> Franck wishes me to tell you that he teaches counterpoint without using any text-book at all, from nothing but his own spoken advice; indeed, he considers all the text-books deplorable. He is hardly acquainted with the treatise of Bazin, who, it seemed to me, does not inspire him with much confidence. Bazin's book is the one prescribed at the Conservatoire. Franck's method with all contrapuntal exercises is to take for themes the Church's chant-tunes: *Stabat mater, Dies iræ, Jesu Redemptor.* He demands that the counterpoint woven round these admirable melodies should (1) sound satisfactory (or, if you prefer the word, 'musical'), (2) be expressive —above all things! This he rightly calls introducing life into a course of study which otherwise is as dry as dust.[1]

In his *César Franck* Vincent d'Indy has painted a vivid word-picture of the Master's teaching methods as his devoted pupil liked to think of them. It fills the last twenty-five pages of the book and sets in relief the unequalled excellence of his pedagogy: to that study it would be both impertinent and fruitless to attempt to make the smallest addition.

Outside the Conservatoire Franck taught the organ at the Institute for Young Blind Persons, a national foundation for which he always showed great interest and affection: he was first the organ teacher there, then superintendent of studies until just before his death. It was for this Institute that he composed his *Psalm CL*; there, too, he directed one of the first performances of his *Mass in A.* He put himself to the trouble to finger all the organ works of J. S. Bach (in the Peters edition) for their transcription into Braille notation; he presided at the annual examinations, and at the prize-givings himself announced the marks attained by the candidates. Two of his Institute pupils, Albert Mahaut and Louis Vierne, the one totally and the other practically blind, have noted down their memories of his teaching in this specialized school. They were delighted with the Master's

---

[1] Lekeu had been introduced to César Franck in 1889 by his old friend Charles Read, secretary of the French Society of Antiquaries. At first Franck refused to take him on as a pupil, since he was heavily overburdened at the time. Then he heard that Lekeu had been working on his own and not at any school or college of music, so he at once gave him a theme of four lines long to develop. After examining the completed exercise, Franck was satisfied and agreed, despite his over-full schedule, to give him some lessons. "Only," he said, "I shall charge him high fees." Guillaume Lekeu was to work with Franck until the latter's death—that is, for eighteen months.

radiant good-nature and even with the aural quality of his voice. "Franck's voice," writes Mahaut,

> always seemed to overflow with kindness. That was how it affected us blind students, so sensitive to the shades of vocal expression. He gave us advice and we listened to him, enthralled. He did not say very much, and always used short phrases, but we immediately perceived the profundity of his mind, his greatness, his vitality, and at the same time his understanding sympathy. Sometimes he would climb on to the organ stool and improvise. Those were feast-days for us, and we used to talk about them among ourselves for a long while afterwards.

Vierne writes in equally warm appreciation of "Franck's voice, so solemn, so sweet-toned, so slow," which gave him "a sensation of physical pleasure, not unmixed with a certain mysterious fear."

CHAPTER XX

The Composer

CÉSAR FRANCK is one of the most easily recognized composers when one meets him in a concert-hall. His music leaps to the mind and can be readily identified at a first hearing, unconfused with the music of any other composer. At most, a listener ignorant of his last piano works—the *Prelude, Chorale, and Fugue* and the *Prelude, Aria, and Finale*—might attribute them to Franz Liszt: certain pages in Liszt's works (notably the variations on the Bach theme of *Weinen, Klagen*) are very close in pianistic style to the two Franck works, which seem almost like a reflection of their precursor.

The long life of César Franck began in his native district of the Walloons, involved several long visits to Germany, and filled out the larger part of its span in France. During its winding course Franck came under many other influences than that of Franz Liszt, profound as it was. Not one of those influences, obvious or debatable, could hinder his personality from expanding until at an early moment it took on a most striking character. We have at this point to ask the question: What were the principal characteristics, the most sharply defined features, of his inspiration and his technical expression thereof? What were the essential elements of his genius, in melody, harmony, counterpoint, and rhythm?

According to Vincent d'Indy's dictum, "in this music everything sings, sings on unceasingly." Franck's abundant melodic vein is rich and fluid; his melodies are personal in their outline and in their inflexions, with a characteristic accentuation of their own. His melodic expression is usually couched in short phrases which do not extend over any great length, but repeat themselves—four-square symmetrical phrases that grow naturally, persist, revolve round themselves with a continual sinuous movement, often taking for a basis a single note as if it were a musical pivot, or forming an ornamental embroidery of mobile intervals round one stable sound. This method of procedure was undoubtedly unconscious, but may be early observed in the trios of his youth, and also later in the most mature works, even the last *Chorales*. Below are these typical examples:

Example 1

from the *Pastorale*, for organ (1862)

Example 2

from the *Quintet* (1879)

Example 3

from the *Symphony* (1888)

Franck's melodies are often very compact, digressing little but capable of extension; they glide along by semitones in what has been called 'undulating melismas,' and readily repeat themselves with bold modulations. Example 2, above, is a striking instance.

Vincent d'Indy asserts that the Master "spent a long time searching for the right melody, but nearly always found it at last." However that may be, it cannot be denied that if Franck sometimes had to ponder awhile melodies poured from his mind in a ready stream, forcing a passage through his pen or through his fingers. His son Georges—as we have noted regarding *Hulda* —recorded that during the half-extempore process of composing his operas he would jot down a number of melodic ideas just as they came into his mind, and would later choose therefrom those he considered the best. In plain truth Franck was easily satisfied with his own ideas; he took small pains to filter and decant the first yieldings of his imagination. That fact partly explains why his melismas, original and spontaneous as they are, and so easy to recognize, are always so alike in their colouring— why his idiom is always so markedly personal and why his melodic phrases show almost too close a kinship one with another.

We find few reminiscences of other composers in Franck's music. One of them however is of capital importance—that is, the famous *Muss es sein?* phrase from the Sixteenth String Quartet of Beethoven (in F, Op. 135), which makes itself very obvious in the *Symphony*, constituting indeed its principal theme. Was this a quotation, one may ask, intended as an act of homage to the great German Master? Vincent d'Indy never dared to pose the question, which raises a Franckist enigma on the top of the original Beethoven enigma. For ourselves, we consider that the reminiscence was quite unconscious: Franck himself had already used a similar theme as the basic idea for the Slave Chorus in his third 'Béatitude.' His lasting interest in this musical idea most likely derives, not from the Beethoven quartet, but from Liszt's *Les Préludes*, the music of which grows up from a similar thematic root.

The melodic invention is continuous; often smooth and tender, usually symmetrical, unremitting in the expansion and contraction of its intervals, the melody seems inexhaustible in its flow, partly because of its constant use—even abuse at times—of an expressive chromaticism, the romantic origins of which we have already traced. There is the risk that this melodic style might at any moment become monotonous; there is no attempt to disguise that modal type of flexibility which arises naturally out of the organist's daily use of the ancient or Gregorian church modes, nor yet to conceal that modulating movement which continually modifies the tonality by almost imperceptible degrees. The second theme quoted opposite is a typical example of melody which progresses with a kind of smoothly gliding movement, which rises only to descend again immediately, by steps reduced to an extreme narrowness, until it reaches the essential central note that has the magnetic attraction of the tonic-note of the key.

Melodically the themes possess a plasticity that is both serpentine and capricious; they superimpose themselves one on the other, they become entangled in an interplay of brilliant diversity. Such melodies cannot but entail a harmonic style equally chromatic with their own. Franck's harmony is the issue of his fluent and masterly counterpoint, born of that parentage spontaneously and almost as if by hazard—a chance birth, but one smiled upon by art! This harmony, with its sliding progressions of chords, gives us chordal combinations that cannot be classified, resolves without harshness all the dissonances involved by the movement of the separate voices, establishes a fixed if somewhat ambiguous tonality none the less firmly because as a whole it is a continuous blending of alternating keys.

The young Achille Debussy while studying the organ with Franck observed (as he did in Wagner) the expressive interest of the frequent successions of fifths and dominant sevenths and ninths that blossomed spontaneously in the soil of his scholarly improvisations. Debussy certainly closed neither his eyes nor his ears to the opening bars of the *Violin Sonata*, where the piano chords at once pose a problem of tonality and modality, a problem soon solved by the composer in the most elegant manner; nor yet to the beginning of the lento movement in the *Quintet*, where the first bars hesitate in the most expressive way, both melodically and harmonically, between various ancient and modern scales.

Upon such foundations, firm yet mobile, coming from a remote or a nearer past, was built up a style of real originality, a style that owed nothing to the ordinary teaching of a harmony traditional to the French Conservatoire, a style that escaped from all the minute regimentation of that rigid and academic science! When César-Auguste studied at Liége, as we have shown in our opening chapters, he was taught (apart from piano) nothing but counterpoint under Daussoigne-Méhul, though the subject of his lessons was officially called 'harmony,' and thus his pedagogic background led him always towards the contrapuntal in composing; at the Paris Conservatoire he never entered the classes where the gymnastics of text-book harmony were practised and where the pupil was taught, according to an exclusive formula, to build up chords on given basses or to add chords below a given treble-part. First Reicha, then Leborne, showed him, as their main task as teachers, the proper horizontal method of progression of simultaneous lines of melody interlacing among themselves with infinite musical potentialities, provided the style of writing was sound; the supreme goal aimed at by this method of teaching was, of course, fugue.

Franck's musical education provided him with one technical characteristic that stood out from among all the others—a special taste for canonic writing. Canons could easily be quoted from a number of his works, but the most striking example is to be seen in the finale of the *Violin and Piano Sonata*. It is true (as Saint-Saëns pointed out in his booklet on *Les Idées de Vincent d'Indy*) that Franck's canons were often spaced at the unison or the octave, "a trick that presents no technical difficulty." Saint-Saëns had proved himself in *Samson et Dalila* and in other works to be an accomplished technician in music, but he was prejudiced, and never held a favourable view of his colleague's essays in fugal form. He expressed the opinion that in the *Prelude, Chorale, and Fugue* the fugue was not strictly a fugue, and that the published music "no more resembles a fugue than a jelly-fish resembles a mammal!"[1]

From the time of his musical training in Liége and Paris César-Auguste cherished his liking for the models of symphonic construction left by the great masters; his instinct leant towards extended compositions built on a vast, firm, and solid plan. This idea of a strong formal plan influenced him in the writing of even his minor works, and 'sonata form' and '*Lied* form' appealed to him as the most suitable bases for his improvisations and elaborations of given themes. Their formal balance, settled a century back, seemed to him to be eternal, and he sought no other, save when at the end of his life in his organ *Chorales* he had the desire to take one or two steps farther beyond the path trodden by Bach himself.

We have written several times in this book about Franck's symphonic form. As a composer he was ever a traditionalist, and was satisfied to accept the old forms consecrated by the genius of his predecessors. Vincent d'Indy may assert as often as he will that his Master was "devoured by a thirst for new forms"; the fact remains that the general plans laid down for the varying movements of a sonata sufficed for his needs, although, after the manner of the later Beethoven, he liked at times to enlarge those

---

[1] Vincent d'Indy did not share in this judgment: see in this connexion our article in *La Revue musicale* of February 1947: "Une discussion Saint-Saëns et d'Indy."

plans, even to dislocate them. John Sebastian Bach was another composer whose patterns he strove to follow, and from Bach he derived his model for the prelude and fugue, adopting it gratefully, but adding to it variations or interrupting it with a chorale. The shape of the chorale as a form Franck expanded with splendid success in his three last organ works, and in this way he paid his deeply felt respect for a broad-shouldered, square-built form of typically Protestant origin, while he seldom seems to have been touched emotionally by the infinite flexibility of the Gregorian plain-chant of the Catholic Church.

The old accepted forms he liked to modify by his own expressive intentions, spontaneously overloading their first design with the continual interpolation of episodes and recapitulations; characteristically, he felt these latter to be a natural method of expansion. We have already shown here how, when an organ student at the Conservatoire was playing a Bach fugue his professor would delight in adding to Bach's text a new entry of the theme. Another story about the same point is told by Pierre de Bréville. On a certain occasion at Duparc's house Franck and Vincent d'Indy were improvising together, at two pianos, a transcription of some of the Strauss waltzes: Franck, with his marvellous intuition in counterpoint, introduced into their extempore version a number of imitative phrases and canons that were as musical as they were unexpected.

One of Franck's natural endowments was an overriding sense of tonality, which gave him scope to reinforce the solidity of structures already well founded. Despite the incessant ambiguity of his style, with its subtle gradations of tonality, an inflexible discipline controls the tonal waywardness and directs it towards the realization of the composer's basic plan with its finely balanced design. Fully to comprehend this sense of tonality it is only necessary to read or reread the many pages devoted to the subject of his Master's technique by Vincent d'Indy, both in his biography of Franck and in his *Treatise on Composition*, and then to examine the full score of *Rédemption* from this particular angle, that work being the first in which Franck systematically put into practice his theories of tonal progression that would lead the music ever upward towards the extreme sharp keys. This planned tonality was of such importance to Franck that, if we may accept the reliable but disquieting testimony of Alfred Cortot, the composer, at least during his latter years, would fix in advance the modulations which would govern a forthcoming piece of music, though he as yet had not decided on its subject or its nature.[1]

Rhythm is not the most remarkable element in Franck's music; it is a long way from attaining the suppleness and variety of his contrapuntal harmony, and often indeed approaches the commonplace. One can of course find in the pages of certain works points of careful elaboration and happy rhythmic touches, but on the whole the rhythm moves along with a regular step and a solid progress of equal beats, unrelieved by unexpected pulses and with the repetitions always identical. The rhythmic accentuation is the slave of the bar and never crosses the bar-lines, though there is syncopation in plenty, which lends a little variety to the over-regular utterance. Possibly this particular weakness, which comes near to producing monotony, is the result of constant practical experience at the church organ, as are the frequent pauses and silence-bars of rests, which cut up the continuity of the music and clearly correspond to those interruptions needed by the organist for modifying or re-establishing the registration.

Innumerable pages have been written about the instinct for cyclical form, which showed itself in Franck as early as his *First Trio*. Many writers have praised on the one hand and criticized on the other a system of musical construction which certain people have liked to hail as new, original, and hitherto unknown, whereas it was really a spontaneous revival of a musical procedure used by Beethoven, Schubert, Schumann, and Liszt, indeed by composers of every period, including that of Gregorian chant. With Franck, was this procedure in truth voluntarily used with systematic intent, as Vincent d'Indy would have us think? Rather, we would suggest, it came out of the spontaneous flowering of melodies of little variety and similar in feeling, or the return to semiconsciousness of kindred themes which, as we have read above, Franck designated by the picturesque term of 'cousins.' In any case, this use of a symphonic leitmotiv system which the composer developed progressively and entirely unmechanically was no more deliberate on his part than were his occasional thematic reminiscences. Franck himself, we fancy, must have been surprised when in the 1880's his disciples disclosed to him what they considered to be the originality of his 'cyclism'!

[1] Alfred Cortot, *La Musique française de piano*, i, p. 87.

Even then he seems to have thought the matter of little importance, as we can discover from the analysis of his *Symphony* which the Master himself wrote to be printed in concert programmes; in this descriptive note—an official pronouncement one might almost call it—there is no allusion whatever, direct or indirect, to that cyclical return of themes, to which, led on by Vincent d'Indy's example, composition teachers and critics have attached a primordial importance during the last sixty or seventy years.

Quite another explanation suggests itself—one that is new and perhaps paradoxical. The suggestion is here made that, like the rhythmic weakness mentioned above and the orchestral quality to be discussed in the next paragraph, Franck's 'cyclism,' whether unconscious or deliberate, was the outcome of his practice of improvising at the organ. Keyboard improvisation is an art which favours, if it does not demand, frequent restatements of the theme, a continual recharging of the musical texture by means of the assertion and reassertion of the principal thematic ideas and their countless 'cousins,' simply with a view to filling up time or drawing attention to a forthcoming new idea. To us it seems in the highest degree likely that Franck was in his innermost soul an improviser, whatever d'Indy may allege to the contrary.

Franck's instrumentation has never aroused admiration, a point we made in connexion with *Rédemption*. Even the most indulgent of his critics, Gabriel Fauré, is aware of certain failings, especially "the wearisome continuity of the basses as if they were in actual fact the pedal-board of the organ." Vincent d'Indy does not analyse Franck as an orchestrator lest he might have to criticize him. But Franck himself had enough of unaffected modesty within him to realize his shortcomings in comparison with Wagner's orchestration, or even that of his pupils. "On all orchestral points," he used always to say, "consult d'Indy; he is far stronger on that subject than I am." After the performance of the *Symphony* at the Conservatoire in 1889 he openly confessed that he had learnt a most valuable lesson from the rehearsal and the concert, especially in the matter of writing for the brass department. The secret of Franck's orchestration is that he played on the orchestra as if it were a three-manual organ, transferring to the composite instrument all his tricks with the solo instrument—in orchestration as well as in general style of composition.

The orchestral *tutti* to him was the full organ, the strings on one side being the foundation stops, the brass on the other the 'great,' with all manner of solo stops entrusted to the wood-wind players.

César Franck's inborn inspiration would burst out in a number of different ways, according to his pupils' reports. Sometimes an idea would unexpectedly flash into his brain in the course of a stroll or while he was giving a lesson—if the latter, then the pupil would watch him break off in the middle of his discourse and scribble down a few bars on a scrap of paper. Under other circumstances he would evince an almost unbalanced craving for the right idea, and would turn in a feverish search to any music handy, his own as well as that of others! Vincent d'Indy tells us that he both saw and heard Franck threshing out at the piano with all his muscular strength the Overture to *Die Meistersinger*, or some other piece by, say, Bach, Beethoven, or Schumann:

> After some time, sooner or later as circumstances dictated, the deafening clatter would die gradually down to a murmur, to a semi-silence, and then to nothing at all. . . . The Master had found what he was seeking.

Franck himself confessed: "In the end, when I want to get hold of some really good musical idea, I once again play over my *Béatitudes*, for it was in that work that I really succeeded in my aims." Charles Bordes, who used to see him in the country during his vacations, has given us a verbal picture of his Master in the semblance of an old lion, caring (it seemed) nothing for regular working-hours and the customary régime of daily living.

> At such moments César Franck was positively orgiastic; it was quite sufficient to come across him (as I did several times) bellowing like a stag at his piano and warming up his inspiration by playing his own published scores so as to key him up for the business of writing some more—quite sufficient, I say, to understand that genius and regularity of living are totally incompatible forces.[1]

This kind of preliminary musical incitement seems to have been often needed by Franck, as we noted in our observations on his improvising at Sainte-Clotilde. On the other hand, the letter quoted above about the composition of *Rébecca* (p. 171) makes it clear that he liked a long period of reflection before undertaking a work of any importance.

[1] *Tribune de Saint-Gervais* and *Mercure musical*, November 15, 1906.

Franck's musical inspiration—so abundant and so seldom hesitant in its flow—appeared to the composer himself in the guise of a divine revelation. Pupils and friends were one day affectionately discussing a certain passage in his works; Franck peremptorily broke in: "That is exactly how I first heard it!" The story is not unfamiliar about how, one Sunday morning on the way to Sainte-Clotilde, he ran into his friend the Marquis de Freycinet; hardly noticing the formal greeting offered, Franck explained himself quite clearly by saying, "Walk along beside me and don't talk! Last night I heard some heavenly voices singing and I don't want to forget them!"

These general observations on Franck as a composer have already been made in the particular study of his works attempted in these pages. Being of a material character, they are of secondary importance. Analyses of so personal an art as that in question have little interest for the ordinary music-lover. He hears the works, and allows his soul to be transported into new worlds by their magic. Critical discussion will never weaken the commanding power, the all-conquering charm, of César Franck's music.

The influence wielded by César Franck is not his least remarkable characteristic. As we look back over his life, we see him first as the young virtuoso-pianist, devoted from his fifteenth year onward to the winning of prizes and honours; then as the humble music-teacher and accompanist in Paris and the provinces, the organist snatched from obscurity by the interest and good-will of Cavaillé-Coll; then there comes the hesitant composer whom for ten or fifteen years of his life his pupils had persuaded to write according to ideas partly of their own formation; lastly, the developed composer, from 1880 to 1890 producing a series of masterpieces.

It was after 1872 that César Franck's influence began to be felt, and began to increase every day. That influence reached farther than the general musical world of France and Belgium; before long it insinuated itself into the hostile circle of the Paris Conservatoire. It even reached that most independent of composers, Claude Debussy. For all his reactions against Franck when he was his organ pupil, Debussy learnt more from him than he liked to admit; in more than one of Debussy's works, especially the string quartet, we find the impress of Franck in certain turns of melody and harmony.

Franck created, or rather (one should write) allowed to be created round him, a doctrine which has been given the name of Franckism. This doctrine arose spontaneously from the Master's work in music and from that of his pupils. Indistinct at first, it gradually became defined and codified by one of those pupils, and spread by him as a gospel in which he had a burning faith. Into French art this doctrine brought a new spirit comparable in more than one way with the parallel doctrine of Wagnerism.

It was Vincent d'Indy's ambition to make Franckism into a kind of musical temple, ever open to all who would accept its ideals; to the Franckist code of musical ideals d'Indy added his own ideas of technique according to the practice of the *Schola cantorum*, that school of the highest moral tenets in art. Franckism, less Franckist than d'Indyist, is to-day somewhat outworn, but it remains an historical fact of major importance to music. It did much to change the whole course of musical life and thought in France by rescuing that country's composers from the too exclusive devotion to the superficial art of opera, and by restoring to them the ideals of the great non-theatrical composers—the ideals of the symphony, that noblest and most independent of all expressive forms.

Note

AN English writer of French stock (recently deceased), Andrew de Ternant, went so far as to publish in England what amounts to an imaginative novel about Franck. Before that he had set down on paper some pretty legends (partly based on fact) about Debussy in London—legends to which we have drawn unreserved attention in our book *Claude Debussy et son temps* (French edition, p. 72; English edition, p. 49).

In various articles in the *Musical Times* and *The Choir* Andrew de Ternant asserts, among other particulars, that César Franck made frequent journeys to England, where he was welcomed by musician friends, and where he visited churches, museums, restaurants, and cafés, all identified with exactitude.

It is necessary to state here that César Franck never once travelled to England, not even for the marriage at Greenwich, in 1877, of his elder son to an Englishwoman whom he had met in Paris. (The whole matter has been exposed by this author in his open letter to *Music and Letters* of October 1947.)

With Franck, as with Debussy, de Ternant's writings show him to have been no more than an imaginative fraud.

Index

ADAM, ADOLPHE, 27, 49, 64, 72, 98, 103, 107
Adam, Louis, 49
Adiny, Mme, 219 n.
Alard, Delphin, 24
Alkan, Charles, 24, 27, 109, 118, 119, 183, 248
Altès, Ernest-Eugène, 91
Auber, Daniel, 16, 49
Auguez, —, 196

BACH, JOHANN SEBASTIAN, 41, 99–101, 104, 113, 114, 116, 120, 127, 146, 163, 173, 184, 193, 198, 203, 226, 233, 236, 241, 243, 256, 263, 269, 270, 273
Bagès, —, 187
Balbreck, Victor, 14 n., 222
Balleroy, Mme, 196
Bannelier, Charles, 162
Baptiste, —, 103
Barbedette, —, 208
Barth, —, 29
Batton, Désiré, 103
Battu, Marie, 139–140
Bazille, Auguste, 103, 125, 230
Bazin, François, 263
Beaulieu, Désiré, 103
Beck, Franz, 100
Beethoven, Ludwig von, 23, 24, 25, 34, 38, 44–45, 49, 50, 53, 54, 66, 70, 95, 119, 120, 144, 155, 184, 190, 192, 193, 203, 220, 222, 223, 226, 233, 236, 239, 267, 269, 271, 273
Bellaigue, Camille, 164, 203, 214–215, 225
Benoist, François, 30–31, 71, 100, 101, 115, 118, 137, 138, 151, 152, 252
Benoît, Camille, 116, 142, 162, 170, 213–214, 223, 226, 228, 235, 261
Bériot, Charles de, 16, 35, 39, 41, 62, 64
Berlioz, Hector, 38, 47, 72, 73, 75, 76, 80, 97, 127, 144, 149, 156, 159, 240, 241, 248
Berton, Henri-Montan, 27, 33, 49

Beyle, Gaston, 196
Bizet, Georges, 151, 152, 153, 159, 183, 193, 210, 254
Björnson, Björnsterne, 173
Blanc, Claudius, 178
Blanchard, Henri, 42–45, 66–69, 72–73, 75–76, 79, 100, 102, 103
Blau, Édouard, 140
Boëly, Alexandre, 100, 101, 103, 104, 114, 244
Bordes, Charles, 116, 117, 168, 177 n., 190, 194, 195, 226, 244, 251, 262, 273
Bordes-Pène, Mme, 170, 195, 196, 197, 200, 202
Borren, Charles van den, 188, 189 n., 218–219
Bosquin, —, 140
Bouchet, Jean-Adolphe, 92
Bouhy, —, 140
Boulanger, General Georges, 250
Boulay, Jeanne, 182
Bourgault-Ducoudray, Louis, 146, 151, 211
Bourges, Maurice, 41, 42, 51–54, 71 n., 103
Bousquet, Georges, 103
Boutarel, Amédée, 202
Brahms, Johannes, 99, 145, 220, 236
Bréville, Pierre de, 23 n., 57, 94, 167, 169, 187 n., 211, 213, 218, 221, 222, 226, 227, 230, 243, 252, 258, 260 n., 262, 270
Brizeux, Auguste, 209, 247
Bruckner, Anton, 126
Bruneau, Alfred, 119, 208, 228–229, 235, 252
Bülow, Hans von, 55, 87, 97, 107, 121–123, 124, 195
Bürger, Gottfried, 154, 175, 176
Bussine, Roman, 134, 135, 140, 174

CAHEN, ALBERT, 225, 235, 249
Carraud, Gaston, 252
Castil-Blaze, François, 61, 103

Castillon, Alexis de, 135, 160, 166, 187 n., 258
Caters, Mme de, 142
Caut, Mlle, 71
Cavaillé-Coll, Aristide, 91, 100–101, 103, 109, 112, 118, 124, 125, 126, 127, 159, 274
Cavallo, —, 103
Chabrier, Emmanuel, 148, 186, 235
Chaminade, Cécile, 172
Chapron, —, 117
Charlot, —, 27
Chausson, Ernest, 192, 211, 218, 221, 226, 249, 261
Chauvet, Charles, 118, 125, 126
Cherubini, Luigi, 22, 27, 28, 31, 33, 49, 91
Chevillard, Paul-Alexandre, 24, 34, 65, 66, 92
Chopin, Frédéric, 35, 42, 49, 109, 241–242, 248
Claes, Balthazar—see Benoît, Camille
Clapisson, Antoine, 49
Closson, Ernest, 18
Cohen, Jules, 151, 158
Colomb, Mme, 160
Colonne, Édouard, 142, 144, 145, 146, 155, 162, 163 n., 176, 178, 203, 223–224, 235
Conrady, —, 14
Coquard, Arthur, 37, 131, 139, 218, 252
Cordier, Mlle, 91
Corneille, Pierre, 91
Cortot, Alfred, 191, 270–271
Cossmann, Bernhard, 108
Couperin, François, 100
Couppey, Félix le, 27, 35
Cundell, Mlles, 35

Dalayrac, Nicolas, 64, 65
Dallier, Henri, 230, 254
Damner, Charlotte, 187
Dancel, Abbé, 92, 101
Daublaine-Callinet, —, 101
Daudet, Alphonse, 209, 247
Daussoigne-Méhul, Joseph, 14, 15, 19, 268
David, Félicien, 71, 73, 76, 78, 79, 97, 166
Debussy, Claude-Achille, 11, 173 n., 182, 187, 191, 192, 199, 248, 254, 256, 257, 258, 260, 268, 274, 276
Delaborde, Élie, 165
Delavaux, —, 14
Delchelvalerie, Charles, 17 n.
Deldevez, Édouard, 76
Delfosse, Bernard, 95

Delibes, Léo, 174, 234, 257
Desbordes-Valmore, Marceline, 247
Deschamps, Émile, 60
Deslignières, Mlles, 120
Desmarest, —, 76
Diémer, Louis, 175 n., 178, 190, 191, 196
Dietsch, Pierre, 91, 103
d'Indy, Vincent—see Indy, d'
Doehler, Théodor, 39, 40, 70
Dolmetsch, Victor, 197
Donizetti, Gaetano, 49, 105
Dreyschock, Alexander, 70
Drouart, Mlle, 24
Dubois, Théodore, 112, 117, 127, 135, 138, 150, 230, 233 n., 257
Dufourcq, Norbert, 112 n.
Dugas, —, 196
Duguet, —, 14
Duparc, Henri, 37, 130, 131, 132, 134, 135, 136, 139, 142, 144, 149, 154, 160, 174, 175, 194, 207, 210, 226, 249, 261, 270
Dupont, Joseph, 157, 187
Duprato, —, 175 n.
Dupuis, Sylvain, 195, 209, 247
Durand, Auguste, 125, 233 n.
Duvernoy, Henri, 27, 29, 31, 33

Eames, Mme, 219 n.
Emmanuel, Maurice, 19, 20, 167, 171, 184 n., 226, 227, 233, 252, 257
Engelfred, —, 189 n.
Erard (piano salons), 38, 60, 66, 72, 79, 84, 155, 194
Ernest, Alfred, 196–197
Ernst, Alfred, 222
Escudier (the brothers), 106
Eugénie, Empress (wife of Napoléon III), 98
Evers, Karl, 70
Expert, Henri, 34, 244

Fage, Adrien de la—see La Fage
Fantin-Latour, Théodor, 186
Fauré, Gabriel, 134, 136, 145, 174, 178, 180, 183, 235, 248, 272
Fay, Amy, 145 n.
Fessy, —, 101
Fétis, François, 42, 100
Feyteau, Blanche, 66
Fischer, —, 198
Fissot, Alexis, 175 n., 230
Forkel, Johann, 100
Fourcaud, Louis de, 204, 209

Fra Angelico, 160, 238, 242
Franchomme, Auguste, 39, 57
Franck, César:
Family of: 11–13, 22, 23 n., 37, 38, 59, 105, 111, 132, 180, 206 n.
Father (Nicholas-Joseph): 12, 13, 15, 16, 19, 20, 21, 22, 24–25, 26, 29, 34, 36, 38, 41, 43, 46, 48–50, 59, 64, 66, 67, 68, 69, 70, 71, 72, 78, 79, 84, 92, 107, 132, 242, 244
Brother (Joseph): 13, 14, 16, 26, 34, 35, 37, 39, 41, 43, 44, 45, 57, 58, 60, 61, 62, 65, 66, 67, 83, 84–85, 93, 98–99, 102, 111, 114–115, 118, 132, 137
Wife: 81–88, 92–93, 94, 130, 143, 144, 169, 206, 242–3
Children: 90, 93, 97–98, 99, 105, 111, 130, 188, 189, 197, 204–205, 206, 208, 211, 217, 218, 231, 233 n., 239, 243–245, 247, 250, 266, 276
Wife's family (Desmousseaux, Saillot, Baptiste, Féréol): 65, 81–88, 92–93, 94, 96, 98 n., 104–105, 111, 171, 230, 234, 235
Compositions:
Aimer, 110
Andantino quietoso, 153
Andantino for violin and piano, 65
Ange et l'enfant, L', 83–84, 153, 196, 209, 223, 249
Ave Maria, 91, 115
Ballade, 16, 64, 66
Béatitudes, Les, 128, 130, 155, 159–165, 169, 176, 185, 188, 190, 196, 203, 205, 206, 211, 215, 223, 229, 239, 246, 249, 260, 267, 273
Cantabile in B, 159, 164
Ce qu'on entend sur la montagne, 90–91, 246
Chanson du vannier, La, 209, 247
Chasseur maudit, Le, 91, 175–177, 178, 196, 201, 203, 218, 240, 249
Chorales, Three, 230, 232–233, 234, 266, 269
Combien j'ai douce souvenance, 84
Complaint of the Israelites, The, 127
Concertos for piano and orchestra, Two, (op. 11), 22–23
Dances de Lormont, 247
Delicieux, Les, 86
Djinns, Les, 91, 176–180, 184, 190, 198, 201, 246, 250
Domine, Domine, 153 n.
Domine non secundum (etc.), 153 n.

Domine salvam fac rempublicam, 94–95
Éolides, Les, 91, 132 n., 154–158, 174, 181, 207, 210, 224, 240, 246, 250
Fantaisie, 16, 23
Fantaisie in A, 159, 164
Fantaisie in C, 119, 126
Fantaisie on airs from Gulistan, 64, 65
Fifty pieces for harmonium, 230–232
Finale, 120, 126
Five Pieces (harmonium), 121
"Freedom," 95
Garde d'honneur, Le, 117
Ghiselle, 189 n., 217–221, 224, 229, 230–231, 239, 240, 243, 247
God Save the King (variations), 64–65
Grand Pièce symphonique, 119–120, 126
Grande Rondo, 16
Hulda, 171, 173, 175, 177, 181, 185–190, 196, 217, 218, 219, 239, 240, 243, 247
Hymne de Racine, 209, 247
Lied, 153
Mariage des Roses, Le, 136, 153
Mass for three voices, 115–117, 122, 164, 181, 201, 225–226, 263
Nocturne, 204, 209
Notre Dame des orages (cantata), 39
O Salutaris, 17
Offertories, 132
Panis angelicus, 116, 164–165, 181, 226
Paris, 131, 132
Passez toujours, 153
Pastorale, 120, 126
Patria, 131, 132
"Patriotic Hymn," 95
Philistin mordra la poussière, Le, 155
Piano fantasy, 39, 96
Prelude, Aria, and Finale, 202–203, 265
Prelude, Chorale, and Fugue, 120, 183–185, 196, 202, 243, 265, 269
Prelude, Fugue, and Variations, 120, 153
Premier Caprice, 43
Prière, 120
Procession, La, 209
Psalm CL, 128, 182, 263
Psyché, 188, 204–208, 218, 224, 239, 243, 250
Quae est ista, Dextera Domine, 153
Quartet, 168, 220, 221–223, 229
Quasi Marcia (harmonium), 121, 155
Quintet, 53, 55, 120, 157, 165, 166–170, 171, 172, 181, 184, 192, 196, 199, 206, 207, 211, 223, 229, 233, 239, 242, 243, 248, 266

Rebecca, 171–173, 180, 181, 201
Rédemption, 89, 128, 140–150, 153, 160, 185, 188, 198, 201, 203, 215
Robin Gray, 86
Ruth, 59, 64, 70–80, 83, 87, 91, 97, 106, 110, 123, 124, 133–134, 139–140, 143, 148, 153, 157, 181, 196, 201, 203, 221, 231, 248, 271
S'il est un charmant gazon, 155
Six Pieces for Organ, 115, 118–121, 126
Solemn Mass, 115
Sonata for piano (op. 10), 22–23
Souvenance, 153
Stradella, 60–61
Sub tuum, 110
Sylphe, Le, 153
Symphonic concertante, 57
Symphonic Variations, 120, 167, 190–191, 196–197, 201, 203, 208, 229, 239, 241, 250
Symphony (op. 13), 22
Symphony, 120, 203, 209–216, 221, 243, 248, 250, 266, 267, 272
Tendre Marie, 117
Tower of Babel, The, 127
Trio-concertante in E flat, 35
Trios (opp. 16 and 22), 22, 39, 40, 41, 42, 43, 48–58, 60, 62, 65, 66, 67, 82, 97, 109, 121–123, 124, 135–136, 165, 166, 194, 210
Trois exilés, Les, 95
Valet de ferme, Le, 105–107, 110, 249
Variations brilliantes on a favourite round-dance of Gustave III, 16
Variations on the theme " Prés-aux-clercs," 16
Veni Creator, 181
Vierge à la crèche, La, 209, 247
Violin Sonata, 168, 195–200, 197–198, 239, 250, 268, 269
Freycinet, Marquis de, 274
Fuchs, Mme, 172
Fursch-Madier, Mlle, 140

GANNE, —, 175 *n.*
Garcia, Pauline Viardot, 16, 49, 84, 103, 110
Garcin, Jules, 134, 135, 211
Gardey, Canon, 234
Gastoué, Amédée, 231
Gautier-Villars, Henry (l'Ouvreuse), 222–225, 225, 229
Gavioli, Mme, 196

Genty, Mlle, 158
Géraldy, —, 23, 61
Gevaert, François, 196
Gibier, —, 222
Gigout, Eugène, 159, 175 *n.*, 230, 233 *n.*, 234
Gilbert, Alphonse, 91
Girac, —, 92
Gluck, Christopher Willibald, 41
Gounod, Charles, 71, 88–89, 103, 146–147, 149, 150, 162, 172, 183, 210, 212, 244, 249
Grand-Jany, —, 175 *n.*
Grandmougin, —, 173, 174
Granval, Mme de, 142
Grégoir, Jacques, 64
Grétry, André, 47, 84
Gros, Aimé, 226
Groz, Albert, 198
Guidé, Guillaume, 195
Guillemin, Alexandre, 71
Guilmant, Alexandre, 124–125, 159, 175 *n.*, 230, 233 *n.*, 235
Guiraud, Ernest, 135, 170, 174, 175, 257, 260

HABENECK, FRANÇOIS, 34, 35, 38, 75
Haincelin, Mlle, 181
Hainl, Georges, 35, 57
Halévy, Jacques, 34, 49, 72, 103
Hallays, André, 147
Hamelin, Abbé, 132
Handel, George Frederick, 34
Haydn, Joseph, 23, 34, 91, 109
Heller, Stephen, 72, 183
Hermann, Ludwig, 124, 222
Hérold, Ferdinand, 16
Herz, Henri, 49
Herz, Jacques, 27, 49
Hesse, Adolphe, 100–101, 103, 114
Heuvel, Van der, 110
Holmès, Augusta, 145, 153, 169, 233 *n.*, 235
Holtzen, —, 91
Hugo, Victor, 38 *n.*, 90, 94, 110, 131, 176–180, 246
Hummel, Ferdinand, 24, 27, 38, 39, 44–45, 203
Huré, Jean, 112 *n.*

IMBERT, HUGUES, 204
Indy, Vincent d', 11, 30, 31, 38, 42, 46, 47, 48, 49, 51, 54, 55, 56, 57, 77, 84, 105, 116, 131, 135, 136, 139, 141, 142, 143,

144, 145, 152, 156, 162, 163 *n*., 164, 167, 168, 169, 174, 175, 176, 180, 183, 184, 187, 188, 189, 190, 191, 192, 194, 196, 197, 198, 202, 204–205, 208 *n*., 210, 218, 221, 226, 227, 229, 232, 235, 237, 238, 239, 245 *n*., 247, 249, 250, 251, 252, 257, 259, 261–262, 263, 265, 266, 269, 270, 271, 272, 275

Jacquard, Léon, 134
Jalheau, —, 14, 21
Jardillier, Robert, 167, 198–199
Jeannin, Paul, 175 *n*.
Jehin, Léon, 219 *n*.
Jehin, Deschamps-, Mme, 219 *n*.
Joachim, Joseph, 99, 108 *n*.
Joncières, Victorin de, 162, 235
Jullien, Adolphe, 143, 162–163

Kalkbrenner, Friedrich, 42, 64
Kant, Immanuel, 245
Kastner, Georges, 65, 71 *n*.
Kayser, —, 175 *n*.
Kiefer, —, 246, 263
Kontzki, Anton von, 40
Kontzki, Charles, 27
Kufferath, Maurice, 187, 195

La Fage, Adrien de, 100, 103, 113
Labro, —, 39
Lacombe, Paul, 165
Laforgue, Jules, 195, 226
Lalo, Édouard, 142, 153, 162, 186–187, 210, 235
Lamartine, Alphonse de, 73, 94
Lamberts, Joseph, 12 *n*.
Lambillote, R. P., 115, 117
Lamoureux, Charles, 157, 181, 196, 203, 210–211, 213, 224–225
Langrand, —, 145 *n*.
Lapissida, —, 187
Laub, Ferdinand, 108
Laurens, Jean-Bonaventure, 99
Laurent, —, 31, 32
Lavigne, Paul, 201
Lavoye, Mlle, 75
Leborne, Aimé, 26, 29, 268
Lebouc, —, 109
Lebrun, Annette, 39
Lecointe, —, 35
Ledent, —, 14
Lefébure-Wély, Louis, 101, 112, 118, 119, 121

Lefèvre, Charles, 175 *n*.
Lekeu, Guillaume, 221, 234, 245–246, 249, 262–263, 264 *n*.
Lemmens, Nicholas, 100, 103–104, 114
Léon, Hermann, 172
Leopold I, King of the Belgians, 15, 48, 50, 60, 62, 63, 79, 98, 99, 104
Leslino, Mme, 196
Lesueur, Jean-François, 91
Leter, —, 117
Letscart, —, 255
Liégeois, —, 222
Lindenlaub, Théodore, 195
Lisle, Leconte de, 154, 156, 158, 240, 246
Liszt, Franz, 16, 17, 22, 24, 26, 47, 49, 53, 54, 55, 56, 70, 72, 73–75, 85, 87, 90–91, 97, 106, 107, 108–109, 110, 121, 122, 124, 126–127, 145, 146, 165, 167, 180, 187, 195, 239, 240, 248, 265, 267, 271
Liverini, —, 35
Louis-Napoléon, 95, 106
Loys, —, 167

Mahaut, Albert, 182, 227, 252, 255, 263
Maître, Abbé, 163 *n*.
Malibran, Maria, 16
Marie, Gabriel, 211
Marmontel, Antoine, 40
Marsick, Martin, 166
Marty, Adolphe, 182, 255
Mason, William, 108 *n*.
Massé, Victor, 27, 151, 170, 259
Massenet, Jules, 134, 140, 141, 142, 144, 150, 151, 153, 172, 193, 228, 248, 253–254, 257, 258
Maton, —, 172
Mauzin, —, 219 *n*.
Méhul, Étienne, 14, 71, 73, 96, 239
Melchissédec, Pierre, 219 *n*.
Mendelssohn, Felix, 41, 43, 87, 97, 99, 109, 120, 162, 215, 240
Mercadante, Saverio, 35
Merklin, —, 164
Messager, André, 170, 172, 234
Messemaker, —, 64
Metternich, Princess, 127
Meyerbeer, Giacomo, 22, 34, 49, 72, 74, 107, 110, 149, 150, 162, 220, 240, 246
Mirbeau, Octave, 146–147
Miroir, —, 100
Moisson, Mlle, 71
Mondonville, Jean, 51
Mondutaigny, Mlle, 71

Montaigne, Michel, 68
Montalivet, Count of, 73–75
Montendre, Count of, 61
Montigny, Mme, 178, 195
Montpensier, Duke of, 79
Moscheles, Ignaz, 42, 72
Mouliérat, —, 162
Mounet-Sully, Jean, 142
Mouret, Jean-Joseph, 51
Mozart, Wolfgang Amadeus, 34, 38, 91
Musset, Alfred de, 244

NAPOLÉON III, 95, 106
Nau, Maria-Dolores, 23
Naumbourg, Samuel, 249
Niedermeyer, Louis, 61
Nisard, Théodore, 99, 115

OBIN, —, 72
Offenbach, Jacques, 86
Oller-Costello, —, 39
Onslow, George, 49, 166
Ortigue, Joseph d', 103, 127
Osborne, George Alexander, 35, 41
Ouvreuse, l', —, see Gauthier-Villars

PALADILHE, ÉMILE, 151
Palestrina, Giovanni da, 117
Pampelonne, Roger de, 245 n.
Panofka, Heinrich, 64
Panseron, Auguste, 49, 103
Pape (piano salon), 24, 41, 44–45, 62
Papot, Mlle, 158
Pasdeloup, Jules, 139, 142, 145 n., 153, 176, 191, 196–197
Pastou, Chevalier, 32, 61
Pastouret, Count of, 39
Paulin, Gaston, 109, 206
Pierné, Gabriel, 175, 226–227, 230, 252, 253, 255–256, 261
Pixis, Johann, 24, 72
Pleyel, Camille, 27, 109, 114, 194
Pleyel, Mme Camille (Marie), 47, 49, 70
Poitevin, Mlle, 170, 180, 185
Ponchard, Louis, 39
Pougin, Arthur, 109, 214, 235
Poujaud, Paul, 208–209, 212, 220, 226, 247
Praslin, — de, 85
Prestat, Mlle, 230
Pugno, Raoul, 230

QUIROT, —, 162

RACINE, JEAN, 87, 209, 244, 247
Radoux, Théodore, 132, 195
Rambaud, Henri, 204
Rameau, Jean-Philippe, 34, 51
Read, Charles, 264 n.
Reber, Napoléon-Henri, 170, 260
Régnier, Léon, 220
Reicha, Anton, 19, 20, 22, 26, 29, 268
Rémy, —, 166, 198
Renan, Ernest, 245, 250
Renaud, Mlle, 158
Réty, Émile, 256–257
Reuchsel, Léon, 225
Reyer, Ernest, 133–134, 140, 144, 146, 259–260
Rignault, —, 41, 58
Rode, Pierre, 16
Rodenbach, Georges, 147, 212
Roger, Gustave, 41, 91
Rollot, Abbé de, 91
Rongier, Jeanne, 186, 237
Ropartz, Guy, 148–149, 198, 208 n., 239, 261
Rossini, Gioacchino, 22, 34, 35, 105, 142, 155
Rousseau, Samuel, 158, 189, 218
Rousseau, Vita, 172
Royer, Alphonse, 105, 106–107
Rudder, May de, 12 n.

SAINBRIS, GUILLOT DE, 172
Saint-Saëns, Camille, 78, 116, 118, 124, 125, 134, 135, 136, 137–138, 139, 140, 142, 146, 150, 151, 153, 154, 159, 165, 166–167, 169, 170, 172, 178, 180, 183, 185, 186, 192, 193, 209–210, 215, 234, 248, 262, 269
Sanches (family), 132 n., 177, 185, 232
Sand, George, 49, 95
Scarlatti, Alessandro, 186
Schad, Joseph, 59
Scheffer, Ary, 74
Schmitt, Georges, 125
Schneitzhoeffer, —, 27
Schubert, Franz, 17, 25, 41, 43, 51, 54, 64, 73, 109, 116, 220, 226, 240, 271
Schumann, Robert, 17, 54, 99, 162, 166, 184, 190, 193, 240, 271, 273
Scribe, Eugène, 240, 246
Scudo, Pietro, 103
Seguin, —, 162
Sejan, Nicolas, 100

Serres, Louis de, 154, 177, 210, 211 *n.*, 212–213, 252, 254, 258
Servières, Georges, 107 *n.*, 189 *n.*
Sicard, —, 204
Simon, Antoine, 103
Soubre, —, 132
Spalding, —, 191
Spontini, Gasparo, 72, 76, 110
Stamaty, Camille, 103
Strauss, Johann, 270

Taffanel, Claude, 134
Tagliafico, Joseph, 44
Ternant, Andrew de, 276
Thalberg, Sigismond, 35, 40, 41, 42, 62, 64, 70, 84, 109
Theuriet, André, 209, 247
Thierry, Gilbert-Augustin, 216, 219
Thomas, Ambroise, 49, 103, 138, 151, 152, 175 *n.*, 177, 229–230, 234, 249, 258–259, 260
Tiersot, Julien, 23 *n.*, 30, 57, 90, 91, 189, 205, 222, 250
Tolstoy, Leo, 250–251
Torchet, Julien, 202–203
Toscanini, Arturo, 218
Tournemire, Charles, 150 *n.*, 227–228, 230, 255
Trémont, Baron de, 49
Trouillon-Lacombe, —, 103

Udine, Jean d', 149
Uhland, Johann, 175

Uhran, —, 49

Vazë, Gustave, 105, 106–107
Vaucanson, —, 44
Verdi, Giuseppe, 187
Vergnet, —, 219 *n*
Viardot, Pauline—*see* Garcia
Vierne, Louis, 227–228, 253–255, 263–264
Vieuxtemps, Henri, 64

Waefelghem, Louis van, 167
Wagner, Richard, 34, 91, 119, 123 *n.*, 149, 153, 156, 163, 181, 184, 187, 190, 191–192, 193, 196, 203, 222, 241–242, 248, 268, 273
Wailly, Paul de, 247–248, 252, 258, 261
Weber, Carl Maria von, 17, 25, 34, 41, 51, 65, 240
Weckerlin, Jean-Baptiste, 106, 109
Widor, Charles, 65 *n.*
Widor, Charles-Marie, 65 *n.*, 124, 125, 151, 235, 252, 253, 254, 255, 259, 272
Willmers, Rudolf, 59
Willy, Colette, 222 *n.*
Wolff, Auguste, 64

Ysaÿe (Eugène, Théodore), 195, 196, 197, 200, 201, 220, 223, 226

Zimmermann, Pierre, 19, 20, 22, 26, 27, 28, 29, 40, 105
Zola, Émile, 228